POWER AND GLORY: COURT ARTS OF CHINA'S

Ming Dynasty

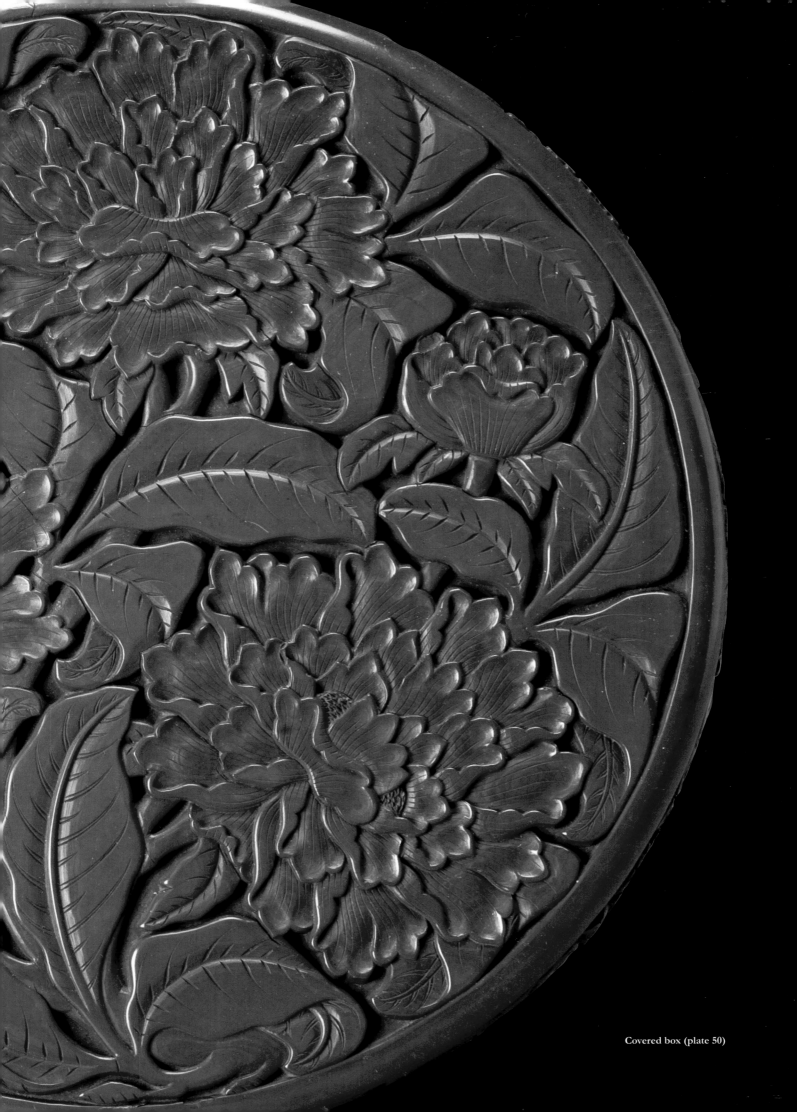

Covered box (plate 50)

POWER AND GLORY: COURT ARTS OF CHINA'S

Ming Dynasty

BY LI HE AND MICHAEL KNIGHT

With contributions from Richard Vinograd, Terese Tse Bartholomew, and Dany Chan

ASIAN ART MUSEUM — CHONG-MOON LEE CENTER FOR ASIAN ART AND CULTURE

The Asian Art Museum–Chong-Moon Lee Center for Asian Art and Culture is a public institution whose mission is to lead a diverse global audience in discovering the unique material, aesthetic, and intellectual achievements of Asian art and culture.

何 鴻 毅 家 族 基 金
THE ROBERT H. N. HO
FAMILY FOUNDATION

This exhibition was developed by a grant from the Robert H. N. Ho Family Foundation. The museum is grateful for additional support provided by the Henry Luce Foundation, the Starr Foundation, and United Airlines. Additional funding is provided by the National Endowment for the Arts.

NATIONAL
ENDOWMENT
FOR THE ARTS
A great nation
deserves great art.

UNITED
It's time to fly.

Published on the occasion of the exhibition *Power and Glory: Court Arts of China's Ming Dynasty*, organized by the Asian Art Museum in association with the Palace Museum, Beijing; the Nanjing Municipal Museum; and the Shanghai Museum, and presented at the following venues:

Asian Art Museum, San Francisco, June–September 2008

Indianapolis Museum of Art, October 2008–January 2009

Saint Louis Art Museum, February–May 2009

Because some objects are light sensitive, not all will be on view at once during the exhibition.

Asian Art Museum books are distributed to the trade by Tuttle Publishing, North Clarendon, Vermont.

Front cover: Cat. no. 147, p. 259
Back cover: Cat. no. 90, p. 154

1 3 5 7 9 8 6 4 2

FIRST PRINTING

This book was written by exhibition curators He Li and Michael Knight, with contributions from Dany Chan, Terese Tse Bartholomew, and Richard Vinograd. Yvonne Kong provided assistance. Michael Knight and Dany Chan prepared the index. John Stucky reviewed and corrected the references. The book was edited by Theresa Duran and proofread by Kristina Youso. Robin Jacobson provided editorial assistance. Editing and production were overseen by Thomas Christensen, who prepared the images on pp. 24, 25, 124, and 125. Jason Jose prepared the maps. The Asian Art Museum's staff photographer, Kaz Tsuruta, took photos of the museum's objects and assisted with image preparation. The book was designed and typeset in Adobe Baskerville and Adobe Garamond by Ron Shore of Shore Design, Brisbane, California. It was printed and bound on 170 gsm silk art paper by Regal Printing, Ltd., Hong Kong.

Images of Ming emperors on p. 264 are courtesy of the National Palace Museum, Taiwan, Republic of China. Models for the illustrations on pages 25 and 25 can be found in Huang Nengfu and Chen Juanjuan, *Zhongguo fuzhang she* (A History of Chinese Costumes; Beijing: Zhongguo luyou chubanshe, 1995). Models for illustrations on page 124 top and 125 can be found in Xiao, Mo, ed., *Zhonggo Jianzhu shi* (Chinese Architectural Art History; Beijing: Wenwu chubansghe, 1999). The model for the illustration on p. 124 bottom can be found in Nagoya Municpal Government, *Zhongguo nanjingshi bowuguan Mingchao wanggogn guizu wenwuzhan* (An Exhibition of Cultural Relics of the Ming Monarch and Aristocracy of Nanjing; Nagoya: Municipal Government, 1989).

CONTENTS

Zheng Xinmiao, Director

The Ming dynasty spanned more than two hundred seventy years, and it left behind a magnificent culture on the pages of ancient Chinese history. Objects that represent the essence of various arts and techniques bring to us the civilization of times past and tell a story from long, long ago.

Here, The Palace Museum, the Nanjing Municipal Museum, and the Shanghai Museum are working with the Asian Art Museum, the Saint Louis Art Museum, and the Indianapolis Museum of Art to share the arts of the Ming imperial court with the American public, from an historical, cultural, and artistic angle, so that our audience might get a sense of China's extensive history and culture and experience firsthand the appeal of these special objects of art.

We believe that this exhibition will certainly take Chinese American cultural exchange to a new level; it will appeal to the aesthetic in you, and touch the heart of each of our visitors.

Finally, to the success of the exhibition!

PREFACE FROM THE NANJING MUNICIPAL MUSEUM
Bai Ning, Director

Power and Glory: Court Arts of China's Ming Dynasty, which is launching at the Asian Art Museum, is a matchless exhibition, and a demonstration of East Asian art and culture.

China is one of the great ancient civilizations, with a long history and age-old culture. The Ming Dynasty, which roughly spanned the fourteenth through seventeenth centuries, came at the end of China's feudal era and enjoyed a period of exceptional prosperity; it has left us with an incredibly rich historical heritage. The Ming dynasty established its capital in Nanjing; after Zhu Yuanzhang founded his capital, he set about its planning — the court architecture, imperial mausoleum, ancient city walls, and shipyard remains still convey the powerful spirit unique to an emperor's capital city. The exquisite objects excavated from the Nanjing-area tombs of noble families reflect the progress and development that characterized Ming society. The objects included in this exhibition represent the essence of the culture of the Chinese people; through them we can experience the farsightedness, wisdom, and creativity of Chinese civilization, the appeal of ancient Chinese art, and see the contributions Chinese culture has made to world civilization.

Through our collaboration with the Asian Art Museum on this exhibition, we are building a bridge between Chinese and American culture, and making efforts to promote friendship among the people of both countries. We believe this exhibition will play an important role in the process of cultural exchange between China and the United States.

To the success of the exhibition!

PREFACE FROM THE SHANGHAI MUSEUM
Chen Xiejun, Director

The Asian Art Museum of San Francisco is known around the world as a premier collector of Asian art. It is especially famous for its collection of ceramics, jades, and bronzes. The Shanghai Museum is honored to have this opportunity to collaborate with the Palace Museum and Nanjing Municipal Museum on the exhibition *Power and Glory: Court Arts of China's Ming Dynasty,* at the Asian Art Museum.

Life at court is an important aspect of traditional Chinese culture, as well as a historical microcosm. Because the Ming Dynasty was a unique and deeply influential period in Chinese history, we believe that this special exhibition, with its exceptional artistic charm and abundance of historical content, will most certainly deeply move our audience.

From the bottom of my heart, I wish the exhibition every success.

PREFACE FROM THE ASIAN ART MUSEUM

his exhibition is the fruit of a collaboration between the Asian Art Museum of San Francisco and three of China's leading museums: The National Palace Museum in Beijing, the Shanghai Museum, and the Nanjing Municipal Museum. The process began in 2001 as the Asian Art Museum was preparing to move from Golden Gate Park to its new facility in San Francisco's Civic Center; it took on final form with the announcement of the 2008 Olympic Summer Games in Beijing. It was a natural for the Asian Art Museum to organize an exhibition celebrating a unique aspect of Chinese culture during this auspicious year. Avery Brundage (1887–1975), whose collection is the core of the Asian's holdings, was an Olympic athlete, president of the United States Olympic Committee as early as 1929, and served as president of the International Olympic Committee from 1952 to 1972. His vision of building a bridge of international understanding and cooperation through amateur athletics and the arts is core to the development of this exhibition. It seemed only right that important Ming ceramics and lacquers from his collection should be included in the exhibition.

He Li, Associate Curator of Chinese Art at the Asian Art Museum, took the curatorial lead and worked closely with the staff of the three Chinese museums. Each of these three institutions provided unique opportunities for this exhibition.

The Nanjing Municipal Museum, directed by Ms. Bai Ning, is the repository of many of the great Ming dynasty objects found in that city and its environs in recent decades. The city of Nanjing served as the Ming capital from the founding of the dynasty until 1420 when Beijing was declared the primary capital. Nanjing remained the secondary capital for the remainder of the dynasty and much of the Ming city remained intact until it was destroyed during the Taiping rebellions in 1854. While the Ming dynasty buildings were destroyed at this time, many of their architectural elements have survived, some in a remarkable state of preservation. These are kept at the Nanjing Municipal Museum and a number are included in this exhibition. Among the most spectacular of these are the glazed ceramic tiles that made up part of the Baoen'si, a temple created in the first half of the fifteenth century.

Like many cities in China, Nanjing has witnessed an economic boom in recent years and the city is expanding dramatically. The Nanjing Municipal Museum has benefited from materials excavated from archaeological sites uncovered during this expansion. Many Ming aristocrats lived and were buried in the Nanjing area. Materials from their tombs included in this exhibition include textiles, jewelry, utilitarian objects, and figurines.

The Asian Art Museum of San Francisco and the Shanghai Museum have had a close relationship since 1982 when the Asian organized the first U.S. exhibition from that museum following the opening of China in the late 1970s. Our thanks to Ms. Zhou Yanqun, head of the Foreign Relations office at the Shanghai Museum; Mr. Chen Xiejun, Director; and the Shanghai Museum staff for their generosity in lending to this exhibition. The Shanghai Museum is renowned for its paintings, and it has added immensely to the exhibition by lending a number of pivotal works by artists active at the Ming court. It has also provided a series of miniature furniture models found in Ming dynasty tombs.

Our primary partner in China for this exhibition was the National Palace Museum in Beijing. We worked closely with Mr. Li Ji, Deputy Director, and Ms. Li Shaoyi, Head of American and European Section, Foreign Affairs Department. Their efforts and those of the staff at the Palace Museum were invaluable in making this exhibition a success.

Beijing served as the primary capital of the Ming dynasty from 1420 to the fall of the dynasty in 1644. By the end of the dynasty Beijing was one of the world's largest cities, and its residents were active consumers of art. Included in this exhibition from the Palace Museum's unparalleled holdings of materials from the Ming dynasty are textiles, paintings, ceramics, lacquers, cloisonné, and furniture.

Dr. Richard Vinograd, Christensen Fund Professor in Asian Art in the Department of Art and Art History at Stanford University has provided a comprehensive essay on Chinese painting at the Ming court for this catalogue. At the Asian Art Museum, He Li, Associate Curator of Chinese Art, has written the essays and entries in the sections on Gold and Jade, Ceramics, and Metal and Cloissonne as well as the entries for the paintings section. Terese Bartholomew, Curator Emeritus of Chinese Decorative Art and Himalayan Art provided the essay and entries on Textiles and Costumes as well as select other entries.

The preparation of this catalogue would not have been possible without the efforts of Kazuhiro Tsuruta for photo preparation, Aino Tolme for photo management, Thomas Christensen for directing this publication, Theresa Duran for editing, John Stucky for vetting the bibliography, Kristina Youso for proofreading, Robin Jacobson for editorial assistance, Ron Shore for design and production, and Yvonne Kong and Dany Chan for general assistance. Sharon Steckline has been invaluable in keeping lists in order. Mark Fenn has provided technical information concerning objects.

The exhibition will travel to two American museums following its presentation at the Asian Art Museum. We are grateful to Jim Robinson, Curator of Asian Art, and Sue Ellen Paxson, Director of

Exhibitions and Special Projects of the Indianapolis Museum of Art, and Philip Hu, Associate Curator of Asian Art and Linda Thomas, Assistant Director for Exhibitions and Collections, of the St. Louis Museum of Art for their interest and their help in bringing the exhibition to an even wider public.

The first financial support for this exhibition came from Asian Art Museum trustees Julia Cheng, Doris Lee, and Sally Hambrecht. They provided funding for the catalogue and for hiring Yvonne Kong as project assistant. Additional early support came from the Harold Brown Charitable Trust.

The Robert H. N. Ho Family Foundation in Hong Kong is the Lead Sponsor for the development of this exhibition and for the presentation in San Francisco. The Foundation provided major support of the exhibition with the largest grant the Asian Art Museum has ever received for a special exhibition. The Robert H. N. Ho Family Foundation is a Hong Kong-based independent philanthropic organization with a mission to foster and support Chinese arts and culture worldwide, in particular cross-cultural understanding between China and the world. We would like to take this opportunity to thank the Foundation's Board and Staff for their generous and important support. The exhibition also received generous support from the Henry Luce Foundation, the Starr Foundation, United Airlines, and the National Endowment for the Arts (both in direct support of the exhibition and its programs and in a federal indemnity to support insurance costs).

Many others, staff and friends of the Asian Art Museum and at our partner institutions, worked hard to bring this exhibition to the public. While we cannot thank each person individually here, we are deeply grateful for their efforts.

MICHAEL KNIGHT
Senior Curator of Chinese Art and Deputy Director of Strategic Programs and Partnerships

MING DYNASTY

Hami
Shazhou
Jiayu Pass
Liangzhou
Taiyuan
Jinan
Qingzhou
Luzhou
Kaifeng
Ruzhou
Fengyang
Yangzhou
Changzhou
Xi'an
Songjiang
Huzhou
Jiaxing
Chengdu
Wuchang
Hangzhou
Shaoxing
Ningbo
Jingdezhen
Wenzhou
Nanchang
Changsha
Guiyang
Quanzhou
Guilin
Zhangzhou
Weijiang
Liuzhou
Guangzhou
Chaozhou
Huizhou
Nanning
Shanhai Pass
Juyong Pass
Shuntianfu

INTRODUCTION

ince the founding of the Ming dynasty, the world has been fascinated by the porcelains produced at the imperially supervised kilns at Jingdezhen—to the extent that "Ming" has become synonymous with fine Ming porcelains. For centuries, studies of porcelain focused on the technology required to make these wares and their methods of distribution. Only in more recent years have scholars begun to study more closely the roles played by these materials in the overall context of the Ming court. The same can be said of other imperially sponsored arts like lacquerware; extensive studies have been undertaken on the materials and methods of production, while studies of their actual use and the roles of both the art and centers of production are relatively new.

A different issue faces those who study paintings of the Ming dynasty. (For a more complete discussion of Ming court painting, see Richard Vinograd's essay in this catalogue.) Starting at least as early as the writings of Dong Qichang (1555–1636), there has been a strong preference for the arts of the educated elite, the so-called "southern school," and a sense of disdain for paintings created by court and professional artists of the "northern school." In recent years this bias has spread; interest in the arts and material culture of the Ming dynasty has focused on those products created by and for the educated elite. The dichotomy between these groups has been emphasized at the expense of what was in fact a dynamic interaction. Each "school" exerted considerable influence on the other: many "amateur" painters were members of the official bureaucracy (Dong Qichang himself served the imperial family as a tutor), while the emperors of the late Ming actively cultivated some elements of the literati lifestyle. The relationship between the arts commissioned by members of the court and those of the educated elite is only one of many that changed dramatically during the Ming dynasty.

THE IMPERIAL CAPITALS

During the middle half of the fourteenth century, a series of natural disasters hit China, adding to the misery of a people suffering under the harsh rule of the Mongol Yuan dynasty (*CHC,* vol. 7, pp. 11–57). Occurrences of social unrest and outright revolt increased, and groups of roving and desperate souls began to band together into larger armies. The leader of one of these groups was Zhu

Yuanzhang (1328–1398), an orphan who had lost his family to an epidemic of smallpox (and who had survived the disease, deeply scarred, himself). Zhu had spent part of his younger years in a Buddhist monastery. By 1368 he headed the army that overthrew the Mongol rulers of the Yuan dynasty. As the Hongwu emperor, he ruled over the dynasty he named *Da Ming* ("Great Brightness" or "Great Hope"), which would last for 276 years.

Primary among the concerns of the Hongwu emperor was to establish the legitimacy of his dynasty; the nature of works of art commissioned by him and other early rulers was largely dictated by this concern. Given the need for an appropriately imperial presence, the painting styles preferred at the early Ming court were based on those that had been practiced at the court during the Song dynasty. Other works of art tended to be large scale, elaborately decorated, meant for use in rituals and ceremonies, and full of auspicious meanings. They served a dual purpose, with their actual function often being secondary to their symbolic value. An example is the preference for the color red for lacquers (see cat. nos. 47, 50, 51, 53–55) and for the decoration on certain types of ceramics (cat. nos. 68, 75). The Chinese term for this red is *zhu*, which was both the surname of the Ming imperial family and the Ming dynastic color. Dragons, phoenixes, and other auspicious symbols of peace, prosperity, and the rebirth of Chinese civilization were also common in court-sponsored arts throughout the dynasty (see cat. nos. 5, 32, 53–55).

More than individual works of art, however, the establishment of a capital city with an appropriately imperial presence was critical to the first emperor of the Ming dynasty. Even before his final conquest of the Mongols, the Hongwu emperor had chosen Nanjing as his capital city and begun to build suitable structures (*CHC*, vol. 7, pp. 55–57). Nanjing lay in the heart of the Jiangnan region, far from the Yuan capital in Beijing, in an area that was China's wealthiest and home to many of the educated elite.

The details surrounding the selection of artisans, commissioning of works, and their delivery to the court during the Hongwu reign are not entirely clear. Later in the dynasty, eunuchs ran a complex system in which different handicrafts and art forms were either created at workshops within the court or commissioned from regional workshops and shipped to the capital. The Hongwu emperor, however, did not trust eunuchs; thus their numbers and influence were smaller at his court.

A labor service levy system was central to the Ming tax structure, and it was the method by which most basic laborers were recruited for the creation of the crafts and other materials destined for the court. (For a discussion of this system see *CHC*, vol. 8, pp. 477–86.) From court records and the remains of the Ming capital in Nanjing, it is clear that this labor service system was put in place during the Hongwu reign, along with an elaborate network to supply construction materials. This exhibition includes a brick (cat. no. 88) ordered from Tongcheng in Anhui province, and a water downspout (cat. no. 94) made of limestone from a source near Nanjing.

Nanjing (literally "southern capital") was the primary Ming capital from 1368 until the reign of the Yongle emperor (1403–1424), who established his capital at Beijing ("northern capital"). Following the move of the primary capital to Beijing in 1420, Nanjing served as the secondary capital with diminishing administrative significance until the end of the dynasty in 1644 (*CHC,* vol. 8, p. 82). Unlike Beijing, it did not serve as a capital during the following Qing dynasty; many of the Ming structures in Nanjing remained virtually untouched throughout the Qing until they were destroyed during the Taiping rebellions of the 1850s.

Zhu Di, who ruled as the Yongle emperor, usurped the Ming throne from his nephew in 1403. While some construction continued in Nanjing during his reign (including the Bao'ensi, or Temple of Gratitude, which was not completed until the following Xuande reign, 1426–1435), the Yongle emperor spent a great deal of the state's resources on building a new capital at Beijing. Zhu Di had been given the title Prince of Yan (the area around Beijing) by the Hongwu emperor, and his center of power was there. Shortly after taking the throne, he began the process of moving the Ming capital to Beijing. Construction began there in 1406 (Naquin 2001, p. 110).

Unlike Nanjing, Beijing was far from China's agricultural, social, and economic center. Almost every necessity had to be shipped to the city. Nevertheless, the Yongle emperor set about building a capital of even grander scale than that of Nanjing. As a usurper whose legitimacy of rule was very much in question, he needed a capital of indisputable imperial qualities and placed great emphasis on monumentality in a cosmologically imperial layout. He drew the materials for his capital from all parts of China. The large columns and beams were made of *nanmu,* the softwood preferred for large-scale, high-level construction, which had to be imported from as far away as Sichuan province. Stone, tiles, and the full range of building materials were brought from areas around China noted for each. This not only meant that the best materials were available for building the imperial capital but also demonstrated the emperor's control over the vast Ming territories. Transportation of this material was extremely challenging until repairs on the Grand Canal were substantially completed in 1415, nine years after construction had commenced. The Yongle emperor placed this massive undertaking of building a new capital, as he did many of the other enterprises of his reign, under the control of the court eunuchs (*CHC,* vol. 8, pp. 21–24).

During the first decades that Beijing served as the Ming capital, the infrastructure was not in place to support massive numbers of workers who would have been employed in imperial workshops. Instead the necessary materials were commissioned from regional workshops and assembled at the palace. For some materials, this established a tradition that was to continue for the rest of the dynasty. For example, the imperial fabric workshops remained in Nanjing, Hangzhou, and Suzhou (see cat. nos. 29, 39, and 42). Other workshops were located near supplies of the raw materials; the porcelains kilns at Jingdezhen,

Jiangxi province, are an excellent example (cat. nos. 67–87). Many other materials were ordered from places of local manufacture as part of the Ming tax structure. Eunuchs were involved in selecting these materials or inspecting them to ensure that they were fit for imperial consumption. Eunuchs also communicated designs and specific requests from the court to these workshops and oversaw production. (See He Li's essay on Ming porcelains in this catalogue for a further discussion of porcelain production and the role played by eunuchs.)

Over time, the infrastructure became available to enable many specialized workshops to move to the capital. By the end of the dynasty, Beijing had an enormous population serving the needs of the imperial family as well as the official bureaucracy. Specialized artisans who worked within the imperial compound were registered, and their services considered part of the service levy. Some estimates place the number of members of the imperial family supported by the state as high as sixty thousand by the end of the dynasty (*CHC,* vol. 8, pp. 24–25). A vast array of objects to serve the needs of the imperial household, from the simplest bowl for eating rice to items used in the most elaborate court rituals, were created by these specialized artisans.

The city of Beijing changed considerably during the 224 years it served as the Ming capital. As mentioned above, the emphasis during the early years had been on legitimizing dynastic rule, and, by necessity, most construction efforts had focused on creating an imperial capital that reflected the power and glory of the Ming court. By the 1500s this phase of building was complete, transportation systems and other infrastructures were in place, and the imperial palaces had come to include large numbers of warehouses, workshops, and housing for eunuchs and artisans. According to Ray Huang, "together they formed a service and supply center that was undoubtedly the largest of its kind in the world at that time (*CHC,* vol. 8, p. 115).

By the end of the dynasty, the major building activities in Beijing were no longer palace or administrative structures but rather temples, many commissioned by eunuchs or imperial family members, and gardens built by the educated elite, often following traditions of the Jiangnan area. (See Naquin 2001, pp. 187–90, on the creation of villas in the Ming capital; and ibid., pp. 280–83, on the sights and nature of the city in the late Ming.) Members of the imperial household were not immune to these trends; they built gardens reflecting contemporary taste and furnished them in contemporary styles. Hardwood furniture and other items normally associated with the taste of the Jiangnan educated elite (see cat. nos. 60–63, 66) were commissioned by members of the court, blurring the lines of distinction between "court" taste and "literati" taste emphasized by studies of Chinese paintings and the writings of late Ming theorists such as Dong Qichang. However, even in these materials there was a greater focus on images suggestive of good fortune and harmony within the state. This was dictated in part by the role of the emperor (cat. nos. 56–58).

FOREIGN RELATIONS

A dichotomy—and often conflict—existed between the role of the emperor and his court and that of the Confucian-educated members of the state bureaucracy. This was especially true in the area of foreign relations. By its very nature, the Confucian bureaucracy was conservative on foreign affairs, preferring to focus on the proper running of the domestic infrastructure. The often difficult relations with neighboring states were left to the emperor, his court advisors (frequently made up of eunuchs), and the military.

With some exceptions, the later Ming emperors tended to devote less time and resources to foreign affairs than the earlier emperors. Combined with the attitudes of the official bureaucracy, this led to an increasingly isolationist point of view during the Ming. By the end of the dynasty, the state was unprepared for the arrival of the West. The small gun in this exhibition (cat. no. 98) demonstrates the Ming decline in military technology. At the beginning of the dynasty, China led the world in the use of gunpowder and related technologies. By the end of the dynasty, they relied on Jesuits to upgrade their outmoded armaments.

Even at the beginning of the Ming, foreign relations were defined by China's view of itself as the "central state" and the emperor as the "Son of Heaven" with a divine right to rule. Within this structure, the Ming court did not trade for goods with foreign powers, but instead received tribute and bestowed gifts of imperial favor. The early emperors, who sought to prove their legitimacy and to secure their borders against the still-powerful Mongol forces, actively sought signs of homage from other states. One example that has recently received a great deal of attention in the West is the explorations of the eunuch Zheng He, which were undertaken at the behest of the Yongle emperor. These were massive expeditions, involving up to twenty-seven thousand men on flotillas of enormous ships (*CHC,* vol. 8, pp. 320–21). The shipyards in Nanjing where these vessels were built have recently been excavated, and examples of the timbers used for these ships are included in this exhibition (cat. no. 65). Although they reached as far as Africa, these journeys were not inspired by a desire to explore, to expand trade, or even to exert direct dominance. Rather, they sought tokens of recognition. They left little incentive for private exploration on the part of those who traveled on them and had little lasting impact on the Ming court, which became increasingly isolationist under the emperors that followed (ibid.).

Examples in this exhibition of works of art presented as signs of Ming imperial favor include a lacquered wood sutra cover (cat. no. 49) and thangka (cat. no. 29), both made at court workshops during the reign of the Yongle emperor. These works were clearly designed to show the superiority of Ming workmanship and, by association, of the dynasty and its emperor. The conspicuous inclusion of the imperial reign mark emphasized this function. Other arts were made for the same purpose or to fit the desires of foreign states with which the Ming emperor sought a positive relationship. The trade in porcelains from the imperially supervised kilns at Jingdezhen has been studied at some length. As He Li points out in her essay, porcelain began to replace metal in a number of ritual uses, and to replace silk as the material most sought from the imperial workshops. Another material favored for presentation was carved lacquer (see cat. nos. 47–55).

In exchange for these presentation pieces, the Ming court sought a variety of items as "tribute." Some were curiosities, like the animals—including a giraffe—brought back from Zheng He's expeditions. (A Ming-dynasty painting of this animal exists in the collection of the National Museum of China.) There was also human trade, including young girls from Korea and eunuchs from various parts of the world, that served the personal needs and desires of the Ming emperors (*CHC,* vol. 8, pp. 291–92). Some foreign materials filled other needs at the Ming court. The mining and casting of bronze had reached such a low point in the Ming that adequate raw material for coinage became a real issue. As He Li points out in her essay on Ming metalwork, the Xuande emperor (1426–1435) went so far as to make special orders of bronze from Thailand for the creation of incense burners and other metal items central to court rituals. Silver, taken in exchange for porcelains, was used for tea items and other luxury goods, and it became important for the monetization of the Chinese economy in the late Ming (*CHC,* vol. 8, pp. 456–57). The sources of this silver varied, but a fair amount was taken by Europeans from native peoples in the Americas.

Ming relations with the Mongols provide insights into the nature of presentation pieces and "tribute." The Ming had continuous problems with the Mongols, particularly with Temur (also known as Tamerlane; ruled 1369–1405), who held forth from Samarkand. But China had a strong desire to trade with Central Asia, where they sought horses, cobalt, furs, and jade (see cat. nos. 1, 11, 20–26). The primary sources for jade, the stone most loved by the Chinese, were in parts of Central Asia controlled by the Mongols or other nomadic people (Asian Art Museum 2007, pp. 37–40). During the early Ming, the trade link for jade was through the oasis of Hami. The Yongle emperor placed great importance on that link, and caravans moved freely and frequently across the old trade routes. The tribute missions came on a regular basis and, since the court bore many of the expenses of their travel and stay, could be a large financial burden for the Ming. The court entrusted much of the foreign trade to eunuchs, many of whom were foreign and Muslim.

After the death of the Yongle emperor in 1424, there was a period of retrenchment as Chinese military power and imperial control over merchants waned. In 1440 Esen became the ruler of the Western Mongols, or Oirats, in the Altai, the mountainous region north of Hami. His missions to Beijing were huge: 2,302 Oirats came in 1442, 1,867 in 1444, and 2,000 in 1449. (For a complete discussion of the relations between the Ming dynasty and states in Inner Asia, see *CHC,* vol. 8, pp. 221–71.) In 1446 he captured most of the oasis on China's borders, and in 1449 he defeated and took captive the Ming emperor. Esen was assassinated in 1454 and tribute began to flow again, but the Chinese complained of the poor quality of the jade. In 1488 Hami fell to powers centered in Turfan which controlled the jade mining regions. Still, tribute continued once a year, fueled in no small part by the Chinese desire for products, including jade. By the end of the 1500s, the Ming court was weak and unable to control trade with Central Asia or other parts of the world. Much of the fine imported jade ended up in flourishing private workshops in Suzhou.

OFFICIAL RELIGION

From the beginnings of the imperial state, China's emperors believed they were bestowed the divine right to rule, thus the common title "Son of Heaven." This right to rule was inherited from their ancestors, but it could be withdrawn at any time and bestowed upon another if Heaven so deemed. Emperors spent a vast amount of time and state resources assuring that this did not occur. Communication with heaven was through the ancestors and through a plethora of rites and rituals.

Worship of ancestors and their role as a means of communication with the cosmos have been foundations of Chinese ritual and religious practice since the Neolithic period. The great works of ceramics, bronze, jade, and other materials found in tombs from the Neolithic period through the Tang dynasty were made expressly for ancestor worship. This practice continued at various levels of society during the Ming. The large set of mortuary figures in this exhibition (cat. no. 96) is an example of goods made expressly for burial, as are the textiles, jades, jewelry, and other luxury materials excavated from the tombs in Nanjing and Beijing (cat. nos. 1–6, 8–9, 11–19, 30–31). The Bao'ensi (cat. nos. 89–92), which is dedicated to an empress, is an example of ancestor worship at the highest level.

Since the emperor maintained the "mandate of heaven" by performing the correct rituals and ceremonies at the right time, the majority of the many festivals and rituals in which the emperor had a central role are seasonal. By the Ming dynasty, there was at least one such festival or ritual every month. (For a more complete discussion of official religion during the Ming, see *CHC,* vol. 8, pp. 840–92. Romeyn Taylor provides a chart of these rituals divided into major, middle, and minor categories on pp. 843–45.) Astrology played a vital role in many of the major rituals, four of which were devoted to the sun (to mark the solstices and equinoxes), four concerned with offering to the ancestors, and others timed to the phases of the moon.

The proper performance and sequence of rituals were sources of frequent conflict between the emperor and the Confucian-educated elite (*CHC,* vol. 8, pp. 783–88). Some of these disagreements had a profound influence on artistic production at the court. For example, the demise of the Ming imperial painting academy has been attributed to the great rites controversy at the beginning of the reign of the Jiajing emperor (1522–1566). (For a description of the controversy, see *CHC,* vol. 8, pp. 851–61; for its impact on the painting academy, see Fong and Watt 1996, p. 364.)

These rituals took on a prescribed form with carefully determined and properly performed dance, movement, and sacrifices (*CHC,* vol. 8, pp. 841, 847–49). Other than general studies on seasonal badges and certain textiles (Simcox 2004; *ZGMSQJ,* vol. 7. pp. 44–46), the exact nature of the art used in each ceremony has not been fully studied. Incense burners (see cat. nos. 102, 109–11) were certainly important since the smoke of the magical herbs burned in them was another form of communication with cosmic forces.

Sacrifices would have been presented on works for which the symbolic value was as great, or greater, than the functional value. Large-scale objects decorated with bold designs with auspicious meaning or symbols of power were preferred over simple utilitarian vessels. Many of the elaborate lacquer plates and vessels (see cat. nos. 47–48), which can have had little practical application, might have been used in such ceremonies. As He Li notes in her essay, porcelains replaced metalwares for many ceremonial functions during the Ming. Again, visual appearance would have played a role equal to the actual function of the vessel in a given ritual. Large pieces decorated with images of good fortune and those that reflected the power and glory of the Ming rulers were certainly required. The large Hongwu-era jar with underglaze red dragon (cat. no. 68) might well have been created for ceremonial use.

CONFUCIANISM

By the Ming, Confucianism had taken on many of the trappings of religion, and the worship of Confucius as a deity was not uncommon. The Hongwu emperor (1368–1398), made great efforts to establish the Cheng-Zhu school of Confucianism as the official orthodoxy. He installed the National Academy in Nanjing, reinstituted the civil service examinations, and even went as far as banning the activities of all other competing religious sects (*CHC,* vol. 7, p. 122). Confucianism also saw imperial favor in the reigns of the Jianwen (1399–1402), Yongle (1403–1424), Hongxi (1425), Xuande (1426–1435), Hongzhi (1488–1505), and Jiajing (1522–1566) emperors. Emperors frequently clashed with their Confucian-trained advisors, as in the major contest over bureaucratic control between the Wanli emperor (1573–1619) and the Donglin partisans.

Various trends in Ming Confucianism have been examined in depth by Benjamin Elman (2001) and can be summarized as following a development from Cheng-Zhu orthodoxy to the Wang Yangming school, and reaching "evidential" (*kaozheng*) scholarship by the eighteenth century.

Art created under Confucian influence can be divided into three broad groups: images of Confucius, narrative illustrations of Confucian principles, and handbooks of court ritual. Confucius has been worshipped as a gentleman, teacher, sage, and deity. By the Ming, his image existed in two major kinds of representations: iconic portraits of him alone or with disciples, and depictions of his figure contextualized within a narrative (Murray 2002, p. 223). Print images and sculptures were favored by the court.

Narrative illustrations of the life of Confucius appeared in print as part of the mid-fifteenth-century popularity of pictorial biographies. The genre had existed in Buddhism and Taoism well before Zhang Kai (1398–1460), an imperial censor, published the Confucian version, *Shengji tu* (Wilson 2002, p. 29). *Shengji tu*, or Pictures of the Sage's Traces, offers a series of annotated illustrations that tell selected life stories of Confucius from his official biography in the *Shi ji*, or Records of History, by Sima Qian (approx. 145–86 BCE). Zhang later had them engraved in stone (Murray 2002, p. 225). The compilation provides insight into the role of the pictorial biography in endorsing orthodox Confucianism. *Shengji tu* focuses on episodes of Confucius's life that exemplify his moral character as a statesman, teacher, and gentleman. No longer extant, this court-sanctioned publication established what would become a genre, as different versions later appeared, some with the same or similar titles, with additional and/or deleted scenes. The later surviving compilations were private and commercial commissions.

Narrative illustrations of Confucius's teachings, depicting general episodes of exemplary moral conduct, ideal governance, and social harmony, were utilized by the court in numerous ways. For example, the emperor might have presented these works to his subordinates either to influence them or to display his own merits. Conversely, court officials might have presented such images to the emperor to influence him. And finally, albums were created for the education of a young emperor or crown prince (Murray 2007, pp. 74–75).

Not unlike Confucius's pictorial biography, these illustrations served didactic purposes. They animated for the Confucian reader obtuse values long expounded solely through texts. To see exemplars in action on the page was then thought to be a more expedient means of gaining knowledge. In the sixteenth and early seventeenth centuries, one school of Confucian thought led by eminent statesman Wang Yangming (1471–1529) came to dominate the mainstream (Cleary 1991, p. xxii). Wang emphasized a person's innate capacity for moral judgment and the mind as the portal to self-cultivation. Craig Clunas (1997, pp. 102–33) makes a case for the Ming belief in a direct link between acts of viewing and knowledge acquisition.

Sculptures of Confucius did not sustain court favor throughout the Ming. In 1530, Grand Secretary Zhang Cong (1475–1539) submitted a memorial to the Jiajing emperor calling for the wholesale destruction of clay images used in sacrificial offerings to Confucius, to be replaced by wooden tablets (*zhu*) bearing his name and title alone (Sommer 2002, p. 126). In the late fourteenth century, the Hongwu emperor had ordered the removal of sculptures of Confucius from the Imperial University (Clunas 1997, p. 101). Not until the late Ming was this decree implemented for the entire realm (save for Confucius's ancestral shrines at Qufu), as the clay images were systematically dissolved in water and the resulting paste used for mural paintings of clouds and mountains (Sommer 2002, pp. 95, 126).

Far from being an act of persecution against Confucianism, this decree signified increasing fervor for the sage's teachings. Offerings to a representation of Confucius (painted or sculpted) had been an imperial practice since the eighth century (Wilson 2002, p. 26); but especially in the sixteenth century, scholars began to question the validity of such idolatry. In what was to culminate in "evidential scholarship" (*kaozheng xue*), they scoured ancient texts for ritual precedents that supported the use of the word over Confucius's image.

The full effect of evidential studies in Confucianism can be seen in the court publications of ritual handbooks. In the early Ming, these compilations contained an abundance of illustrations. For example, the 1370 compendium entitled *Da Ming ji li* (Collected Rituals of the Great Ming) provides charts and diagrams of the schematic layouts of ritual paraphernalia and participants (Clunas 2007, p. 53). Another noted publication was the treatise compiled by the Ming crown prince Zhu Zaiyu (1536–1611) on *jikong yuewu,* the ritual dance and music performed in Confucian temples and during sacrificial offerings to Confucius (Lam 2002, p. 134). In it are diagrams of dancers demonstrating each step of the dance sequence.

Such handbooks consisted primarily of illustrations that inventory and describe the whole material apparatus of court rituals (Zito 1997, p. 8). Devoid of discussion or theory of ritual, they focus instead on the performance, advancing the rationale that "correct movement is correct practice" (Clunas 2007, p. 54). And for evidential scholars, correct movement was established in antiquity, calling for empirical investigations of classical texts.

BUDDHISM AND TAOISM

Both Buddhism and Taoism were actively supported by a number of Ming-dynasty emperors. However, their role in these religions was less central than in the state religion, and involvement varied from emperor to emperor. The drama of works like the large thangka (cat. no. 29) and the lacquered sutra cover (cat. no. 49) are clear evidence of the interest of the Yongle emperor in Tibetan Buddhism. This

The Forbidden City, Beijing

interest was based in part on politics, as well as on diplomacy and religious belief. He also supported Taoism, particularly the worship of Zhenwu. By the Ming dynasty, Buddhism had infiltrated the personal beliefs and lives of every level of Chinese society, including the imperial family. Many members of court were important patrons of Buddhist sites and temples in and around Beijing. (See Naquin 2001, pp. 19–48, for a complete discussion of Buddhist and Taoist temples in Ming-dynasty Beijing and the role of the imperial family in supporting them.)

Several emperors were castigated by the Confucian elite for the depth of their involvement in both Buddhism and Taoism. Both the Chenghua and Jiajing emperors were criticized for allowing Taoism to interfere with their running of the state. The influence of Taoism can clearly be seen in works produced at the imperial kilns during these two reigns (cat. nos. 77, 80–82, 85).

Ming was an appropriate title for a dynasty whose 276 years of rule were marked by stability, economic strength, and a dramatic flourishing of the arts. The influence of the Ming court rose and fell with the power and interests of each individual emperor, a rise and fall that can also be observed in the arts they commissioned. By the end of the dynasty, the imperial capital in Beijing was one of the largest cities in China and a center of great artistic creation and consumption. The imperial family, however, had lost its ability to rule, and the systems of governance they inherited from the first emperor were no longer adequate in the face of a rapidly changing world.

MICHAEL KNIGHT AND DANY CHAN

Pair of eardrops in the shape of the Herbal Goddess (plate 9)

Gold and Jade

HE LI

Within a short period of time, early Ming rulers evolved their own institutional guilds and structure. Their administrative support of arts and crafts resulted in ambitious productions of luxury goods. The dynastic founder Zhu Yuanzhang (1328–1398), having risen from the lowest peasant class, made some attempts to do away with the system of a hereditary ruling class. Immediately after being enthroned in 1368, Zhu implemented a practice that he had always advocated, reviving the traditional codified appearance of major imperial and political officials. These customs had long-standing importance. At the heart of the imperial autocracy lay a profound sense of principles and precise codes of etiquette reflecting the hierarchical social order. With a complex and extensive repertoire of dynastic elements, the imperial system of attire and headdress employed the whole body to signify hierarchy. A proper appearance served as political and socioeconomic expression among the nobility. Like Ming bureaucratic structure, Ming official attire drew heavily from the influences of the Tang (618–906) and Song (960–1279) dynasties.

The initial establishment of the attire and headdress system (1370–1379) was a function of the growth of the government. With complicated principles and highly detailed, exacting restrictions, the system was modified throughout the Ming dynasty by the Ministry of Rites. Each change and revision caused existing regulations to be more specific and refined.

Administrative planning, designing, ordering, manufacturing, collecting, and purchasing fell to the eunuchs in the Directorate of Palace Attendants, the principal institution governing the production of luxury goods and fine arts and crafts. The eunuchs were divided into twenty-four agencies by their respective subjects, such as the Bureau of Silver Works, the Bureau of Weaving and Dyeing, and the Clothing Service. In close cooperation with the eunuchs were the female servants in the Palace Women's Six Bureaus, founded in 1367. With a total staff of sixty, this service team initially included seven women for crown and jewelry, and ten for cloth. It was reorganized and enlarged several times with the expansion of the Directorate of Palace Attendants (*Mingshi*, chap. 2 and 74, pp. 167–168).

Throughout recorded history in China, gold and jade were considered the most ancient and luxurious materials at all levels of society. Their powerful and beautiful natural appearance was enhanced through the creation of forms connected with human life. Reflecting long-standing traditions, amber, rhinoceros horn, silver, and ivory were also desirable materials for use in art and adornment. Artworks and crafts making use of these materials served strikingly different functions and audiences: religious, funereal, political, military, and cultural. Luxury items awarded by the emperor to his subjects, concubines, and foreign envoys included jade belts, gold tables, pelts of marten, paintings, scholars' objects, and jewelry such as hairpins and earrings (*Mingshi*, chap. 63, p. 141).

Official attire was specified for various state functions, from sacrificial ceremonies to festival celebrations and the issuance of imperial edicts. Many measures were taken to differentiate among ranks. Specific regulations applied to material, color, and design, including a ban on the use of Mongolian-styled cloths. The Ming system of attire particularly emphasized

unity among the three major categories of dress: headdress (diadem, crown, and hat), belt (accessories), and cloth (see the introduction to the Textiles and Costumes section).

One of the first articles of clothing to be associated with the upper class was the headdress. A gold diadem with dragons was worn only by an emperor at grand ceremonies. A black silk hat was worn on a common day. On the top of this hat were two crescents resembling the Chinese character for "kindness" (*shan*), an element known as the "crown with wings of kindness" (see cat. no. 147). A formal jade or gold crown was limited to use by aristocracy during official audiences. Across the top of such a crown, raised ribs numbering from one to eight indicated official ranks (cat. no. 11). More commonly worn by officials was a black hat with a rectangular gauze wing on each side (cat. nos. 124–125). Crowns and caps, worn by both men and women over the hair bun or coil, were held in place with hairpins (cat. no. 12).

Lady Bi, wife of crown prince Qiyang Li Wenzhong (1339–1384), wearing a crown with phoenix ornaments, after a portrait.

The type of headdress worn by the empress and noblewomen during major ceremonies was a phoenix diadem (see cat. no. 146). Excavated phoenix crowns from Ming tombs reveal elaborately splendid manufacture. One crown could be inlaid with more than 5,000 pearls and more than 100 precious stones. Such a crown was worth 500 to 600 taels of pure silver, enough to purchase roughly 140,000 *jin* (154,000 pounds) of rice at that time. Less formal but still elaborate types included "floral" and "jewelry" crowns, adorned with a variety of designs and materials excluding imperial emblems (cat. nos. 6, 13).

Belt plaques in various shapes were attached to a leather belt wrapped in silk for display. Their number, medium, and decorative motifs distinguished grades of kinsmen and imperial civil servants. There were nine grades, with grade one being the most senior, or highest. Belt plaques were worn in sets of fourteen, fifteen, sixteen, or twenty, the last indicating the highest grade. Together with other twenty-belt sets unearthed from dated Ming tombs in Nanjing, the set included here (cat. no. 2) attests to a standardized system, in which thirteen of the twenty ornaments were arranged in the front and seven in the rear (Nanjing Municipal Museum 2000, pp. 24–48). In terms of medium, the first grade is distinguished by jade (cat. no. 1), the second by rhinoceros horn and gold with decoration, followed by plain jade or gold, silver, rhinoceros horn, and for the lowest rank, ivory and iron. The five-clawed dragon surrounded by auspicious clouds represented the authority of the Son of Heaven (the emperor), whose nobility could never be surpassed.

Strings of waist ornaments, after a woodblock book.

More common than these imperial luxury objects are small jewelry items for the forehead, chest, ears (cat. no. 9), fingers, arms (cat. no. 7), and waist (cat. no. 8); tools (cat. no. 17); and decorative additions for combs (cat. no. 10), headdresses (cat. no. 4), and clothes (buckles). Only an empress was allowed to wear up to twelve gold accessories; by contrast, wives of the lowest-ranking civil servants (grades seven, eight, and nine) were allowed to wear at most three such ornaments (*Mingshi,* chap. 66, p. 147).

The production of goldwares primarily involved techniques like smelting, casting, hammering, welding, beading, engraving, and filigree. To decorate the surface of gold objects, the most common methods employed were punching, chasing, embossing, tracing, engraving, and inlay. The group of ornaments from Nanjing exhibits mastery of goldsmithing from repoussé to chiseling, soldering, and joining separate parts by riveting and polishing (cat. nos. 13, 19). Some of these techniques were derived from those used for ancient bronze work, while some others were brought from western Asia.

Yellow gold is generally divided into two categories, "mountain gold" from mineral rocks, and "sandy gold." From a physical standpoint, gold does not oxidize, rust easily, or dissolve in acid or alkaline, and it has a high level of extensibility. Because silver does not possess these qualities to the same extent and is more readily available as a natural resource, it was far less precious than gold.

Mining jade, gold, and silver in China was the exclusive monopoly of the government. (For a recent study on Ming jade, see Asian Art Museum 2007.) Eunuchs played principal administrative roles in mobilizing these resources. Under imperial oversight the beginnings of a system evolved wherein eunuchs operated state affairs in return for the power, wealth, and trust given to them by the emperor. This system made possible the collection of gold, pearls, and treasures from all over the country and overseas, which made their way into the Forbidden City.

For example, every year from 1538 to 1577, the court sent eunuchs to Yunnan, Sichuan, Shandong, or Hebei, to collect and oversee the mining of silver, copper, and iron. The yearly "silver taxation" collected was about 4 to 4.5 million *liang,* or 200,00 to 225,000 kilograms (Zhang Xikong and Tian Jue 1987, p. 582). The government established offices along the southeastern and southern coasts to collect pearls in Zhejiang and Guangdong. The importance of these localities rested on their agricultural produce and above all on pearls, which had been used as tribute for centuries. A regular inventory of pearls collected (largely by eunuchs) in 1557 counted 90,000 pieces from Guangdong and 40,000 from Zhejiang (Zhang Xikong and Tian Jue 1987, p. 553).

Two-ridged official headdress, after an album of paintings.

Another source of gold and gems was tributes given from neighbor states that succumbed to the Ming's forceful coercion. In addition, the court purchased large amounts of these precious materials from Sri Lanka and India.

Local skilled artisans included tailors, jade cutters, leather makers, carpenters, and gold-smith craftsmen, among others. Government control over these artisans was codified by the drawing up of official registers. One type of imperial labor service demanded that these registered artisans pay "military dues." This service was organized by a rotation system, in which each artisan was obligated to work in the capital in shifts of three to six months during certain years. A 1525 memorandum to the Jiajing emperor appealed to reduce artisan recruits, based on current figures of such laborers that included 2,165 in the Bureau of Weaving and Dyeing, and 9,350 in the Directorate of Palace Attendants (Zhang Xikong and Tian Jue 1987, p. 510). The memorandum's criticism of the excessive cost of lavish life in the inner palace went mostly unheeded.

The imperial court asserted the prerogative of controlling and utilizing all aspects of the attire system. Elements worn by the royal classes that were taboo to civil servants and common people included certain colors, like blue (for ritual use), yellow (cat. no. 32), and purple; fine textiles such as brocaded silk and satin with gold threads (cat. nos. 31, 33); emblems of the five- and four-clawed dragon, and the phoenix; and materials of gold, jade, agate, amber, and coral (*Mingshi,* chap. 67, p. 149). When households with illicit goods were exposed, the owners were charged with committing the crime of placing themselves as superior to the emperor by secretly crafting belts and robes.

Seven-ridged official headdress, after a woodblock book.

From the late fifteenth century onward, some vassals, princes, titled military commanders, and eunuchs grew covetous of supreme titles. They frequently solicited the emperor for per-mission to own such precious and highly valued objects as the four-clawed-dragon robes. To address this embarrassing situation, the court reformulated an imperial edict in 1490 to prohibit submitting such requests (*Mingshi,* chap. 67, p. 149). Taking this as a provocation, numerous noblemen and eunuchs took matters into their own hands. Disregarding the ordinances, they commissioned massive jade belts and robes with royal emblems for their own private collections. These eunuchs and holders of power had come to dominate the court. Their manipulation of emperors for their own ambitious and nefarious purposes was the climax to the long financial decline in government, which eventually resulted in the dissolution of the Ming dynasty.

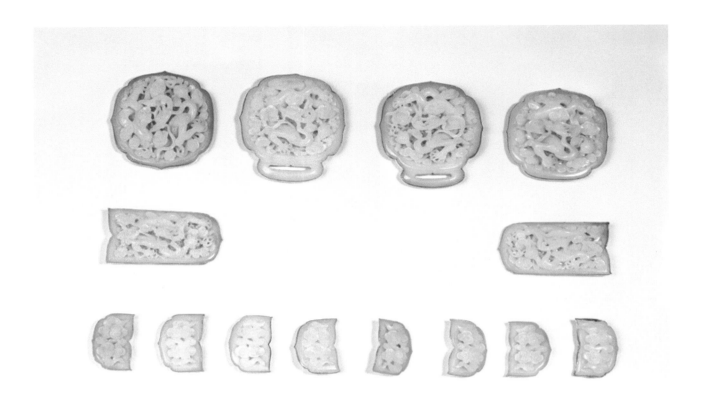

1

明洪武四年(1371年)　南京中央門外張家洼汪興祖墓出土　白玉鑲金托　龍雲帶十四塊

Belt ornaments of fourteen dragon plaques, buried 1371 (above, right, following two pages)

From the tomb of Wang Xingzu, outside the Central Gate, Nanjing

Reign of the Hongwu emperor (1368–1398)

Whitish nephrite with relief on gold mounts

H. 39 cm (15.35 in.), W. 62.2 cm (24.49 in.) (total, laid out)

Nanjing Municipal Museum

This is the only known set of jade-on-gold belt ornaments with five-clawed dragons from early Ming excavations. All of the fourteen sections were worked out of the best quality of white jade from Hetian, Xinjiang, in northwest China, each set into a form-matched gold mount. Probably because it was executed before 1393, when the Hongwu emperor issued a complete costume system to distinguish ranks, this belt set bears some irregular characteristics. Only fourteen sections were made—less than the Ming belt standard of twenty. The foliage outlines are distinctive compared to the more usual rectangular or square shape. Six main plaques are decorated with a running dragon amidst clouds; eight smaller ones with whirling clouds are accessories to the main ones. Making the best use of

available materials, the design is rendered in a generous portion of a high-relief dome, rather than the flat surface or thin body of the majority of Ming belt sets.

The two lobed medallions, each with a slit at the lower section, were probably the central pieces. They derive from a traditional design for the rear belt, from which small implements would have hung. The two rectangular plaques with one finial functioned on the opposite side as the end of the front belt. The eight small fittings would have flanked the main plaques.

Coming from an important excavation in 1972 (*Kaogu* 1972, no. 4, pp. 31–33), the whole set was found in the tomb of military general Wang Xingzu (1338–1371), whose foster father, Zhang Desheng (died 1360), posthumously known as the Duke of Cai,

was a famous navy commander. Wang himself achieved power under Xu Da (1332–1385) by competing with northern rivals for control of the Ming territory. Having proven his fighting ability on both land and water, Wang was appointed chief military commissioner of Shanxi. In the Ming expansion toward Sichuan, he fell in battle from an attack of thrown stones. His death was honored by the Hongwu emperor, who named him Marquis of East Triumph. Wang was granted privileges of nobility, including the right to use an emblem that was the emperor's monopoly—the five-clawed dragon. Considering his honest character, Wang would not have secretly violated the prohibition on using the five-clawed dragon. The set would very possibly have been a reward from the Hongwu emperor. HL

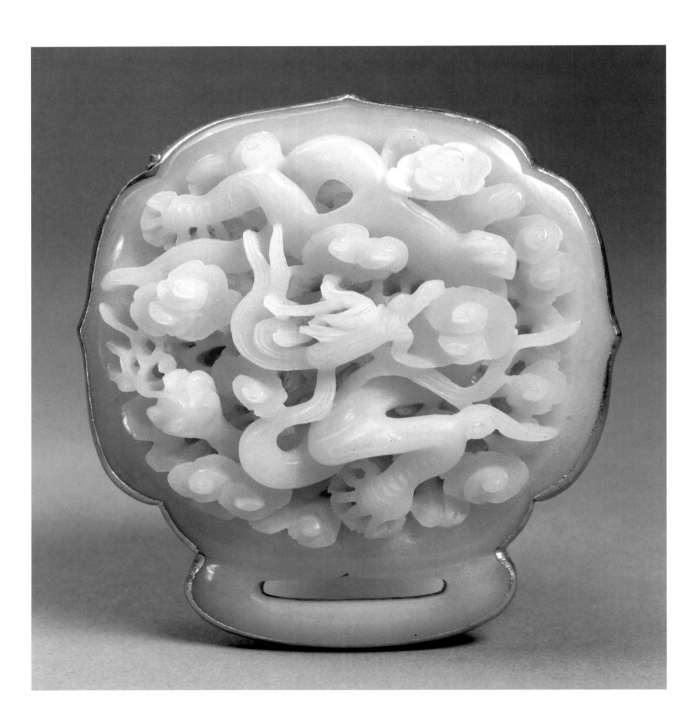

2

晚明　南京太平門外板倉出土　金製　雲蟒紋帶二十塊

Belt ornaments of twenty dragon plaques, approx. 1567–1619 (below, right, and page 30)

From an unidentifiable tomb at Bancang, outside the Taiping Gate, Nanjing

Gold with punching and repoussé designs

H. 33 cm (13 in.), W. 86.5 cm (34.06 in.) (total, laid out)

Nanjing Municipal Museum

Among all Ming archaeological finds from Nanjing, this golden belt set is unique. According to the Ming belt system issued in 1393, thirteen of the total twenty sections would have been worn at the front, and seven at the rear. Beautifully executed in model-pressed techniques, with gold sheets hammered around the edges to create thin borders, the set consists of six peach shapes, eight rectangular sections, four narrower rectangular ones, and two tails with domed ends. To affix the sections to a belt, they have serrated edges, small holes, or lugs at the rear for strapping or tying mounts.

The surfaces are embellished with the four-clawed dragon, *mang*, cavorting through cloudy oceans. With hair blowing and a curvy fishlike tail, the dragon has its mouth open to spew flames. The two sections bearing a front-facing dragon would have been the central pieces at the front and rear of the belt; the rest, with profiles, would have been facing each other opposite from the central piece. The four-clawed dragon was second in significance after the five-clawed dragon, reserved for imperial use. The former was used to indicate a high rank equivalent to prince, duke, or the like (*Kaogu* 1999, no. 10, pp. 40–41, pl. 1).

This set came to light in 1987 from an anonymous tomb between two grave clusters of illustrious families—those of Xu Da (1332–1385) and Li Wenzhong (posthumous Prince of Qiyang, 1339–1384). The Hongwu emperor chose his grave at a hill called Dulongfu, to the south of Purple Mountain (Zijinshan), and allocated the adjoining lands for cemeteries for his core subjects. No stone stele was found to determine the date or identity. Judging by the tomb's location and the person's high status indicated by the four-clawed dragon, the deceased was probably a descendant of either the Xu or the Li family. The latest date found on items from the tomb corresponds to the reign of the Longqing emperor (1567–1572). The burial time would likely have fallen in a period not later than the next reign, that of the Wanli emperor (1573–1619). HL

Front

Back

32

3

明洪武三年（1370年）　南京中央門外康茂才墓出土　金碗

Bowl, buried 1370

From the tomb of Kang Maocai, Duke of Qi, outside the Central Gate, Nanjing

Reign of the Hongwu emperor (1368–1398)

Gold

D. 8.3 cm (3.27 in.), H. 3.1 cm (1.22 in.)

Nanjing Municipal Museum

This bowl was created by hammering a round body with a slightly concave base and a raised line circling the waist. With no decoration on the surface, the bowl is striking in its simplicity and well-proportioned shape. Paired with a golden dish, the bowl came to light from the tomb of Kang Maocai (1313–1369), posthumously known as the Duke of Qi (*Kaogu* 1999, no. 10, pp. 14–15, pl. 5–15, 6–11). Kang was a mid-ranking officer in the service of Yuan Mongols. He was known as a Confucian scholar and dutiful son of his mother. Holding out against the Ming army at his base in Jiqing (Jiangsu province), he was forced to surrender. Kang then entered Ming service as a naval commander. Recruited by Xu Da (1332–1385) in the conquering of the northwest in 1368, Kang died the next year on the way back to Nanjing.

Under the Ming government, the trade of gold was prohibited for private possession. This ban has been verified by modern archaeology, for excavated gold items have come mainly from royal or noble tombs. Three-dimensional gold items are quite rare. Only two such examples have been found in Beijing: a round basin with a five-clawed dragon design from the Wanli emperor's tomb, Dingling (*ZGMSQJ*, vol. 10, p. 88, pl. 169), and a set of octagonal cups on a round dish from the tomb of the Chenghua emperor's father-in-law, Wan Gui (Shoudu Bowuguan 2001, pp. 112–15.). The latter, with designs of Eight Immortals over the Eastern Ocean surrounding the character for "longevity," presents the Taoist concept of immortality. In Taoist alchemy, stretching back into the third century, various utensils were used to make and drink elixirs—including bowl-and-dish sets, such as the one to which this item belongs. The presence of such utensils in a grave was significant because they reflected the values of the people they served in the afterworld. HL

4

明正德十二年（1517年）　南京太平門外板倉魏國公徐俌墓出土　銀製　雲托日月紋飾件一對

Pair of hair ornaments with the characters for "sun" and "moon," buried 1517

From the tomb of Duke Xu Fu, outside the Taiping Gate, Nanjing

Reign of the Zhengde emperor (1506–1521)

Silver with embossed and repoussé design

H. 3.75 cm (14.76 in.), W. 6.5 cm (25.59 in.)

Nanjing Municipal Museum

This pair was discovered beneath Xu Fu's head, suggesting an association with a headdress. The ornaments were produced by hammering silver sheets. Both are embossed with characters that mean "sun" and "moon." Together the two characters make up *Ming*, meaning "bright," the wording for the dynastic symbol. Xu Fu (1450–1517) was hereditary Duke of Wei. As a military commander, he rendered valuable assistance to the southern capital government in its attempts to improve legal and administrative measures. His honest fervor reflected a moral commitment to political governing in his quest to serve two emperors. As one of Xu Da's descendants, he inherited the privilege of using the grave land allotted by the Hongwu emperor; thus the shared tomb of Xu Fu and his two wives is located one hundred meters east of Xu Da's, in the outskirts of Nanjing (*Wenwu* 1982, no. 2, p. 30).

Worth mentioning is the cloud-head design, which was treated artistically, as well as philosophically, as the sacred fungus *lingzhi*, the magic plant on Taoist islands. For their sought-after magical powers, both clouds and fungus were revered in China from ancient times. As common motifs in art from the tenth century onward, they became alike in form. In gold and silver ornaments, the motifs were often embossed onto small petals for a headdress, with or without the characters "sun" and "moon." Various uses for character-containing ornaments are suggested by the positions they were buried in when found in tombs. An earlier gold pair was found being held by both hands of the mother (buried 1365) of Zhang Shicheng, self-proclaimed King of Wu in Suzhou (*Kaogu* 1965, no. 6, p. 289). A later pair was sewn on a cotton-padded mattress under the body of Lady Sheng (buried 1540), wife of a late Ming minister (*Dongnan wenhua* 1999.2, p. 30). Principally, however, the cloud-head ornaments were worn as emblems of the auspicious manifestation of heavenly eternity. HL

5

明正德十二年(1517年)　南京太平門外板倉魏國夫人、徐俌妻朱氏墓出土　金製　鳳凰雙飛髮簪一對

Pair of crown ornaments with phoenix on cloud, buried 1517

From the tomb of Duchess Xu at Bancang, outside the Taiping Gate, Nanjing

Reign of the Zhengde emperor (1506–1521)

Gold with granulations and filigree designs

L. 23.25 cm (9.15 in.), W. 6.5 cm (2.56 in.)

Nanjing Municipal Museum

Exhibiting the social prominence of the wearer, this pair of gold crown ornaments was meant to symmetrically adorn the upper component of a "phoenix crown," a traditional headdress for noblewomen. Mirroring those on Lady Shen's crown (see cat. no. 146), each ornament is formed of a long hooked pin with a phoenix-on-cloud finial. A long string of jewelry would have been suspended from each phoenix's mouth, falling over the shoulders. The phoenix's head and claws consist of a series of soldering granulations; the feathers, tail, and cloud employ intricate filigree work, giving the phoenix a sense of flying, to embody the old phrase "noble phoenix goes toward the sun." The ornaments were found inside the coffin of the former Duchess Xu, known as Lady Zhu, from a wealthy family. Lady Zhu, who died prior to her husband, was granted an equality to share the tomb with Duke Xu Fu, as well as with his subsequent Duchess Xu. Attesting to her first position among Xu's wives, her coffin was placed next to her husband's (*Wenwu* 1982, no. 2, pl. 4, fig. 2).

The wearing of crowns by women was very fashionable during the Northern Song period (960–1126), coming later than a parallel trend among men. In a ceremonial scene depicted on wall frescoes in an 1100 tomb in Henan, women are wearing large domed crowns with conical horns at the front and rear (Su Bai 1957). It was said that with such oversized crowns, women could not easily move around. Consequently, for practical purposes, female crowns were improved to be smaller in size and to use lighter materials. Still, for formal occasions Ming women wore splendid crowns that were heavy and sumptuous, often with long suspensions from the two upper components that bore the dragon, phoenix, or peacock accordingly by rank. Archaeological evidence reveals that the owners of this type of phoenix ornament included empresses, duchesses, and wives of ministers. HL

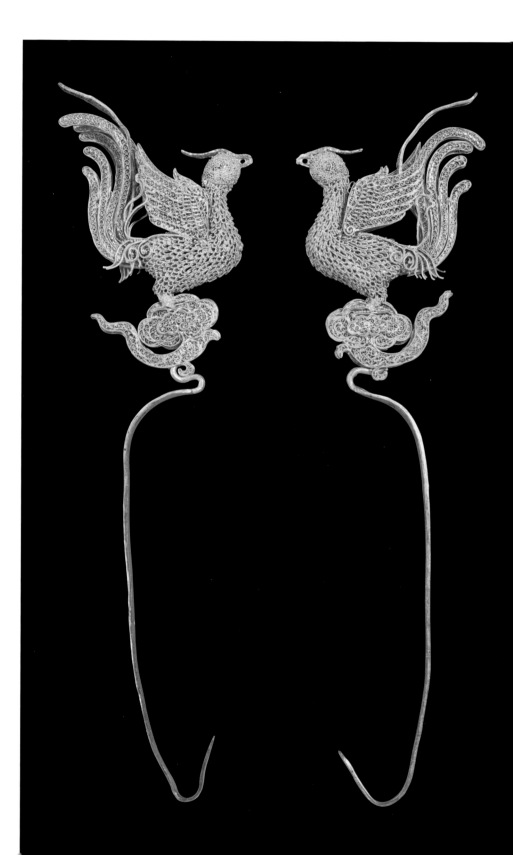

6

明正德十二年(1517年)　　南京太平門外板魏國夫人、徐俌妻王氏墓出土　　金製　　嵌寶石花葉冠飾

Hair ornament with gemstones, buried 1517

From the tomb of Duchess Xu at Bancang, outside the Taiping Gate, Nanjing

Reign of the Zhengde emperor (1506–1521)

Gold with repoussé design and gemstone inlay

H. 8.25 cm (3.25 in.), W. 6.5 cm (2.56 in.)

Nanjing Municipal Museum

This gold ornament with gemstone inlays was made for the second Duchess Xu, Lady Wang, who would have used it for her hairdo (*Wenwu* 1982, no. 2, pp. 32–33). The piece successfully converts a decorative design found on crafts and porcelain into a triangular openwork suitable for a female crown. The solid triad in the center creates an auspicious symbol; it resembles the triangular-leafed arrowroot (*cigu*), whose first character is a homonym for the word "compassionate" (*ci*). The openwork sets the foliate scrolls. Framed either by a filigree sunflower or beading, the ten gemstone inlays display a colorful arrangement: a central yellow topaz above a small malachite; a red ruby glimmering at the top and bottom; two blue topaz (aquamarine) sitting symmetrically on both sides; and four missing gems, probably pearls, which set off the four corners.

Chinese goldsmithing with green-colored gemstone inlays goes as far back as the Bronze Age (approx. 1300 BCE). Beginning in the Han dynasty (206 BCE–220 CE), influenced by exotic fashions from the Hellenistic world that entered China by the Silk Road, metal ornaments were inlaid with multiple gemstones, showing red and green against gold. The best examples from eighth-century tombs assemble six or seven colored materials. During the Ming period, gemstones were mainly supplied from Sri Lanka as a result of Zheng He's expeditions to Southeast Asia (see cat. no. 65). According to the imperial house inventory, the presents from Sri Lanka to the Yongle emperor included gemstones. Ming author Huang Sheng in his record on foreign tributes verified "six precious gemstones" including blue topaz from Sri Lanka. Due to their precious nature—and often exotic sources—gemstones were found to be much less in use than gold. This ornament is an impressive example of the admiration and enthusiasm that the Ming upper class felt for gemstones. HL

7

明中期　金製　"尚官局"　監造銘文款腕釧　南京市博物館

Gold spiral bracelet with inscription, approx. 1500–1550 (above and right)

Discovered on the outskirts of Nanjing

D. 7.0 cm (2.75 in.)

Nanjing Municipal Museum

This is one of six gold spiral bracelets excavated from Ming sites in Nanjing, carrying the inscription translated below (Nanjing Municipal Museum 2000, pp. 155–58). The bracelet was made by coiling a narrow hammered strap into ten circles, which are secured with tensely wound wires at both ends. Engraved on the interior at one end, the inscription is a specific record of its crafting. It was commissioned by the Imperial General Service, obviously for a court lady, and was crafted at a workshop supervised by Zhang Si, who may also have been a craftsman himself. General Service was the leading agency of the Palace Women's Six Bureaus, among which the female staff were distributed. These agencies were responsible for managing the ceremonial

and everyday needs of the court. Established during the Hongwu reign, the Six Bureaus (or Six Services) were later reorganized by the Yongle emperor to be under the supervision of the palace eunuchs, or Palace Domestic Service as referred to in the inscription.

Writings before the year 600 define bangles as "arm circles." During the Tang dynasty (618–906), the term "hand bangles" appears in literature. Because of the precious material, gold bangles and bracelets are rare in comparison to other ornaments. The earliest known gold bangles were found in the Pinggu district of Beijing, datable to the late Shang dynasty (approx. 1600–1050 BCE; *Wenwu* 1977, no. 11, p. 6). Early works were fashioned in a single circle. Spiral

bracelets have not been seen prior to the Ming discoveries. The only pair from a dated tomb were buried with Lady Wang in 1517 (see cat. no. 6). The six known Ming spiral bracelets vary in number of circles, from seven to ten, twelve, and thirteen. Three have plain surfaces; the other three are adorned with repoussé designs of seasonal flowers. All contain stylistic qualities of the time.

Inscription: *To General Service / made of 90 percent gold / each costs ten liang [1.76 ounces] / supervised by Zhang Si and others / Head of the workshop under Palace Domestic Service*（尚官局玖成金每只壹十两内使監造作頭張四等）．HL

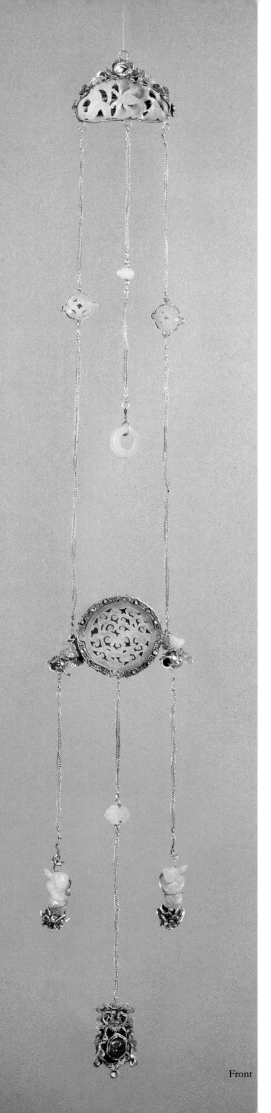

Front

8

明中期　南京太平門外板倉魏國公徐達家族墓出土　金鑲嵌寶石青玉佩
玎璫綬

String of waist ornaments, approx. 1450–1550 (left and immediate right)
From the tomb of a descendant of Xu Da, outside the Taiping Gate, Nanjing
Nephrite, gemstones, and gold with punched, inlaid, and repoussé designs
H. 485 cm (17.71 in.)
Nanjing Municipal Museum

Another discovery from a tomb of one of Xu Da's descendants (see cat. nos. 2 and 4), this string of ornaments was meant to be worn around the waist, trailing down the symmetrical sides of a dress (*Wenwu* 1993, no. 2, p. 68, fig. 22). As frequently documented, these waist ornaments would make crisp sounds as the wearer walked; the heavy weight of gold and jade would prevent a well-behaved wearer from hurrying and scurrying around. For such purposes, waist ornaments were variously referred to as a "prehensile stride," "jingle jangle," and "hanging" in Ming official records. With distinguishing colors of green, yellow, red, or purple, executed in jade or gold, a hanging of ornaments would indicate the social status of the wearer.

This set represents a traditional style of waist strings conveying a Taoist concept— longevity. Its fine manipulation integrates techniques of goldsmithing and stone carving. The set is assembled with three parts: a head pendant, a waist pendant in the middle, and three long chains. The head pendant, in a cloud-head shape with golden filigree borders, has inlays on one face of two rubies and a blue gemstone,

and on the other, floral openwork in green nephrite. A top loop was used to affix the set to the waist; three rings on its lower edge suspend the gold chains. Each of the chains is further accented by small pendants in a gold frame with green nephrite or ruby inlays, forming a gourd, a butterfly, a double lozenge, and a boy standing on a lotus pedestal. The two side chains are attached to the round waist pendant, which has an inlay of green nephrite with a fungus design symbolizing immortality. The central chain is cut off by the waist pendant; its upper section suspends a ring, and the lower section has inlays on both sides, showing a red ruby amidst gold leaves and a green nephrite leaf.

The earliest known images of women wearing waist ornaments of this kind appeared on the outer slabs of the stone coffin found in the tomb of Prince Yide (682–701) in Xi'an, on which were carved two court ladies standing face to face (*Wenwu* 1972, no. 7, p. 27). The waist pendants they wear stylistically match their hair ornaments and formal clothing. Clearly, waist ornaments of the Tang dynasty were the prototypes for this example. HL

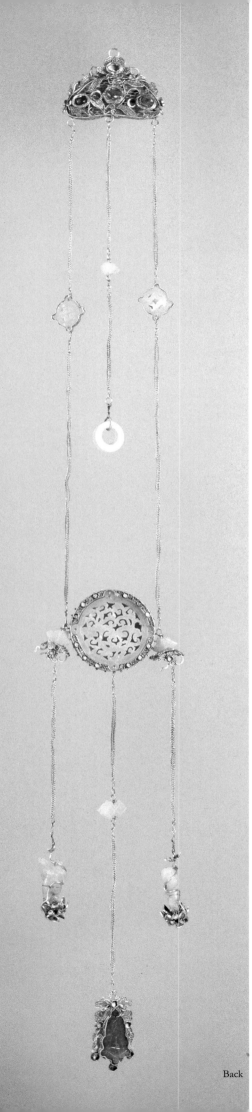

Back

9

明中期　南京太平門外板倉魏國公徐達家族墓出土　金製　藥仙採靈芝耳墜一對

Pair of eardrops in the shape of the Herbal Goddess, approx. 1500–1600
(detail above and page 22)
From the tomb of a descendant of Xu Da, outside the Taiping Gate, Nanjing
Gold with inlays of gemstones
Figure: H. 5 cm (1.97 in.), W. 1.8 cm (0.71 in.)
Overall: L. 10.75 cm (4.23 in.)
Nanjing Municipal Museum

Among extant Ming eardrops, this exuberant gold pair stands out in its originality and quality. Borrowing from ancient images of the Herbal Goddess, the design combines the female adept and a classical S-shaped ear hook into highly finished, three-dimensional masterpieces. Here the Herbal Goddess, who was worshipped as a Taoist adept since the Tang dynasty, is identified by her backpack containing the magical fungus *lingzhi,* the essential diet of immortals. She is dressed in a shawl and a skirt, both made of double-layered lotus petals. Her hair is neatly swept up and held in place with a foliated crown. Above the goddess is a four-layered, lotus-shaped umbrella with six kernel-shaped filigree compartments and inlays of red and blue gemstones. She stands on a lotus with inlays of gemstones and pearls that are missing, leaving only gold circular frames. Again, such fine work revealing incredibly complicated goldsmithing came to light from a tomb of Duke Xu's family (*Wenwu* 1993, no. 2, p. 67, fig. 16).

The ancient term *erzhen,* literally "ear-jade," was gradually abandoned; instead, the new terms "earring" and "eardrop" became popular after the 400s. The latter two were considered in Ming sources to be interconnected with crown accessories. One Ming statistic shows that of 267 eardrops and earrings registered, about 30 percent were eardrops (*Wenwu* 2001, no. 7, p. 79). About twenty-some pairs of eardrops have been unearthed from Ming aristocratic tombs in six provinces. Those with Taoist motifs depict gourds, flowers, clouds, and paradise with palaces. The introduction of gold-smithing among these examples was primarily due to the influence of Islamic culture. A Tang dynasty gold eardrop found in Yangzhou, a seaport on the east coast, was presumably of Western Asian origin (*ZGG JWWJ* 1996, p. 126, pl. 114); the methods it employs—punching, chasing, ring matting, embossing, and inlaying—would all become Ming goldsmith applications. HL

10

明中期　南京中華門外長崗村出土　金製　鴛荷塘池紋梳背

Comb-spine cover with mandarin ducks, approx. 1450–1600 (above)

From Changgang village, outside the Zhonghua Gate, Nanjing

Gold with repoussé design

L. 9.5 cm (3.74 in.), W. 1.5 cm (0.59 in.)

Nanjing Municipal Museum

This adornment was created to cover a comb spine. A thin gold sheet was formed into an arch-shaped trough to hold the spine. The outer surface is rendered with a repoussé design depicting a pair of swimming mandarin ducks on alternating lotus blossoms and foliate scrolls. By tradition, mandarin ducks were regarded as beneficent creatures; a pair of them was associated with a loving couple. The lotus was an emblem of fertility, standing for numerous progeny. Thus the pictorial iconography embodies symbolic meanings representing an old saying, "a happy marriage with many sons."

Early bone and jade examples of comb-like hairpins with coarse teeth have been unearthed from Shang dynasty tombs of important people (approx. 1600–1050 BCE). Their upper ridges or comb spines were often adorned with bird or animal forms for decorative and expressive effect.

Surviving combs from the Han through Tang dynasties increasingly used a variety of materials, including metal, ivory, and wood. They often depicted, on their upper ridges, scenes from classical mythology. Archaeological evidence reveals that the highly decorative style of Tang combs changed during the Song dynasty to a simple, plain, semispherical form. It is rare to see excavated comb-spine covers separated from combs datable before the Ming dynasty. Ming combs became shorter and rectangular in form, with or without an arch ridge (*Kaogu* 1985, no. 6, p. 542). Still, the majority of Ming combs were discovered without covers. Less than ten in number, Ming comb-spine covers have been discovered mainly in the Nanjing area. Similar in form, the repoussé decorations on them tend to be feminine, such as lotuses, plums, peonies, bamboo, and chrysanthemums (Nanjing Municipal Museum 2000, pp. 151–54). The fad for gold comb-spine covers was fashionable only for a short period among Ming upper-class women in the metropolitan area. HL

11

明天启五年（1625年）　南京將軍山黔國公沐昌祚墓出土　金製　六梁束
髮冠—碧玉簪

Six-ridged court headdress and jade hairpins, buried 1625 (below left)

From the tomb of Mu Changzuo at Mount Jiangjun, Nanjing

Reign of the Tianqi emperor (1621–1627)

Gold with repoussé and openwork designs

Crown: L. 10.25 cm (4.04 in.); hairpin: L. 10.3 cm (4.1 in.)

Nanjing Municipal Museum

Different from daily casual scarves and hats, this gold headdress was used to show the social status of a noble-man. The hollow cap was designed to enclose a topknot of long hair, as Chinese men did not cut their hair until modern times. The upper crown is divided by six raised ribs into seven lobed bands. Each side is enclosed with a large opening to hold a feather or ornaments, and a small hole for a hairpin to penetrate. The hat brim was encircled by horizontal ribs. The pair of dark green nephrite hairpins have a domed head and taper to a rounded tip. They were found in the tomb, inserted halfway in the holes on the crown's sides (*Kaogu* 1999, no. 10, p. 46, pl. 4).

A headdress, with high petals around the brim and raised ridges across the upper cap, was a formal ridged crown for imperial civil servants to wear in the court. The number of ridges distinguished the three titles of nobility and nine ranks of civil servants. An eight-ridged crown denoted a duke; seven ridges, a marquis, count, or grade-one civil servant; and six ridges, grade two. More often seen in archaeological evidence from Ming burials are simplified forms without high petals around them, probably worn outside the court. Yet the number of ridges might not exactly match the rank of the tomb occupant. As in the case here, the six ribs were more modest

than the eight allowed for the hereditary title Duke of Qian, which the Mu family had won.

Jade hairpins have been in use since the Neolithic period. From the Han dynasty onward, hairpins were put to a practical use when the hair-crown became part of the uniform system worn by officials at court. Hair-crowns of gold, silver, jade, agate, amber, bamboo, and wood have all been unearthed from burials, though crystal and ivory were also used as materials according to descriptions in Ming texts. HL

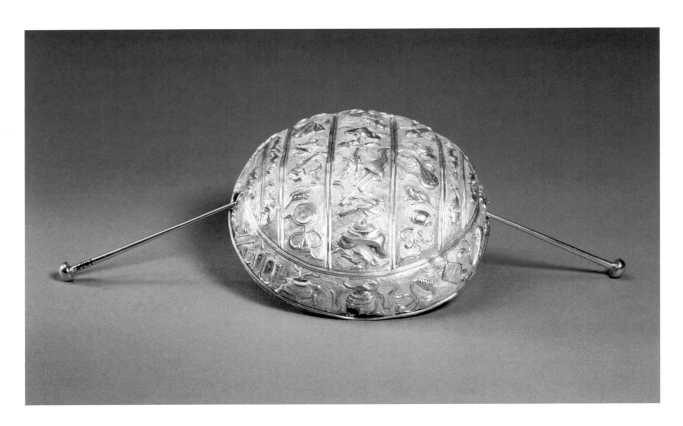

12

葬於清朝順治年間　南京中華門外鄧府山佟卜年夫人陳氏墓出土　金製　雜寶紋包髻

Hair clasp with a design of various treasures, approx. 1647–1658

From the tomb of Lady Chen, wife of Tong Bonian, in Dengfushan, outside the Zhonghua Gate, Nanjing

Gold with repoussé design

D. 9.2 cm (3.62 in.)

Nanjing Municipal Museum

A round hair clasp was a type of female headdress to enclose a coiled topknot of hair. Made of gold and adorned with distinctive designs, this particular piece was worn by a noblewoman on formal or special occasions. The dome top is divided by ribs into seven bands, each with chased designs in shallow relief. Two holes for hairpins are placed on opposing sides of the rim frame. The designs present more than ten motifs drawn from Taoism and popular belief. Treasures—a conch, horn, sacred mushroom, drum, vase, incense burner, ingot, book, fan, painting,

crane, peacock, instruments, ribbons, and clouds—are all blessing symbols with multiple meanings of long life, wealth, nobility, and prosperity.

Along with the piece of heart-shaped amber (cat. no. 19) and another 137 items, this piece was found in the tomb of Lady Chen (1589–1647), close to her head (*Kaogu* 1999, no. 10, p. 57). An inscription on a stone stele attached to the tomb gate states that her coffin had previously been moved five times; she was finally reburied in Nanjing. The inscription was written by her son-in-

law, who died in 1658. It is possible that this piece was commissioned by her son upon relocating her burial place sometime between 1647 and 1658.

Wives of noblemen were not allowed to wear the ribbed crown worn by their husbands (cat. no. 11). On their headdresses, therefore, materials and designs served as important indications of social status. In keeping with the luxurious tastes of Ming nobility, this hair clasp with a complex design is a unique example among excavated golden headdresses of the early seventeenth century. HL

13

明天启五年（1625年）　南京將軍山黔國公沐昌祚墓出土
金製　牡丹花金飾件

Ornament in the shape of a peony blossom, buried 1625

From the tomb of Mu Changzuo at Mount

Jiangjun, Nanjing

Reign of the Tianqi emperor (1621–1627)

Gold with filigree designs

D. 20.5 cm (8.07 in.)

Nanjing Municipal Museum

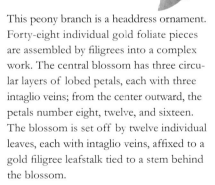

This peony branch is a headdress ornament. Forty-eight individual gold foliate pieces are assembled by filigrees into a complex work. The central blossom has three circular layers of lobed petals, each with three intaglio veins; from the center outward, the petals number eight, twelve, and sixteen. The blossom is set off by twelve individual leaves, each with intaglio veins, affixed to a gold filigree leafstalk tied to a stem behind the blossom.

Along with the gold hair-crown (cat. no. 11), the piece was discovered in the left chamber of the couple's shared tomb, where Mu Changzuo's coffin was placed (*Kaogu* 1999, no. 10, pp. 46–47, pl. 4). Comparing it with a gold flower from his wife's chamber on the right suggests the two ornaments probably were intended as a pair for the Mu couple. The other flower, with longer stemmed leaves, seems more suitable for a female hairdo, while this one, bundled on a thick stalk, could adequately be affixed to a male's hat or crown.

Because of his connection to the imperial family, Mu Changzuo possessed the hereditary title Duke of Qian (Yunnan and Guizhou). In 1584 he was granted another premium title, Grand Guardian of the Heir Apparent. He ruled the south frontiers, under the official name of Qian. Due to a serious health problem in 1595, he abdicated the title to his son Mu Rui (see cat. no. 15), who later was tried as a conspirator against the Ming sovereign and stripped of his honors. The court allowed Changzuo to retake the title and did not castigate him as being involved. Moreover, Changzuo, his wife, and even Rui himself retained the privilege to be buried in the Mus' grave, near those of the monarchs on the outskirts of Nanjing. Such special treatment from the court proved the Mus to be true beneficiaries among Ming aristocracy.

Based on a 1370 regulation for the empress's crown, the court readjusted details of crown accessories in 1405. The specifications covered sixteen types of iconographies—including the dragon, phoenix, clouds, and flowers—and their presentation, particularly by medium, such as gold, feathers, jades, and gems. According to these guidelines, the golden peony blossom was supposed to be positioned at the front and rear of the crown. This popularized the use of gold peonies in hair ornaments among the upper class. HL

14

明天启五年（1625年）　南京將軍山黔國公沐昌祚墓出土　金製　護身鏡

Plaque for exorcizing, buried 1625

From the tomb of Mu Changzuo at Mount Jiangjun, Nanjing

Reign of the Tianqi emperor (1621–1627)

Gold

D. 15 cm (5.91 in.)

Nanjing Municipal Museum

This plaque was produced by hammering a gold sheet. With three punched holes along the edge, the roundel was designed to affix onto metal, textile, or leather armor, or a military uniform. Together with a hundred other articles, it came to light from the tomb shared by Mu Changzuo (died 1625) and his wife, in the left chamber where his own rotten wooden coffin was found on a brick platform (*Kaogu* 1999, no. 10, p. 46). A ninth-generation descendant of Mu Ying (see cat. nos. 100–101), Mu Changzuo participated in compiling state policies for preserving the Ming court, unlike other Mu family members who conducted military duties. He was granted the title Grand Guardian

of the Heir Apparent, one of the Three Preceptors responsible for the education of the heir apparent, which only distinguished academicians could fill. Unseen in other Mu family burials, this special form, which must have belonged to Mu Changzuo, is identified as the "gold mirror of heart protection" in modern archaeology.

As a symbol of the sun, the roundel is often used in Taoist art to represent constellations. Within the shiny circle, the key constellations that fill the corresponding section of the sky are depicted. Used as an exorcising tool since the Six Dynasties period (386–589), a round form began to be placed on military armor. At that time,

as suggested by written documents and excavated clay figures, armor (or "brightly shining armor") was characterized by roundels in parallel or in a triangle on the front of the chest. This fashion once constituted most of the armor of the Tang dynasty (618–906). From clay tomb guardians to forceful figures on metal vessels, warriors were depicted wearing striking armor with two embossed roundels. The style was maintained in Taoist art but not for the weakened Song dynasty troops or the Mongol cavalry from the tenth through the thirteenth centuries. By the Ming dynasty, a single mirror was used for the purpose of symbolically exorcizing evil. HL

15

明天启七年（1627年） 南京將軍山黔國公沐叡墓出土 金製 "黔甯王" 遺訓牌

Hereditary medallion of Duke of Qian Tranquility, buried 1627 (above and page 48)

From the tomb of Mu Rui at Mount Jiangjun, Nanjing

Reign of the Tianqi emperor (1621–1627)

Gold plaque with engraved inscription

H. 13 cm (5.12 in.), W. 11 cm (4.33 in.)

Nanjing Municipal Museum

This gold medallion inscribed with authoritative commands was an heirloom of the Mu family whose key figure, Mu Ying, was granted by the Hongwu emperor the posthumous title Duke of Qian Tranquility in 1392. Engraved on both sides, the commands stress the moral importance of educating offspring. A lobed crown, with two divergent leaves defined by veins, sits atop the medallion. The central hole is for affixing a ribbon.

The plaque was discovered in 1974 in the tomb of Mu Rui (died 1609), the son of Mu Changzuo (see cat. nos. 13–14), on the outskirts of Nanjing (*Kaogu* 1999, no. 10, p. 50, pl. 5). Taking the family's hereditary title Duke of Qian (present-day Yunnan and Guizhou) in 1573, Mu Rui served as Vice Commissioner-in-Chief. His later involvement in a political revolt against the Ming court disgraced the honorable family, which had a connection to the royal throne through the marriage of a Mu ancestor to Princess Chang Ning (1386–1408), a granddaughter

of the Hongwu emperor. The court deprived Mu Rui of his official seal and all titles, and shut him in prison where he died in 1609.

One of the mysteries of Mu Rui's life concerns this gold medallion. It is a unique piece, one of a kind among all funeral articles found in Ming noble tombs. How and when did the family get it? No conclusion about its origin has been determined.

However, a court record may provide a clue. In 1408, the Yongle emperor held a banquet to celebrate a successful battle against Annam, in which Mu Sheng was the chief commander (see cat. no. 103). The emperor is said to have awarded to the guest of honor, Mu Sheng, items including the emperor's own handwritten poem, a jade belt, and a golden plaque (*Mingshi*, chap. 126, p. 7397); the latter was most likely the surviving medallion here. With the commands possibly engraved by Sheng, it must have been passed down as a family heirloom to later generations. Unfortunately,

two hundred years later, its orders were sullied by Mu Rui. Eighteen years after his death, the family was able to conduct Mu Rui's funeral. By burying the prestigious medallion with him, they announced the end of the legendary name of Mu, which had once been glorified for its support of the Ming court.

Inscription. The front shows inscriptions in standard script in three columns. The double line of five characters in the middle is entitled *Commands from Prince [Duke] of Qian Tranquility*, and flanked by a single line of four characters at each side, reading from right to left: *This plaque must be used as an identity seal carried by a ribbon.* On the rear, the inscription in five columns reads vertically: *To all of my descendants who must wholeheartedly dedicate themselves to the country; must act with prudence and care; and treat colleagues in modest and amiable ways. A special moral behest to be heeded as an exemplar.* HL

16

明天启七年(1627年) 南京將軍山黔國公沐叡墓出土 金錠

Golden ingot, buried 1627

From the tomb of Mu Rui at Mount Jiangjun, Nanjing

Reign of the Tianqi emperor (1621–1627)

Gold

H. 2.5 cm (0.98 in.), L. 5.7 cm (2.24 in.), W. 4 cm (1.57 in.)

Nanjing Municipal Museum

Along with over 180 articles, a large container with three gold ingots was also discovered from Mu Rui's tomb (*Kaogu* 1999, no. 10, p. 50). In contrast to the common shape of coins, a solid ingot is a three-dimensional form with a fine ridge at top. It was visually identified with wealthy nobility.

Gold was always in insufficient supply throughout the Ming dynasty. Whether it came from foreign countries' tributes or from mining within the nation, gold might or might not have reached the treasury on a reliable basis. During the early years, the Ming government strove to implement policies for healing its economy after the preceding turbulent years. While controlling the mining, storage, and distribution of precious materials, the court prohibited private trade of gold and silver. Taxes in kind meant that instead of grain gathered by regional governments, other forms of payment such as gold, silver, money, cotton, or particular products were also accepted—even after the Ming government issued paper currency in 1375, which was based on the paper money begun in the tenth century.

By the mid-fifteenth century, the imperial treasury could hardly supply enough gold to support the extravagant ways of court life. The well-known Huguang governmental mining company (present-day Hunan and Hubei), established by the court in 1474, produced only 30 *liang* (52.8 ounces) in gold at the cost of 550,000 laborers and many deaths.

From the mid-Ming dynasty, gold, as well as tax collections, increasingly fell into the hands of local officials or delegates and eunuchs from the central government who exploited opportunities to obtain luxuries. That resulted in large amounts of gold held in private households outside the court. High-ranking people, landlords, eunuchs, and merchants gained status by amassing gold. Although he came from one of the most eminent Ming families, Mu Rui was no exception. He collected more than a dozen types of gold items, ranging from belts to utensils to ornaments, by means of reinforcing imperial statutes. HL

17

明天启七年（1627年）　南京將軍山黔國公沐叡墓出土　金製　四事件（耳挖，牙籤，鑷子，藥勺）

Tube with four tools (earpick, toothpick, tweezers, and spoon), buried 1627

From the tomb of Mu Rui at Mount Jiangjun, Nanjing

Reign of the Tianqi emperor (1621–1627)

Gold with engraving and filigree designs

Overall: L. 4 cm (15.75 in.); tube: L. 8 cm (3.15 in.)

Nanjing Municipal Museum

A set of mini tools, this one consisting of an earpick, a toothpick, a spoon, and tweezers for grooming the beard or hair, would have been carried by men of the Ming dynasty. This ingenious design consists of a hollow cylinder threaded with a long chain, which is tied at one end to the four mini tools and to a round cap for sealing the tube; at the other end, the chain is attached to a wire-work cloud head that can be hung down from a belt. By pulling the chain from the cloud head, the entire set can be enclosed inside the tube. Its exterior is traced with grooves outlining a landscape. The suspension chain consists of a series of interlocking filigree.

Made of metal, animal bone, jade, or a mix of any of these, mini tool sets vary in numbers of tools, ranging from one to two or more. The earliest individual earpick was found at a late Shang dynasty site (approx.

1300 BCE), and the earliest tweezers a Western Han tomb (175 BCE) in H (Hunan Provincial Museum 1973, p. Later, when waist ornaments becar fashionable during the Tang dynasty of multiple mini tools were made to by a chain from a belt; some sets com as many as ten items. More often see Ming burials are chained sets compr an earpick and a toothpick. Parallel string, the two items were commonl merged into a simplified hairpin, set each of the ends on a long stick. Of mini-tool sets excavated from ninetee burials, this one, from Mu Rui's tom the only gold set of four (*Kaogu* 199 10, p. 50, pl. 4). Another Mu membe probably of a minor rank, who was in Yunnan, was entitled to use a silv of four (*Kaogu* 1965, no. 4, p. 188).

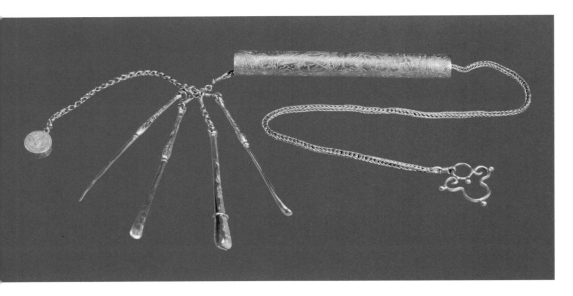

18

明天启七年（1627年）　南京將軍山黔國公沐叡墓出土　琥珀　漁翁戲荷杯

Cup in the shape of a lotus leaf pulled by a swimming fisherman, buried 1627

From the tomb of Mu Rui at Mount Jiangjun, Nanjing

Reign of the Tianqi emperor (1621–1627)

Amber

H. 5 cm (1.97 in.), L. 12.7 cm (5 in.), W. 7.6 cm (2.99 in.)

Nanjing Municipal Museum

Known as the largest piece among ambers found in Ming tombs, this fisherman is also from Mu Rui's tomb (*Kaogu* 1999, no. 10, pl. 61). A single block of semitranslucent crimson amber was carved into a three-dimensional lotus-leaf-shaped cup with a fisherman-shaped handle. The semi-clothed fisherman stretches his body in a 45-degree angle, with his right hand pulling the cup at the rim and his heel braced against the lower section. In his left hand is a fish entwined with a series of openwork lotus stems. The entire work depicts a scene of a smiling fisherman who caught a fish while swimming in a lotus lake.

In ancient China, the upper class was fascinated by amber accessories, and doctors made medicine out of it. Compared to nephrite, fewer amber objects have been found in burials. An early burial contained amber ornaments appropriate to the deceased, dated to the late Shang dynasty (approx. 1300 BCE). Written knowledge of amber, as early as the Han dynasty (206 BCE–220 CE), recognized its physical, chemical, and magnetic properties, as well as its origins in the western region (Near East) and the southern tribes (present-day southwest Yunnan and north Burma). The latter had been the major supplier to mainland China for centuries. A

long period of mining had, by the Ming dynasty, caused an exhaustion of Yunnan amber. Without the tax income from the 200 *jin* (220 pounds) of amber from the court of the Wanli emperor (1573–1619), Yunnan's finances fell into the red. In the early seventeenth century, the price for the best quality of amber was estimated at five times that of gold (Song Yingxing 1637, chap. 2). The evidence of several amber pieces from the Mu family tombs reflects the fact that the family was able to obtain the material conveniently because of its governorship in Yunnan. HL

19

葬清朝順治年間　南京中華門外鄧府山佟卜年夫人陳氏墓出土　金製，琥珀　雙龍戲珠冠帽飾

Two dragons presenting a heart-shaped amber, buried 1647–1658

From the tomb of Lady Chen, wife of Tong Bonian, in Dengfushan, outside the Zhonghua Gate, Nanjing

Amber and ruby; gold with repoussé and filigree designs

H. 6 cm (2.36 in.), W. 5 cm (1.97 in.)

Nanjing Municipal Museum

A brightly colored crown ornament creates a rich interplay of gold, ruby, and amber. The heart-shaped amber can be affixed to a headdress through a hole in the central top. The amber is flanked by two three-clawed dragons by means of gripping it with tongs at their heads, rear legs, and overlapped tails. At the rear surface a gold cloud stretches eight filigree wires to secure the amber by clipping its edges. Around the dragons float a few whirling clouds that are further inlaid with a ruby at top and bottom. Representing the symbolic color of the Ming dynasty, the red heart implies a metaphor of royalty.

This piece came to light from the tomb of Lady Chen (1589–1647), wife of Tong Bonian (died 1625), who, according to Ming biographies and the inscription carved on the stone stele found in Chen's tomb, was commissioned to monitor activities of the Denglai army (Shandong). Tong was arrested on an unjust accusation by a political tribunal. He died a few years later in prison in Hubei. After his death, Lady Chen spent her remaining years as a homeless widow and mother. Years later after her death, the couple's son and son-in-law were recruited to the Qing government (1644–1911). Using their connections, they were able to wipe out the incorrect ruling against Tong Bonian. Lady Chen was granted the posthumous title Lady of Chaste Beauty. Her coffin was allowed to be reburied sometime before 1658, in a Nanjing tomb from which 139 items of gold, silver, amber, porcelain, and bronze have been unearthed (*Kaogu* 1999, no. 10, p. 59, pl. 8). The sumptuous burial by Tong's son indicates the importance he placed on restoring the family name. HL

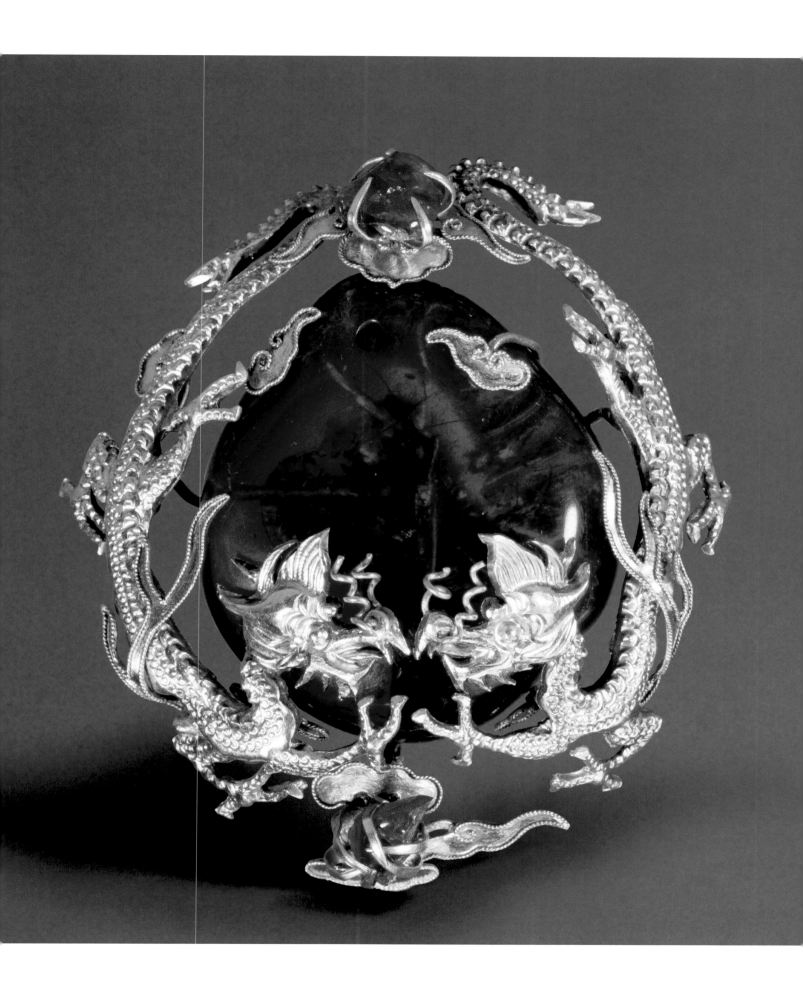

20

明初期　金托，和田白玉　鷺鷥荷塘紋擺件　南京市博物館

Ornament depicting a lotus pond (above and right)

Nanjing, Jiangsu province

Green nephrite on a gold mount

H. 7 cm (2.76 in.)

Nanjing Municipal Museum

This exquisite ornament presents, in a complicated three-dimensional form, a scene of a lotus pond. Beneath two large lotus leaves, four egrets stand amidst aquatic plants. Their postures are varied and naturalistic. Long, thin, triangular leaves are rendered in carefully descriptive as well as realistic detail. The base is mounted into a circular gold pedestal that is borrowed from Buddhist art, consisting of two vertical symmetries of lotus petals supported on cloud-head-shaped aprons.

The scene was based on a Yuan prototype designed by thirteenth-century jade carvers. Evidence of this is a green nephrite that was found in the 1351 tomb of a Yuan official, Ren Ming (1286–1351), in Shanghai, which has comparable features in a similar composition (Shanghai WWGWH, 2001, p. 150). The style, a mannered classicism inflected by intriguing openwork, exhibits the influence of ancient jade. In scholarship, this type of three-dimensional openwork in jade is usually identified as being used for knobs on the top covers of incense burners.

Debates on the function of such jade began in the early seventeenth century, when renowned author Shen Defu (1578–1642) recorded in his encyclopedia that Mongol noblemen wore large-brimmed hats with a jade top "button" that could reach up to five inches high. Because Ming society was deeply disturbed by Mongol fashions, it abandoned Yuan hats; however, the jade hat knobs were reused as appliqués on covers of vessels, due to the value placed on their precious materials and crafting. Taking Shen's view, some modern scholars are irresolute in distinguishing between a lid knob and a hat knob. Meanwhile others have challenged the reliability of Shen's theory based on one example from a Yuan tomb: a gold-mounted jade knob on a large-brimmed hat, whose jade was only three centimeters high (*Wenwu* 1982, no. 2, pl. II, fig. 1).

Except for a few excavated jades of this type found in Zhejiang and Jiangsu, several similar jades are preserved in the imperial collections, now in the Palace Museum, Beijing, and the Palace Museum, Taipei. The mystery surrounding them will no doubt continue to be debated. But this should not blind us to the beauty of these jades, which have survived to dazzle our eyes. HL

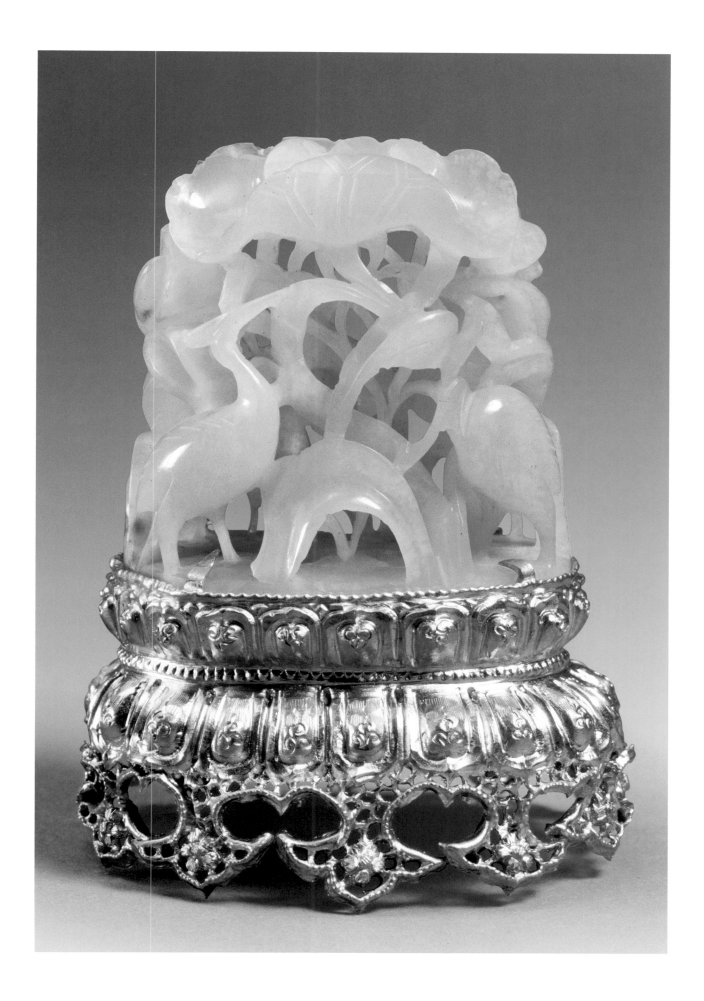

21

明中期　青玉　仙人福祿壽龍紋磬　北京故宮

Chime (*qing*) with immortal gods and dragons, approx. 1550–1600

Hetian nephrite on gold-gilded metal chains with silk tassels

L. 48.5 cm (19.09 in.), W. 21 cm (8.27 in.), D. 1.3 cm (.51 in.)

Palace Museum, Beijing

A hanging chime, called a *qing*, represents the Three Star Gods and celestial dragons in a paradise under pine trees, celebrating happiness, good fortune, and longevity. Surrounding a stag in the center, the Three Star Gods in human form, with their standard iconographical elements, stand at the points of a triangle. The God of Good Fortune, wearing an official crown, presents an official tablet on his right arm. Opposite is the God of Happiness, lifting a peach in his right hand. At the top center, the elder God of Longevity, featuring a peach-shaped head, holds a Taoist element, a wish-granting scepter, or *ruyi*. Two of the Eight Immortals face each other at the lower sides, amidst cranes, a doe, sacred mushrooms, and rocks. The other side of the chime depicts two three-clawed dragons, tumbling on a cloudy ocean with a flaming ball.

A piece of green Hetian jade was worked into a four-lobed plaque form with designs in relief and intaglio. On a rectangular jade ornament with openwork of two facing dragonets, it is suspended through top corner holes by two gold-gilded, loose-ring metal chains. The composition is further balanced by two small bats at the middle chains and, hanging from the jade openwork, yellow silk tassels below knitting of an endless knot and four-lobed flowers.

The chime was one of the essential instruments used in a ritual ceremony known from the Bronze Age. Its use can be likened to that of continuous bell ringing. Made of stone or bronze, a set of chimes numbering from one to a dozen or more were arranged on a wooden rack. The tone a chime emitted depended on its size and thickness, and whether it was struck in the center or sides. Beginning in the Ming, high-quality jade was used for chimes. A jade chime with elaborate designs often serves as a symbolic ornament. HL

22

明中晚期　青玉/渡金內套/木座　陸子崗款丹鳳雙罌萬壽合巹杯　北京故宮

Incense vessel with poems and a phoenix and dragonets

By Lu Zigang (active 1550–1600)

Hetian greenish nephrite; metal cores with gold-gilded tops

H. 11 cm (4.33 in.), D. (at mouth) 5.8 cm (2.28 in.)

Palace Museum, Beijing

This vessel represents an ancient form consisting of a pair of identical vessels from which a married couple drank wine, side by side at a wedding. Made of a single large block of greenish jade, it has been worked using various techniques, showing intaglio, openwork, hollowing, and shallow and high relief. Two cylindrical barrels, resting on short animal-head lugs, are tied together using two cords around the upper and lower bodies. Between them, attached at one side, is a phoenix unfolding her curly split tail onto each of the barrels. Facing her on the other side is a lock-shaped seal mark with the characters for "long life" in clerical script, flanked by two dragonets, one creeping over the barrel edge and the other walking toward the seal.

A poem by Zhu Yunming (1460–1526) is carved on each of the barrels in vertical columns of clerical-script calligraphy. On one barrel, a four-word verse reminds the reader of the Confucian virtue that values the superpower of jade in sacred rites, politics, warfare security, and medical prescriptions.

Smooth jade stone from the Chu [a state centered in present-day Hubei] *offers benefits, and can be worked as well. Whether jade liquid or stone syrup all provide wide pleasures.* —Zhu Yunming

On the other barrel, a five-word verse alludes to the vessel's function as an incense holder, emitting fragrance with divine will.

Nine nations diffuse auspicious smoke from the incense vessel, Thousandfold fragrance blesses the sun with brilliance.
Wish Your Majesty a life of ten thousand years, and amuse yourself to your heart's content at Phoenix Castle.

The combination of the calligraphy of Zhu's poem with a magnificent presentation makes this piece one of the most important examples contributing to our knowledge of Ming jade and the Suzhou jade master Lu Zigang.

Inscription. Engraved around the outer mouth, above the cord design, are the jade cutter's signature, *Produced by Zigang*, and the given identification, *Interconnected cup*.
HL

23

明中晚期　青玉　八仙慶壽紋帶蓋執壺　北京故宮

Covered ewer in the shape of a teapot, approx. 1500–1600

Hetian nephrite

H. 27.5 cm (10.83 in.), D. (at mouth) 12.7 cm (5 in.)

Palace Museum, Beijing

This decorative pot is worked from a single block of greenish jade. Rising from a high foot ring into a compact body, it tapers inward and slightly flares out to a short, straight mouth rim, over which a tightly matched lid tapers to a sculpted knob featuring the elderly God of Longevity on a deer. On an S-shaped handle stands a celestial dragonet. Opposite from the handle, a long, curved spout stretches upward from an animal mouth, and its upper spout is connected to the neck of the pot by horizontal openwork forming an auspicious cloud.

Scenery depicting the Eight Immortals' Gathering extends from one side of the pot to the other: four immortals with their magical attributes—a crutch, a sword, a

fan, and a lotus—form a procession on rocky islands in the ocean, surrounded by pine trees, dancing cranes, and sacred mushrooms. The other four—identified by a flute, a fish-drum, a pair of wooden beaters, and a mushroom—enjoy peach blossoms on high peaks. Above them, a five-word poem in raised calligraphy of cursive script notes that the depiction takes place by Jade Pond:

The tribute vessel through a thousand-mile journey presents to the king
sacred peaches with five colors in even gradations.
An upcoming year accounts from the time when cranes ascend a height
and the palace in ocean rises colorful clouds.
Lasting spring.

A luscious banquet undertaken by Jade Pond favorable illumination revolves round the Purple Tenuity's Pole.
All together, immortal gods gather at the celebration to bless life with eternal immortality.
Life forever.

Emerging from the Complete Realization sect of Taoism, the Eight Immortals grew in popularity from the thirteenth century. This piece is distinguished by a complete rendering of the legendary account in high and shallow relief, difficult to execute on a three-dimensional work. HL

24

明　和田白玉　仿古銅饕餮夔龍紋蓋觶　北京故宮

Vessel in the shape of an ancient bronze zhi, approx. 1475–1644

Hetian nephrite

H. 12.5 cm (4.92 in.), D. 7 cm (2.76 in.)

Palace Museum, Beijing

This white Hetian jade, or "mutton fat," is among the best quality of its kind. The covered vessel is a rather accurate copy of an ancient bronze vessel, *zhi*, used to serve ceremonial wine. With an S-shaped profile, a low-waisted elliptical body rests on a relatively high foot ring. The design on the body consists of four corresponding friezes in relief. Each side of the center part presents a large animal mask with detailed, thickly curved eyebrows, bossy eyes, cloud-shaped ears, and snout and mouth in shallow relief against an intaglio meander-patterned background. Two parallel bands above set off the mask. A narrow circle around the mouth rim consists of

united pairs of facing dragonets on an intaglio meander background. On the neck are two dragonets flanking a cloud. On the lid stands a short circular ridge; inside the ridge are intaglio clouds, and outside, the same relief pattern of dragonets on a meander background. The foot ring is surrounded by slightly raised dragonets. The interior of the cup and foot is left plain.

Excavated bronze *zhi* vessels, with or without a lid, have been concentrated in the central lands of the Shang culture (approx. 1050–600 BCE), present-day Anyang in Henan province. Zhou people from the north-west carried on the Shang's ritual tradition and produced bronze *zhi*

in their homeland, present-day Shaanxi province. One of the popular décors cast on them was the mask against the meander background, which was well documented as representing evil greed. In the Iron Age since 200 BCE, this pattern was abandoned as were many ceremonial vessels. Not until the eleventh century did the ancient ritual forms return, owning to the monarchs' patronage of classical ceremonial formations. Not limited to metals, they were produced in many other mediums. *Zhi* vessels were frequently worked out of jade and ceramics. HL

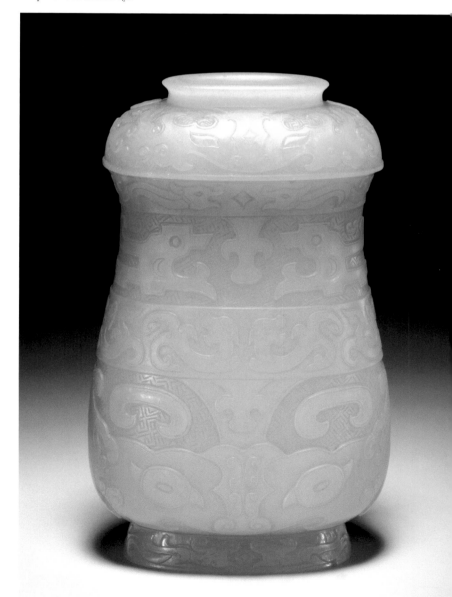

25

明 青玉　雙螭耳鈎雲六方扁瓶　北京故宮

Hexagonal flask with dragon and clouds, approx. 1550–1600

Hetian nephrite

H. 11.5 cm (4.53 in.), D. 3.3–5.8 cm (1.3–2.28 in.)

Palace Museum, Beijing

This hexagonal flask shares stylistic similarities with classical bronze vessels for the drinking of ceremonial wine. Surfaces are divided into six vertical sides and four horizontal sections, decorated with successive friezes. Starting from the top downward, four friezes reveal a section that consists of traditional C-shaped clouds; a series of ear-shaped cloud heads; the principal motif of paired dragonets facing each other among clouds; and stylized lotus petals circling the bottom section. Corresponding to the principal motif, each side has an upright dragonet on the neck, and a dragon looking back at a dragonet whose body is attached to the dragon's tail. The inside pot and base of

a high foot ring are hollow and polished, with no decoration. Given an elaborate execution, the piece is distinctive for the refined raised lines on its dividing borders, clouds, and lotus petals, for which large areas of the background had to be removed with great care.

The maker of this vessel was influenced by ancient designs for bronze ritual vessels. During the late Bronze Age (approx. 771 BCE) a new quadrilateral form for bronze flasks emerged in the Henan and Shanxi areas in the central lands. As Taoist beliefs regarding the four cardinal directions were conceptualized during the Han dynasty (206 BCE–220 CE), a four-sided composition of either a rec-

tangular or diamond arrangement became widespread in ceremonial vessels. Another common number, six, developed in many perspectives of Taoism, for its links to the following: six gods, all representing *yin* (the negative energy corresponding to earth, and the counterpart to positive energy, or *yang*); six directions (heaven, earth, and the four cardinal directions); six pitches in music; and six unions among the ten heavenly stems corresponding to the Juniper star. The use of six divisions for a ritual vessel indicates the increased importance of the number and its symbolism in Taoism, which became pervasive in the Ming. HL

26

明中晚期　和田白玉　褶斑蟠枝带柄桃式洗　北京故宫

Basin in the shape of a peach branch, approx. 1550–1644

Hetian nephrite

H. 3.2 cm (1.26 in.), D. (at mouth) 7.6 cm (2.99 in.), D. (at base) 11.4 cm (4.49 in.)

Palace Museum, Beijing

This elegant basin is a half-peach-shaped form with an openwork branch handle. It would have served as a water container on a scholar's table. Water in the basin could have been used to wash a writing brush or poured out from the tip of the peach onto an inkstone (see cat. no. 63), on which ink is produced by grinding an ink stick. A high-quality single block of jade is worked into a sculpture with designs rendered in openwork, intaglio, and shallow relief. The lustrous white body is treated with apricot-yellow dyes, especially evident on the branch and leaf edges. With no other symbolic elements the peach represents abundance and long life.

More often made of ceramics and metals in early times, water vessels for scholars' tables were increasingly made of jade, agate, and crystal from the seventh century onward. Partly because the wide extent of the Tang dynasty (618–906) reached most of the Central Asiatic territory, there arose an effective transport for jade supply to the mainland. Concurrently the number of educated scholar-officials grew with the economic expansion, as the position of the aristocracy was challenged by the civil bureaucracy. The engagement of members of this bureaucracy in collecting art and in intellectual pursuits such as writing and painting stimulated production

of scholars' objects. Water basins and cups from the tenth through the twelfth centuries with floral, branch-shaped, or cloud-shaped handles survived as inspiration to later jade cutting. An early jade peach basin came to light in excavations from a thirteenth-century tomb in Wuxi, Jiangsu province (*ZGYQQJ* 1993, vol. 5, pl. 188). Its half-peach-shaped form, openwork branch handle, and curved leaves supporting the bottom, as observable on this piece, exemplified a stylized model of the kind. HL

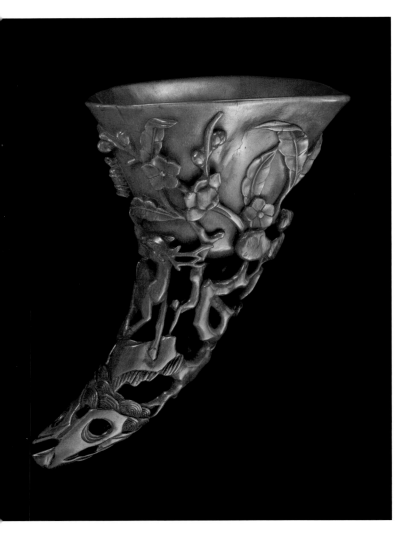

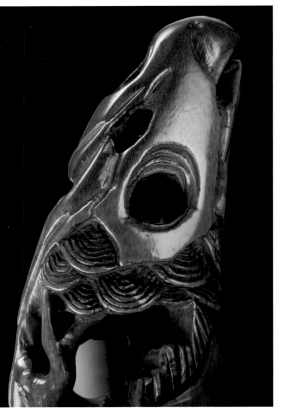

27

晚明　犀角　花束形杯　金山亞洲藝術博物館

Goblet in the shape of a bundle of flowers, approx. 1600

Rhinoceros horn

H. 26 cm (10.25 in.), W. 11.4 cm (4.25 in.)

Asian Art Museum, The Avery Brundage Collection, B65M21

Utilizing the entire horn, this cup has a tapering base carved in openwork. The cup itself is shaped like a magnolia blossom. Below it, the openwork section shows a peach tree bearing flowers and fruit, growing from a rock in the sea. A deer with its head turned emerges from the rock. The back shows a camellia bush with a single blossom. A crane flies above, and another one perches on the rocks below. Chained to the cup is a carved bell with interlocking rings.

A peach tree growing from rocks bring to mind the Ming dynasty motif "mountain of longevity and sea of blessings" (*shoushan fuhai*).

This motif is accompanied by more symbols of longevity, such as the deer and crane. Popular for birthdays, this longevity motif is often found in Ming-dynasty porcelain designs.

The horn on a rhinoceros is not attached to its skull and is different from that of a sheep or antelope. The horn is composed of compressed keratin fibers, similar to the substance found in human fingernails and hair. The rhinoceros horn was believed to have powerful medicinal uses, such as the ability to detect poison.
TTB

28

晚明　犀角　人物山水杯　金山亞洲藝術博物館

Cup with figure in landscape, approx. 1600

Rhinoceros horn

H. 11. 8 cm (4.65 in.), W. 12.4 cm (4.88 in.), D. 17.5 cm (6.88 in.)

Asian Art Museum, The Avery Brundage Collection, B65M23

Cups carved out of rhinoceros horn are mentioned in Chinese literature as early as the Han dynasty. They were once credited with the faculty of revealing poison by sweating. Extant rhinoceros horn cups are mainly from the Ming and Qing dynasties. While some horn cups follow the traditional bamboo root carving by depicting landscapes and floral motifs, others are in the shape of archaistic vessels.

Shown on this cup are sheer cliffs, rocks, and gnarled old trees with their roots exposed and with clinging vines hanging from their branches. A boat on a flowing river appears diagonally under an arching branch of a

tree. The handle of the cup is formed by the intertwining branches of two trees. One of them, a pine, and the other with palmate leaves, extend their branches over the rim.

When the poet-official Su Dongpo (1037–1101) was banished to Hubei province, he twice visited the Red Cliff with his friends, and wrote two odes to commemorate his trips. There are actually two Red Cliffs in Hubei province. The most famous one, in Jiayu county, was the site of the famous battle of 208, in which the weaker armies of Liu Bei and Sun Quan vanquished the mighty army of Cao Cao. The Red Cliff that Su Dongpo visited was a different

one, in Huanggang county. Shown on this cup is the scene of Su Dongpo (wearing his characteristic tall hat) and two of his friends viewing the Red Cliff from a boat. They are accompanied by an oarsman and a young boy warming wine on a stove. Su Dongpo visited the Red Cliff twice. This cup depicts his first visit, which took place on the sixteenth day of the seventh month, 1082. Basking in the gentle breeze and sailing in calm water, the poet and his friends drank wine and enjoyed the moon, composing poetry and singing together TTB

Bright yellow silk with dragons, material for a court robe (plate 32)

Textiles and Costumes

TERESE TSE BARTHOLOMEW

When the war with the Yuan dynasty ended, the economy of China was in a state of decline. In order to boost the country's economy, the Hongwu emperor (1368–1398) strongly encouraged the growing of mulberry (the main source of food for silkworms) and cotton. As a result, the textile industry flourished, and the development of Chinese textile arts reached great heights in the Ming dynasty.

Commoners wore cotton during the winter and hempen cloth during the summer. The upper class wore silk as outer garments, and cotton as undergarments. The officials and the court wore elaborate court robes according to the sumptuary laws of the Ming dynasty. Only the emperor and empress could wear robes depicting five-clawed dragons. Other officials were allowed to wear the *mang,* a four-clawed dragon; *feiyu,* a dragon with fish fins and tail; or *douniu,* a dragon with bovine horns. Badges embroidered with the mythical creatures *qilin* and *baize* (said to understand human speech) were for dukes, marquises, earls, and imperial sons-in-law. Civil officials were identified by a rank badge bearing a bird, while animals decorated the rank badges of military officials. With minor variations, the system of using birds and animals as rank badges was continued by the subsequent Qing dynasty. Special festival badges were created and worn by officials during specific annual festivals.

The court was actually the major consumer of fine textiles, and the Jiangnan coastal area became the main center of silk weaving. The Ministry of Works set up internal textile bureaus to supply silk and satin for the imperial family, while an external textile bureau was responsible for producing textiles for court officials. A special bureau in Nanjing was established just for the silks used for rituals and worship. Textile bureaus were established in various prefectures all over China, in the provinces of Zhejiang, Jiangxi, Fujian, Sichuan, Henan, and Shandong, with Suzhou and Hangzhou prefectures being the largest in scale.

According to the official history of the Ming dynasty, in the thirty-third year of the reign of the Wanli emperor (1605), the Ministry of Works reported that the court used over 43,600 bolts of satin (*duan*) for imperial robes, wedding costumes, and other paraphernalia (*Ming shilu, shencong wanli shilu*). In 1977, the Nanjing Institute for Brocade (*Yunjin*) Research copied some of the robes excavated from the tomb of the Wanli emperor. The weaving process revealed that one bolt of silk (ranging between thirty to fifty Chinese feet) was enough for only one imperial robe. When Ding Ling, the tomb of the Wanli emperor and his two empresses, situated on the northern outskirts of Beijing, was excavated in 1956, it revealed a treasure trove of six hundred items of clothing and 177 bolts of silk (IA-CASS, vol. 1, p. 383). These items have given us a very good idea of the robes and preferred fabrics of the Wanli period.

Ming-dynasty robes reverted back to the styles of the Tang and Song dynasties. Large and roomy, the robes were altered from the traditional three-piece skirt to a single garment resembling a curtain. The dragon robes (cat. nos. 31, 34) show the large persimmon calyx, or four-petal motif, around the neck, enclosing dragons inside. On formal occasions the emperors would wear the *gunfu* bearing the twelve imperial symbols. The decorations on the robes were woven or embroidered.

The formal clothing of the empress was also large like the dragon robes. For informal occasions royal ladies wore short jackets and long skirts. Jackets had square openings or overlapping collars. (Interestingly, in Chinese paintings from the Ming dynasty until the present, men and women are often shown wearing the overlapping collar garments of the Ming dynasty.) Vests were worn over the robes and jackets. The example included here (cat. no. 33) is a sumptuously embroidered red and gold vest (*bija*) made for the birthday of Empress Dowager Li, mother of the Wanli emperor. Although the common people were not allowed to wear gold embroidery in their clothing, the members of the court certainly used a large amount of gold in what they wore. Two imperial jackets embroidered with the "hundred boys" motif were discovered in the coffin of the Xiaojing empress (died 1612) at Ding Ling. The boys, playing various games, were intricately embroidered, and on the same jackets were couched gold dragons and large golden characters (IA-CASS 1990, vol. 1, pl. 234a-b; vol. 2, pl. 45–63).

Civil and military officials of the Ming wore many different types of attire, including ritual, court, official, and everyday wear. Sumptuary laws governed what one should or should not wear, either in general or on specific occasions. For example, in the early Ming, eunuchs were forbidden to wear headdresses and scarves, as well as official (*gongfu*) and ritual attire (*jifu*). However, these restrictions were lifted when they came to power later on.

Commoners were not allowed to wear the color yellow or use gold embroidery. They wore plain boots with no decoration. Women wore half-robes, short jackets, capes vests, and skirts. According to regulations, women could wear only one type of silk, a purple coarse variety that resembled linen. Light colors like purple, green, and pink were allowed for upper garments, but raven black, vermilion, and yellow were forbidden.

Ming-dynasty textiles continued the ancient traditions of the Tang, Song, and Yuan dynasties, but with new innovations. The blue wrapping cloth with precious symbols (cat. no. 45) is a fine example of the clamp-resist dyeing technique known as *jiaxie,* which was invented in the Tang dynasty. This technique continued to be used in the Ming dynasty, especially for decorating the thin silk for covering Tibetan thangkas. Some of the intricately woven textiles of the Ming dynasty are the "heavenly splendor" weaves (*tianhua jin*) for wrapping special objects (cat. no. 38) and decorating the covers of sutras (cat. no. 40). This is a continuation of the Song-dynasty lampas weaves. Others include the *zanghua jin,* a type of *yunjin* or "cloud brocade" (cat. nos. 39, 42) woven in Nanjing. There is much use of gold in these textiles, continuing the tradition of Yuan-dynasty gold brocades. These elaborately woven textiles with supplementary weft designs are woven from specially constructed tall looms that require two weavers. One person works out the design on top, and the other one does the actual weaving on the bottom.

Besides real and imaginary flowers, the Ming textile repertoire included the Eight Treasures (a variable collection of precious symbols such as rhinoceros horns, elephant tusks, coral branches, coins, ingots, lozenges, tablets, and heads of the wish-granting scepter), and the Eight Auspicious Buddhist Symbols (wheel, conch, parasol, standard of victory, lotus, vase, fish, and endless knot). Certain auspicious characters are used as motifs, such as *fu,* which literally means "blessings," *shou* for "longevity," and the auspicious swastika (*wan*) to represent "ten thousand." Rebuses or pictorial puns representing auspicious phrases began to appear in textiles as well as porcelains, such as the swastika and *shou* character together to represent *wanshou,* or "ten thousand longevities" (cat. no. 33).

Embroidery also reached great heights during the Ming dynasty. The birthday vest (cat. no. 33) and the thangka of Raktayamari (cat. no. 29) are masterpieces showing the combination of various embroidery stitches including satin stitch and gold couching. These luxurious and magnificent examples are contrasted by the subtle and scholarly embroideries of the Gu family (*guxiu*), whose style displays a successful attempt to "paint" with needle and thread. It utilizes a variety of needle-work stitches, in combination with pale ink or light color washes to enhance the embroidery. The work, done on plain satin, resembles a painting of the literati style.

The Yongle emperor invited a number of high monks from Tibet to come to China, and these visits resulted in lavish gift giving. The monks included the Fifth Karmapa (1384–1415) of the Kagyu, Kunga Tashi Gyaltsen (born 1349) of Sakya, and Sakya Yeshe (1354–1435) of the Gelug order of Tibetan Buddhism. The monasteries of Sakya, Tsurphu, Sera, and the Potala kept many of these gifts in pristine condition. Besides gilded bronze images, porcelain, paintings, and gilded lacquer sutra covers (cat. no. 49), there are sumptuous examples of embroidery (cat. no. 29) and slit tapestry, or *kesi* (cat. no. 35). One of the important treasures of the Sera Monastery of Tibet is a kesi portrait of its founder, Sakya Yeshe, wearing a cloak with a typical Ming-dynasty design of dragons and *ruyi* clouds. The monk had cured the Xuande emperor (1426–1435) of certain illnesses, and in return he received this cloak as a gift from the emperor (Bowers Museum 2003, cat. no. 10).

The textile arts of the Ming dynasty epitomize the height of Chinese weaving and embroidery. This achievement was no doubt due to imperial patronage and to the creativity fostered by 276 years of peace.

29

永樂朝　緞地彩繡　紅地永樂款唐卡　美國私人收藏

Thangka of the Buddhist deity Raktayamari, the Red Conqueror of Death

Reign of the Yongle emperor (1403–1424)

Silk satin with embroidery

H. 335 cm (131.89 in.), W. 213 cm (83.86 in.)

Private Collection

During the reign of the Yongle emperor, superb textiles such as this example, imperial porcelains, superb sets of sutras with lacquered covers, and fabulous images of gilded bronze were made in the imperial workshops as gifts to the high lamas of Tibet. The dry climate of Tibet preserved these gifts in pristine condition.

This large embroidery depicts the god Raktayamari and his consort in sexual embrace, representing the union of compassion and wisdom. They trample on a god of egotism, who is lying prone upon the back of a buffalo that crouches upon a lotus pedestal. Raktayamari is a wrathful form of Manjushri, personifying enlightenment as the conquest of death. He grants his devotees freedom from premature deaths

and obstructions to their lives. The god brandishes a club (*khatvanga*) above his head, topped by three heads in various stages of decay, surmounted by a half thunderbolt; he has a skull cup in his left hand. The goddess Vajravetali carries a skull bowl, and her hand held behind the god would have held a chopper. The gods are surrounded by a large halo of flames, shown against a green background of stylized scrollwork in the Newari tradition. The body and limbs of the images show a gradation of color, similar to the shading technique used in thangka painting, revealing the fact that this embroidery was actually based upon a thangka prototype.

The seven gods on the top level, from left to right, are as follows: (1) Yama, a guard-

ian of the law and god of death, (2) the yellow buddha Ratnasambhava, (3) the blue buddha Akshobhya, (4) the white buddha Vairochana, (5) the red buddha Amitabha, (6) the green buddha Amoghasiddhi, and (7) Manjushri, bodhisattva of wisdom. Below them are the goddesses of compassion, Green Tara and White Tara. A red legend, embroidered in gold, appears below the White Tara and reads, "donated in the reign of the Yongle emperor (*daming yongle nianshi*)." Below the main images are seven dancing goddesses, carrying various offerings.

The previous owner of this thangka was an Englishman who received this as a gift from the Chogyal of Sikkim in the 1940s. MK

30

弘治朝　南京中華門外皇族王志遠墓出土　暗花緞　祥雲纹長袖褶袍

Tunic with woven clouds

From the tomb of Wang Zhiyuan, outside the Zhonghua Gate, Nanjing

Reign of the Hongzhi emperor (1488–1505)

Silk satin damask

L. 141 cm (55.51 in.), W. 233.5 cm (91.93 in.)

Nanjing Municipal Museum

A tunic made of a top sewed to a skirt was typical of casual clothes worn by men. The original yellow color of this tunic has faded to brown. The lustrous satin textile was woven with the same colored, matted patterns forming cloud heads. Stylistically, it is seen as a top with wide collar trims, right placket, and a sewed-on pleated skirt; the tunic was called a pleated robe. In general, pleats were elasticized by two distinct approaches: evenly folded pleats were often seen on clothes for imperial member (cat. no. 34), while pleats on subjects' robes were random, as done here. Pleats could be arranged all around the waist or like this, densely elasticized on the left and right sides symmetrically. The distinctive form with relatively narrow, bag-shaped sleeves, along with a wide skirt that was a commonly tailored Ming costume, provides convenience for activities. In Ming paintings, men dressed in such tunics are depicted riding horses or playing sports.

Ming tunics of this style have been found in the tombs of the Wanli emperor, Beijing, and those of wealthy and high ranking people in Jiangsu and Guangdong (Chang Shana 2000, vol. 4, pp. 201, 238–39). Those for imperial members would have had colorful emblems of dragons or the like on the shoulders and skirts. They were sometimes granted by emperors to family members or subjects who could otherwise use only plain or low-grade motifs. This piece was discovered in Wang Zhiyuan's tomb, a relative of Lady Wang (died 1517), the Xiaozhen empress to the Chenghua emperor (reigned 1465–1487). Other excavated tunics of this type from Nanjing were also made of monochrome textiles with small woven patterns in the same color. Decorations reveal conventional motifs of water waves, treasures, corals, and clouds (Nanjing Municipal Museum 2000, pp. 224–227). HL

31

明正德十二年(1517年) 南京太平門外板倉魏國公徐俌墓出土 素緞織錦補子 麒麟紋補服(常服)

Long-sleeved robe with woven mythical beast designs, buried 1517

From the tomb of Duke Xu Fu, outside the Taiping Gate, Nanjing

Reign of the Zhengde emperor (1506–1521)

Brocaded silk satin

L. 138 cm (54.33 in.), W. 250 cm (98.43 in.)

Nanjing Municipal Museum

This ankle-length robe was hand-tailored from a single layer of satin without lining. With a round collar, right placket, and square insignia, the robe exemplifies a standard style of an insignia uniform, or regular uniform, of Ming civil servants. The uniform, which included a rank-matched black silk hat and belt, was worn to meetings, offices, and banquets on regular workdays. An imperial civil servant's badge of rank, with a specific insignia, was either appliquéd or woven on both the front and rear of the robe. Rank was also indicated by motifs and

colors of textiles, as well as by decorations on the belt. A regular uniform was tailored in a certain size, with the length of the robe and sleeves meeting the standards for rank issued in 1390.

Here on this robe, with gold thread woven on plain yellow satin, an insignia that is thirty-nine centimeters long presents a crouching beast, identified as the mythical *qilin* or *baize*; both were specified by the court to represent grades of duke, marquis, prince, and count. Surrounding the beast in a stylized landscape are symbols of

prosperity and longevity: peony branches, cloud heads, fungus, ocean waves, and rocks. Of eight robes from Duke Xu Fu's tomb, two regular uniforms carry an insignia (*Wenwu* 1982, no. 2, p. 30). Another is adorned with a celestial deer, an auspicious beast not denoting any rank. Xu Fu's employment of two different insignias verifies the prevalence among Ming officials of using emblems that marked a higher or lower rank than that which they actually held. HL

32

萬曆朝　緞地補洒線繡　黃云龍花卉攢龍袍料　北京故宮

Bright yellow silk with dragons, material for a court robe (above and page 64)

Reign of the Wanli emperor (1573–1619)

Silk satin damask with embroidery

H. 148 cm (59.2 in.), W. 157 cm (61.81 in.)

Palace Museum, Beijing

The Ming court robe is full and flowing, using a lot of material. In the following Qing dynasty, the court robe became tight fitting, with opened front and back seams for ease in riding.

This sumptuous imperial yellow damask woven with dragon medallions among clouds bears an embroidered design also of dragons among clouds. This yellow hue is solely reserved for the emperor. The embroidery is enclosed within a four-leaf design that covers the front, back, and shoulders. Inside this "persimmon calyx" (*shidiwen*) or four-leaf pattern are two golden dragons with their heads facing front and back. They

appear against a background of flowers and leaves, including morning glories, peonies, camellias, hibiscus, chrysanthemums, and pomegranate blossoms, implying a wish for a wealth, honor, longevity, and male offspring.

Typical of the Wanli period, the dragons have white horns, a white spiky beard and eyebrows, white claws, and rainbow-colored hair. Their bodies are embroidered with scales of gold, with a white spiky ridge on top and rainbow hues beneath. Below the dragons are rocks, in typical vertical shaft form, and waves, among which float some of the Hundred Treasures such as

jewels, coral branches, gold coins, and heads of *ruyi* (wish-granting wands). The same pattern of rocks and waves appears on the remaining three sides. It represents auspicious wishes associated with the emperor, for peace in the four seas (*sihai shengping*) and one united rule (*jiangshan yitong, shanhe yitong*).

The workmanship is superb. The embroidery shows a combination of various stitchings including satin stitch, cross stitch, stem stitch, looping, knotting (known variously as Chinese knots or French knots), special stitching for scales, and net stitching. TTB

33

萬曆朝　緞地彩繡　紅地鏽龍紋壽字女朝褂　金山亞洲藝術博物館

Empress's court overvest, 1595 (below and page 74)

Reign of the Wanli emperor (1573–1619)

Silk satin embroidered in canvas and satin stitching, over-embroidered in silver and gold couching

H. 139.7 cm (55 in.)

Asian Art Museum, 1990.214

The shape of this sumptuously embroidered vest continued Yuan-dynasty imperial fashion, but the decoration is typical of the Wanli reign (Asian Art Museum 1994, p. 144). Two dragons, rising from the rocks and waves strewn with jewels and coral branches, ascend a sky filled with wish-granting clouds. Biting the flaming pearls between their teeth, the dragons clutch the clouds with their five-clawed paws. These dragons of the Wanli period are characterized by white horns and white spiky eyebrows and whiskers. Their rainbow-colored hair sweeps back beneath their horns. They have white spines and rainbow underbellies, and their snouts resemble the *lingzhi* fungus near their tails. Four *lingzhi* fungus are shown between the sea and sky, each bearing six little leaves on their crowns, another Ming dynasty characteristic. Two golden *shou* (longevity) characters appear before the clouds and mist, with golden swastikas above them. The swastikas and *shou* characters form the rebus for *wanshou,* or "ten thousand longevities," a birthday greeting that could be used only for the emperor and empress.

Twenty smaller dragons decorate the front and side seams. The design is slightly different in the back. The pearls of the two large dragons appear above them, and there is only one *shou* character with two swastikas. Below the large *shou* character is a conch holding rock and waves, with a descending bat above it. Two dragons are on the front of the collar, and one at the back. Behind the collar at the back are two longevity peaches.

The embroidery is done on red silk gauze, completely covered with canvas stitching. The larger decorative elements are embroidered above the canvas stitching, in a variety of stitches including satin stitch and gold couching. The garment is thinly padded with silk floss.

An embroidered inscription inside the lapel reads, "Made on the fifth day of the eleventh month, twenty-third year of the reign of the Wanli emperor [equivalent to December 5, 1595]. Length four feet, two *liang* [slightly more than two ounces] of silk floss [for padding]." This particular day was just two days before the fiftieth birthday (by Chinese count) of the most powerful woman of the period, the Empress Dowager Li, also known as *Cisheng Huangtaihou,* "Benevolent Blessed Empress Dowager." She was the mother of the Wanli emperor. This elegant vest of superb workmanship was most probably made for the occasion of her fiftieth birthday. TTB

　Detail

74

34

明朝　單紗妝花　黃色雲肩通袖雲頭地海濤雜寶紋褶袍　北京故宮

Yellow robe with mang dragons amidst clouds and waves, approx. 1500–1600 (above)

Silk gauze damask and double weave

L. 152 cm (59.84 in.), W. (at hem) 254 cm (100 in.)

Palace Museum, Beijing

Although the top part of the robe bears a four-leaf persimmon design similar to that of a regular dragon robe, the bottom part is pleated with twenty-two pleats in front and nineteen in the rear. Within the four-leaf persimmon design is a single four-clawed dragon called a *mang*. The dragon is surrounded by clouds, depicted in various colors, and waves, depicted in green with a white outline resembling froth. The dragon's head is similar to those of the Wanli period, except for the eyebrows and beard, which are less spiky than the preceding examples (cat. nos. 32–33). Two panels extending from the collar to the sleeves each contain a four-clawed dragon among clouds and waves, with the same color scheme as the larger dragon. The band across the pleats bears more *mang* dragons, frolicking between clouds and waves.

The thin gauze is woven with a design of linking *ruyi* clouds, shaped like the head of the wish-granting wand, along with various treasures (*zabao*) such as the double lozenge, branch of coral, and heads of *ruyi* scattered in the background. Within each cloud are four *ruyi* heads; thus the motif is named *sihe ruyi*, or "having one's wishes granted in the four directions," a very auspicious motif indeed.

A painting in the National Museum of History, Beijing, shows an official wearing a similar robe, belted at the waist. Instead of having a *mang* dragon design, it has a *feiyu*, a dragon with fins (Zhou Xibao 1984, p. 391, fig. 7). TTB

35

明朝　緙絲　杏黄地彩戲珠片　北京故宮

Yellow tapestry with *mang* dragons chasing a pearl

Silk slit-tapestry (kesi)

L. 84 cm (33.07 in.), W. 37.5 cm (14.76 in.)

Palace Museum, Beijing

In muted colors of yellow, blue, brown, and green, two *mang*, or four-clawed dragons, confront each other in the sky, chasing a single flaming pearl. The dragons have a few spiky hairs hanging in front of their jaws. The rest of their hair sweeps backward, forming halos behind their heads. They have bulging eyes and snouts shaped like the head of a *ruyi*, or wish-granting wand. They appear in the sky among *ruyi*-shaped clouds, and below them are waves and mountains.

During the Ming dynasty, only the emperor could wear the motif of a five-clawed dragon. A dragon with four claws or less is called a *mang*. Aside from the number of claws, *mangs* and dragons look alike. There are actually two other variations on the dragon motif besides the *mang*. *Feiyu*, or flying fish, is a dragon with fish fins and tail, and *douniu* is a dragon with the horns of a buffalo.

Kesi, or slit tapestry, is woven from silk. The Uighurs introduced this technique to China before the Tang dynasty, and it continued to be woven throughout the succeeding dynasties. It is basically a tabby weave with discontinuous wefts of the color required for a specific design area. A tiny slit occurs when two colors abut each other. TTB

36

明朝　天華錦　紅地方棋朵四合如意錦　北京故宮

Red silk with geometric designs and fungus heads, approx. 1450–1600
(page 76), Double weave
L. 208 cm (81.89 in.), W. 76 cm (29.92 in.)
Palace Museum, Beijing

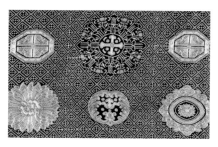

37

明朝　織錦　藍棋子地填花獸面袷袱　北京故宮

Blue wrapper with animal-mask designs (page 77, top)
Brocaded tabby
L. 40.5 cm (15.94 in.), W. 41 cm (16.14 in.)
Palace Museum, Beijing

38

明朝　天華錦（改机）　紫地龜背如意紋裱片　北京故宮

Purple silk with tortoiseshell-patterned design (page 77, bottom)
Double weave
L. 72 cm (28.35 in.), W. 37 cm (14.57 in.)
Palace Museum, Beijing

One type of fancy silk production during the Ming dynasty was the revival of a particular type of lampas weave from the Song dynasty known as "Song brocade" (*song jin*). Called "heavenly splendor brocade" (*tianhua jin*) in the Ming, this textile is based upon geometric patterns such as the circle, square, lozenge, hexagon, and octagon. The design, also known as latticework (Feng Zhao 1999, p. 248, fig. 08.04), is not unlike the architectural designs one finds in ceiling patterns. Within these geometric shapes are various patterns, including larger flowers. The phrase "adding flowers to brocade" (*jinshang tianhua*) aptly describes such sumptuous material.

During the Ming dynasty, this type of fancy textile with an antique flair was used to make wrappers such as the blue example. Traditionally, they decorated the front portions of handscrolls, album leaves, and sutras. They were also used as covering cloths for antiques and were quilted into storage cases (*qin nang*) for the musical instrument *qin.*

In the red example, green lines dissect the red ground at right angles, forming squares. Lozenges shown at alternating squares contain stylized flowers known as *baoxianghua,* an imaginative composite flower created with elements taken from various flowers. The remaining squares contain medallions with flowers, single blossoms, and a design made up of four *ruyi* heads. The *ruyi* is the wish-granting wand that grants one's wishes. Four *ruyi* heads facing the four directions make up the auspicious phrase *sihe ruyi,* or "may your wishes be granted in the four directions." In the corners of the squares holding the lozenges, the *ruyi* heads appear singly.

The blue and gold example shows rows of floral and geometric patterns, alternating with decorative peach-shaped motifs and large medallions with eight spokes resembling the Buddhist wheel of law. These bold patterns appear against a background of blue lozenges intersected by golden lines. The fancy wrapper is attached with ties of the same material, and comes with a bright yellow lining, indicating that it was once used inside the palace.

In the double-layered purple example, the technique is more complicated. It shows alternating lines of ovals and rectangles against a background of tortoiseshell patterns. The oval motifs are similar to the ones in the red example. Each one bears four heads of *ruyi,* making up the auspicious phrase "may your wishes be granted in the four directions" (*sihe ruyi*), also expressed in the red example. A floral motif in the center appears against a lighter background, and around it are four golden coins (one of the Eight Treasures) woven in purple. TTB

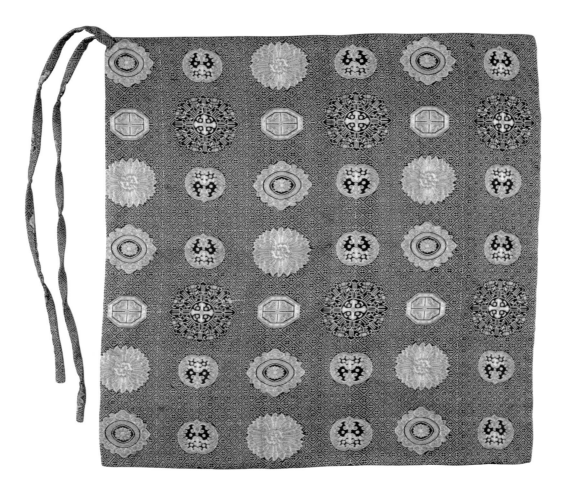

39

嘉靖朝　粧花緞　墨綠地折枝花卉裱片　北京故宮

Dark green satin with floral sprays

Reign of the Jiajing emperor (1522–1566)

Swivel-weave satin with gold thread

L. 51.9 cm (20.43 in.), W. 54 cm (21.26 in.)

Palace Museum, Beijing

Peony, peach, and *baoxianghua,* a stylized flower associated with Buddhism, decorate this piece of brocade. Scattered among them are the Three Abundances (*sanduo*), represented by the Buddha's-hand citron, peach, and pomegranate, symbolizing an abundance of blessings, longevity, and male offspring. The petals are woven in two shades of colors, and the petals, leaves, and veins are outlined in gold.

This type of material is called *zhuang-huaduan,* or swivel-weave satin, which is a type of *yunjin,* the famous "cloud brocade" woven by the official textile workshops in Nanjing during the Ming dynasty. In swivel weaving, colored wefts are employed to form the pattern on a fabric. The fabric has a satin ground and a colorful warp-faced pattern bordered by a woven edge in flat gold thread.

Such brocades were woven on a patterning loom, a tall, complicated structure. It required two people to do the weaving: one seated below to throw the shuttle and do the actual weaving, and another one seated above, known as the "figure-thread lifter," to lift up certain warp threads that control the design. TTB

40

明朝　織金緞　藍地落花流水游鱼佛經包皮
北京故宮

Sutra cover of blue satin with flowers, waves, and fish, approx. 1420–1500
Silk satin lampas with gold thread
L. 31 cm (12.20 in.), W. 12 cm (4.72 in.)
Palace Museum, Beijing

Carp, identified by their long whiskers, swim among waves scattered with branches of chrysanthemum, pomegranate blossoms, and camellia. They are woven in gold, against the blue satin background. This piece of satin was once used as a sutra cover. Many volumes of the Buddhist canon, *Dacang jing,* were produced during the Ming dynasty; following Tibetan custom, it was the practice to stack the pages of each volume between two boards covered with finely woven brocade.

"Fallen blossoms on flowing water" (*luohua liushui*) was a popular motif for brocades of the Song dynasty, showing single peach blossoms scattered among wave patterns. This motif was inspired by a Tang dynasty poem describing peach blossoms on the flowing waters, thus creating an otherworldly realm. The motif continued to be used during the Yuan and Ming dynasties. Later on, the single blossoms evolved into branches of flowers. In this example, carp have been added to the standard motif. The fish are shown in various poses facing different directions, creating a dynamic pattern. Because the word for "fish" (*yu*) is a pun for "abundance" (yu), they add a symbolic meaning to the motif.
TTB

41

萬曆朝　粧花緞　黃地纏枝牡丹蓮花紋裱片　北京故宮

Yellow satin fabric with peonies and lotuses (right)

Reign of the Wanli emperor (1573–1619)

Silk satin damask

L. 84 cm (33.07 in.), W. 37.5 cm (14.76 in.)

Palace Museum, Beijing

42

明朝　粧花緞　絳色纏枝蓮花紋裱片　北京故宮

Brown satin fabric with lotuses, approx. 1522–1600
(below)

Silk satin damask

L. 90.5 cm (35.63 in.), W. 40 cm (15.75 in.)

Palace Museum, Beijing

These sumptuous examples exemplify the work of the official weaving establishment of Nanjing. Known as *zhuanghuaduan*, or swivel-weave satin, this material is a type of *yunjin*, the famous "cloud brocade" woven by the official textile workshops in Nanjing during the Ming dynasty (see also cat. no. 39). The design in the yellow example shows alternating rows of four repeating peonies and lotuses, enclosed within meandering leaf scrolls. The flowers are identical, but the color treatment is different. Each flower and leaf, including the veins, is outlined in gold, and two colors decorate each petal.

The red example depicts rows of lotus blossoms enclosed within curling vines with colorful leaves. The lotus blossoms in varying colors bear plump seedpods filled with seeds, a symbol for numerous male offspring. The petals, leaves, and vines are outlined in gold.

Woven on a patterning loom (draw loom), a tall and complicated structure, such brocades required two people to do the weaving: one seated below to throw the shuttle and do the actual weaving, and another one seated above, known as the "figure-thread lifter," to lift up certain warp threads that control the design. Such material was used as curtains and hangings in the Ming palace, and for covering sutras. TTB

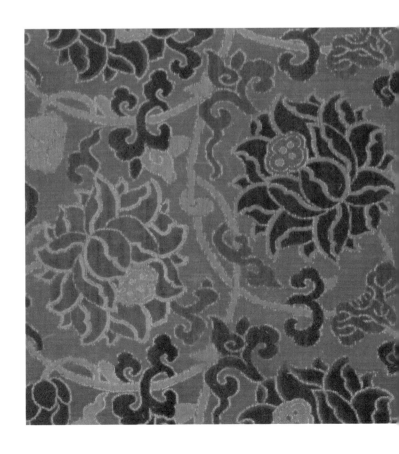

43

萬曆朝　潞綢　綠地折枝花卉紋裱片　北京故宮

Green fabric *(Luchou)* with gold motifs of flowers and plants

Reign of the Wanli emperor (1573–1619)

Silk tabby *(chou)* with supplementary weft design

L. 53.5 cm (21.06 in.), W. 41.5 cm (16.34 in.)

Palace Museum, Beijing

The textile is woven with alternating rows of botanical motifs. One row consists of a repeating design of three bunches of golden bamboo leaves with a single blossom, interspersed with ingots. The other row shows a *baoxianghua* with lozenges. *Baoxianghua* is a stylized flower that was widely used in Buddhist art during the Tang dynasty. It is not a real flower, but a made-up motif based on real flowers such as the lotus, peony, and chrysanthemum. It became a popular design in Yuan and Ming decorative arts. The ingots and lozenges are among the "miscellaneous treasures" *(zabao)*.

This type of silk textile is called *Luchou,* named after the prefecture of Luan fu in Shanxi province. Luan fu (modern-day Changzhi) was an important center of weaving in northern China. It was home to at least one thousand weaving families during the Jiajing and Wanli reigns of the Ming dynasty, with over nine thousand looms producing silk textiles for the court. Because the city is too far north to rear silkworms, its weaving characteristically used silk from Sichuan province. The silk is known for the brilliance of its color and its firm texture. Besides serving the Ming court, these textiles were sold all over China and exported to Japan, the Malay Peninsula, and other countries in Southeast Asia *(Mingshi*, chap. 82, pp. 184–85). TTB

44

明朝　織金緞集錦　各色花卉藏教集錦　北京故宮

Ritual cloth

Pieced silk with gold supplementary weft designs

L. 98 cm (38.58 in.), W. 98 cm (38.58 in.)

Palace Museum, Beijing

Precious silk textiles were seldom wasted in China. Even scraps of material could be used creatively to create works of art.

The ritual cloth is a fine example of pieced work. Variously colored silk, some plain, some patterned, woven with gold supplementary weft designs of blossoms and fruit, had been cut into triangles and sewn together into a square. Four squares consisting of eighteen triangular pieces form the central design, bordered with two rows

of alternating strips of red and yellow brocade with nicely mitered corners. Notice the way the design is fitted together; the same colors are never directly sewn next to each other.

Piecing has a long history in China. When a son was born, his family would go around to a hundred households and ask for a scrap of cloth. From those scraps, a "hundred families robe" (*baijia yi*) was pieced together. A baby wearing that garment would have the protection of a hundred

families and grow up healthy and strong.

This type of textile is used in Buddhist rituals, either to cover cymbals or to be placed underneath ritual implements such as the thunderbolt and bell. It continues to be made in Bhutan today, where it is typically used for covering cymbals. This form was most probably introduced by her neighbor Tibet, who in turn was influenced by Ming dynasty embroidery style. TTB

45

明朝　夾纈綢　藍地雜寶紋袱袱　北京故宮

Blue wrapping with precious symbols

Silk with polychrome clamp-resist dyeing

H. 56 cm (22.05 in.), W. 54 cm (21.26 in.)

Palace Museum, Beijing

As indicated by the broken tape sewn in one corner, this fabric was once used as a wrapping cloth. It is decorated with a white conch, wheel, branch of coral, and pair of crossed tablets, in the cool color scheme of yellow, green, and blue. While the conch and wheel are part of the Eight Auspicious Symbols of Buddhism (*ba jixiang*), the branch of coral and crossed tablets can be found variously in the groupings of Seven Treasures (*qizhen*), Eight Treasures (*babao*), or miscellaneous treasures (*zabao*). These objects are Buddhist symbols which came into China when Tibetan Buddhism was introduced during the Yuan dynasty. The Eight Treasures

(which often include pairs of circular and lozenge-shaped earrings, rhinoceros horns, elephant tusks, and the head of the *ruyi*, or wish-granting scepter) began to appear in Yuan dynasty art and became a popular motif during the Ming dynasty, especially in textile design.

This clamp-resist dyeing technique, known as *jiaxie*, was invented in the Tang dynasty (618–906) and was especially popular during the Song (960–1279), Liao (907–1101), and Xixia (or Western Xia, 997–1227) periods (Feng Zhao 1999, p. 242, fig. 08.01). This technique continued to be used in the Ming dynasty, especially for

decorating the thin silk for covering Tibetan thangkas. The process consists of folding the fabric into layers (as indicated by the horizontal and vertical fold lines of this example) and clamping it between a pair of wooden panels with engraved (intaglio) designs. When placed in the dye bath, the dye runs through the grooves, coloring only the sections of the patterns. To create a complex design with multiple colors, the process is repeated with different boards and different dyes. Besides Buddhist motifs, other designs include fruit and vegetables, and Chinese and Tibetan characters. TTB

46

晚明　緞繡加彩繪　顧派繡觀音羅漢圖集冊　北京故宮

Album of Guanyin and the eighteen *luohans*, approx. 1600–1644

Satin with embroidery and painted colors

H. 32.5 cm (15.80 in.), W. 26.5 cm (10.43 in.) (single page)

Palace Museum, Beijing

This elegant form of embroidery resembling a Chinese painting is known as *guxiu*, or "embroidery of the Gu family," named after such a family in Shanghai. The patriarch Gu Mingshi obtained his *jinshi* degree in 1559 and built a garden estate named Luxiang Yuan (Dew Fragrance Garden); the family's embroidery is also named after this garden. One of Gu's grandsons was a talented painter who studied under the great master Dong Qichang, and his wife Gu Ximeng was a noted exponent of this style of embroidery. As these examples show, the embroidery is a successful attempt to "paint" with needle and thread. It utilizes a variety of needlework stitches, in combination with pale ink or light color washes to enhance the embroidery. Done on plain satin, each work resembles a painting of the literati style. This elegant embroidery heavily influenced the work of the Suzhou needleworkers.

The album depicts a popular subject in Chinese art: *luohans*, also known as arhats, who are the disciples of the Buddha Shakyamuni entrusted with propagating and protecting the Buddhist faith. As foreigners, they are often shown with exaggerated features such as large noses, lots of facial hair, and earrings. In this set of embroidery, some of the *luohans* have sinicized features. They are typically placed in a Chinese landscape among trees and rocks, but some of them are depicted in the act of crossing the sea. This pose may be a takeoff on the iconography of the Indian monk Bodhidharma (Damo), who crossed the Yangzi River standing on a reed. TTB

Following are descriptions of the nineteen scenes included in the album.

46a. *Guanyin* **with attendant**

Guanyin (Avalokiteshvara), Goddess of Mercy, is shown as a compassionate lady seated on a brocade mat in a bamboo grove wreathed with clouds. Her attendant, the Golden Boy (Jintong, *Zhancai tongzi*) stands before her, carrying her attribute, a vase containing a willow branch, placed inside a blue glass bowl. Her parrot flies above her, with its head turning to face the goddess. The embroidery on the opposite page pays homage to the great compassionate deity, who had acquired great meditational achievement (*samadhi*), and who grants all wishes.

Typical of Gu-style embroidery, the work, executed on thin satin, resembles a painting, especially in the way the garments are shaded. The embroidery employs a combination of techniques, including a variety of satin stitches, knotting, and couching. A rolling stitch is used for the willow leaves, giving it a twisted and tensile effect. Guanyin's hair shows examples of couching, and net stitching is used for the brocade mat. Pale ink accentuates the line work.

46b.

46e.

46c.

46f.

46d.

46g.

46h.

46i.

46j.

46b. Meditating *Luohan* under a pine

Under an arching pine tree, a *luohan* meditates on his animal hide, holding a fly whisk in his right hand. He stares intently at the incense smoke rising from his alms bowl. The whisk and hide are accented in ocher. The depiction of the pine tree, with its needles shown in characteristic clumps and with a wash giving it volume, is no different from the way a pine would appear in a regular Chinese painting.

46c. *Luohan* chanting prayers

A *luohan* chants prayers in moonlight as he holds his hands in a gesture of respect (Chinese: *heshi*, Sanskrit: *Anjali mudra*). Two palm trees appear behind, and the opened sutra lies on a flat rock in front of him. His reed mat is accented in brown; its fringes, embroidered in satin stitch, present a naturalistic touch.

46d. *Luohan* riding a buffalo

A *luohan* calmly reads a large sheet of paper as he is carried on the back of a buffalo, dashing across a stormy sea. The way the waves is embroidered is similar to how an artist would depict waves in a painting.

46e. *Luohan* mending a garment

Seated under a willow tree wreathed with clouds, a *luohan* mends his garment. His features are Chinese. His face and the lining of his robe have been tinted with pale colors.

46f. *Luohan* with a brocade bag

A *luohan*, grinning happily, stands on his brocade bag as he travels over the waves, with wispy clouds embroidered above. Exposing his torso, the *luohan* fingers his prayer beads while supporting a staff on his shoulder, with his garment billowing in the breeze. The staff is a natural tree trunk or limb; hanging from it are a smaller brocade bag, a rolled-up scroll, and a fly whisk. The large brocade bag identifies the figure as Budai Heshang, the monk with the cloth bag, a form of the future buddha Maitreya. Usually Budai Heshang is shown seated and surrounded by little boys. In this elegant Gu-style embroidery, the clouds and waves are lightly tinted with ink, and the *luohan's* robe shows excellent shading with satin stitch. The brocade bag, embroidered with net stitch, shows the typical design of a Ming-dynasty brocade with latticework motif.

46g. *Luohan* riding the waves

A *luohan* crosses the sea on a green plantain leaf, carrying a seven-story pagoda. As in the other embroideries showing *luohans* among waves, the fine line work of the waves and clouds are lightly tinted with color.

46h. *Luohan* riding a deer

Carrying a smoking incense burner, a *luohan* rides a spotted deer while turning backward to glance at an auspicious lotus falling from the sky. The deer, raising one front leg, is making its way up a slope toward a rocky outcrop with a Chinese parasol tree (*wutong*).Wispy clouds complete the composition.

A pale wash has been applied to accentuate the clouds and rocks. The robe of the *luohan* shows a nice gradation of colors.

46i. Meditating *Luohan* between plantains

A *luohan* meditates with his head covered with his shawl and his hands hidden inside his sleeves. He sits on a woven reed mat above a stone seat. Two plantains of different heights balance the composition.

46j. *Luohan* blessing a child

A smiling *luohan* bestows a blessing on a young boy by laying his left hand on the child's head. In his right hand is an alarm staff, a stick with an ornamental finial attached with loose metal rings; the sound generated by the rings during the motion of walking is believed to scare insects away from one's path. The child is held by his father, an official who wears a jade belt. Stalks of bamboo grow from a rocky outcrop; in the distance the rocky summits are wreathed in clouds.

46k.

46n.

46l.

46o.

46m.

46p.

46q.

46r.

46s.

46k. *Luohan* with attendant

A *luohan*, wearing a cloak and a grass hat on his back, walks sedately downhill. He holds in his right hand what appears to be a rolled-up scroll or thunderbolt. His dark-complexioned, foreign-looking attendant is carrying a large stack of sutras on his stick, together with a round object that may be a drum and a fly whisk. A short alarm staff (see scene 10 below) is coming right at him in the sky above. The stitching on the *Taihu* rock behind him closely resembles the shading done in Chinese painting.

46l. Meditating *luohan*

A *luohan* draped by a shawl of subtle colors meditates while seated on a mat, embroidered in the style of a Song-dynasty brocade with geometric designs. Incense smoke rises from a tripod incense burner, placed on a rustic stool made of rock. Arching over him are a palm tree and a *Taihu* rock, named for the distinctive cavity-riddled limestone dredged from Lake Tai in Jiangsu province.

46m. *Luohan* playing with his lion

Sitting with his legs crossed on a rock and holding a bamboo staff, a *luohan* plays with his lion cub. Just as it would be depicted in a painting, the old tree shading the *luohan* has its roots exposed. Other vegetation includes bamboo and clumps of small grass.

Gu-style embroidery is noted for its painterly effect. Nice shading is found on the tree trunk, rocks and robes of the *luohan*. The lion is embroidered with various styles of stitches to give its fur a naturalistic appearance

46n. *Luohan* with a white ape

A *luohan* sits in a relaxed pose on a rock, holding a scroll in his left hand. An auspicious white ape, standing in front of him, offers the *luohan* a peach of longevity. Shading the *luohan* is a Chinese mahogany, *Toona sinensis* (*xiangchun*); exposing its roots, it grows horizontally from the rocky cliff above. There is beautiful shading on the rocks and garment. The satin stitch covering the ape's body gives the fur a shimmering quality.

46o. Meditating *luohan* under a peach tree

A *luohan* is seated in meditation on a spotted animal skin under a fruiting peach tree, a symbol of longevity. He holds a ritual instrument in his left hand, a large thunderbolt representing compassion. His robe has been enhanced with light color washes.

46p. *Luohan* with a sutra

Balancing a sutra on his head, a *luohan*, with his eyes closed, chants prayers and fingers his wooden prayer beads as he travels over the waves standing on a *ruyi*, or wish-granting wand. The rolling waves are accentuated with pale ink; the style in which they are depicted, with little breakers over the *ruyi*, is similar to depictions of waves shown in Chinese painting. The buddha Amitabha, Buddha of Boundless Light, is seated on a visionary cloud issuing from the sutra. Mountain crags wreathed in clouds appear in the distance.

46q. *Luohan* subjugating the dragon

Crossing the waves supported by an upside-down alms bowl churning up a miniature storm, a *luohan* offers a pearl to a dragon flying among the clouds, in his effort to tame the mythical beast. The *luohan*'s face is lightly tinted with colors; gray washes enhance the clouds and waves.

46r. *Luohan* riding a tiger

A heroic-looking *luohan* sits erect on the back of a tiger, as he rides down hill. He steadies himself by pressing his right hand to his thigh, his arm straight, while his left hand grasps his weapon, an iron ring. A tree with clusters of small leaves, growing sideways, forms a canopy over his head.

46s. *Luohan* riding a carp

His sleeves and robe billowing before him, the *luohan* Ashita fingers his long eyebrows as he rides the waves standing on the head of a giant carp. The carp is tinted green and brown, and its whiskers also fly in the breeze. A distant peak wreathed in clouds balances the composition.

Lacquer, Wood, and Bamboo

MICHAEL KNIGHT

The objects grouped together as lacquers share the common feature of being coated with a durable substance derived from the sap of the tree *Toxicodendron verniciftuum*. This sap contains very high concentrations of urushiol, a material that, under the right conditions, forms a natural polymer. The final product has many of the properties of modern plastics, including being impervious to water and to many chemicals, and being stable throughout a range of temperatures. The Chinese have long valued the durability of this material and admired its inherent beauty. The earliest known Chinese lacquered vessel is a cup excavated in 1978 from a site of the Neolithic Weizhi culture at Yuyaohe, Zhejiang province (*Wenwu*, 1982, no. 4, p. 70).

Lacquer technology was well developed by the Ming dynasty. Due to its decorative appeal, broad range of applications, secular and religious functions, and associations with prestige and luxury—developed over thousands of years of use—it was favored at court for a wide variety of objects. The Ming dynasty court used prodigious amounts of lacquer; in addition to applications in furniture and in ritual and utilitarian objects, it was used as paint in many court and religious buildings. The amount used is all the more remarkable considering that the production of lacquer is a time-consuming and difficult process.

Primary among the concerns of the first emperor of the Ming dynasty was to legitimize his right to rule and establish a stable governmental infrastructure. This included the building of an imperial capital in Nanjing and the commissioning of objects for use in an array of imperial rituals and objects to be presented as signs of imperial favor. Lacquer played an important role in these functions, in part because of past associations and use but also for more specific reasons. Red is one of the primary colors used in lacquer and one that predominates in lacquer objects made for court consumption (see cat. nos. 47, 50, 53–55). The Chinese character for this red is *zhu*, the same character as the surname for the Ming imperial family. Red was also the dynastic color for the Ming dynasty. Ease of carving and technical developments in cores and other aspects allowed objects to be decorated with a variety of symbols representing the power and glory of Ming rule (cat. nos. 53–55).

The proximity of the first capital in Nanjing to sources of the requisite raw materials and established lacquer workshops is another possible reason for the widespread use of lacquer at court during the beginning years of the Ming. The tree from which lacquer is gathered thrives in relatively warm, damp climates, and traditionally most groves were located along the Yangzi River basin, as far west as Sichuan and Yunnan provinces. There were two schools of lacquer at the beginning of the Ming, one in Yunnan province, the other in Jiaxing, Zhejiang, not far from Nanjing.

During the Song and Yuan dynasties, carved lacquer production was centered mostly on the lower reaches of the Yangzi River, in large cities such as Wenzhou and Hangzhou, close to sources of raw lacquer. Because of the tradition of putting shop names on lacquers produced during these periods, many of the artisans are known. Famous craftsmen of the Yuan like Yang Mao and Zhang Cheng came from the town of Xitang near Jiaxing in present-day Zhejiang province. It was from the descendants of the artisans from these centers that the Hongwu emperor (reigned 1368–1392), the first ruler of the Ming dynasty, drew his higher-level lacquer workers.

93

The details surrounding the selection of artisans, commissioning of works, and their delivery to the court during the reign of the Hongwu emperor are not clear. Later in the Ming dynasty, eunuchs ran a complex system in which different handicrafts and art forms were either created at the court or commissioned from regional workshops and shipped to the capital. The Hongwu emperor, however, did not trust eunuchs; thus their numbers and influence were smaller at his court. A labor service levy system was central to the Ming tax structure, and it was the method by which most basic laborers were recruited for the creation of the crafts and other materials created for the court. (For a discussion of this system see *CHC*, vol. 8, pp. 477–86.) According to records of the Hongwu reign, a new group of lacquer artisans came to the palace every four years, each group numbering as many as 5,137 people (Ch'ien Chai 1992, p. 78). These artisans came for the portion of the year required under their labor service obligations and then returned to their home villages.

Great numbers of very fine lacquers were created during the reign of the Yongle emperor (1403–1424), including a continuation of the carved styles that had come into vogue during the late Song and Yuan dynasties, but also a variety of uses that reflected the emperor's individual tastes and interests, such as the cover for the Tibetan Buddhist sutra (cat. no. 49).

In 1406 the Yongle emperor began the move of the imperial capital to Beijing. As with the creation of the original Ming capital in Nanjing during the reign of the Hongwu emperor, this move created a great demand for objects to furnish the imperial palaces and temples. The Yongle emperor also had issues of legitimacy—in his case because he had usurped the throne. A telling example of the Yongle emperor's concern with legitimacy can be found in the marks applied on works created at the imperial workshops. Whereas the lacquers of the Song and Yuan often carried the names of the family that managed the workshops, the Yongle emperor began a tradition of incising his reign title on the base of lacquers created at the imperial workshops. This practice, similar to the application of marks on the base of porcelains produced at the imperial workshops at Jingdezhen, was to continue through the end of the Qing dynasty.

The Yongle emperor was deeply concerned with establishing appropriate relationships with neighboring countries. Presenting silks, porcelains, lacquers, and other luxury goods as gifts to representatives from these countries played an important role in solidifying these relationships. Evidence of the use of lacquers as presentation pieces can be found in the Japanese diary "Records of Entering Ming," written by Japanese Buddhist monks in the sixteenth century. It mentions that the Yongle emperor presented gifts, including carved red lacquer (*tihong*) and red lacquer with gold paint, to the Japanese emperor on several occasions. A total of 203 lacquer items were given in exchanges that occurred in 1403, 1406, and 1407. Among them, the fifty-eight carved red lacquers given in 1403 are of particular interest since some, if not all, must have been produced during the Hongwu reign (Li Jingze and Hu Shichang 2001, pp. 56–71).

Beijing presented a situation very different from that in Nanjing for the production of lacquer. The project of building the Imperial City spanned the reigns of the Yongle, Xuande, and Zhengtong emperors, and was not completed until the tenth year of the Zhengtong reign (1445). During that time, most of the construction in Beijing focused on refurbishing and expanding the buildings that had survived from the Yuan dynasty and creating new administrative, palace, and ritual structures. Building an infrastructure to support imperial workshops was not an immediate priority, and thus many workshops remained in their traditional locations. For example, the textile workshops remained in Nanjing and Suzhou, furniture in Nanjing, and porcelain was to remain in Jingdezhen for the duration of the dynasty.

Whereas Nanjing was close to the traditional centers of lacquer production and the sources of raw materials, Beijing was at a great distance. The Grand Canal had fallen into disrepair through the end of the Yuan and early parts of the Ming. It was not completely functional until

1415, nine years after construction of the capital in Beijing had begun (*CHC*, vol. 8, pp. 597–99). Prior to that time, the grains, raw materials, and finished works produced in the Jiangnan area destined for use in the capital were either shipped by a maritime route or transshipped over land and by sections of the existing canal. How the massive amounts of lacquer material necessary for the projects in Beijing were packaged and transported from the Yangzi groves to centers of production is unclear—particularly if the lacquer was shipped in a raw state. Raw lacquer is caustic, unstable, and can cause severe dermatitis if handled. The sap also requires a consistently warm and moist environment in order to cure. Such an environment existed in the Jiangnan area but was hard to duplicate in Beijing, with its extremes of very cold, dry winters and hot, humid summers. These constraints had a bearing on the location of the imperial lacquer workshops during the early Ming and the types of objects that could be created there (Li Jingze 2007, pp. 37–38).

The infrastructure for supporting large imperial workshops within Beijing did not exist during the city's early years as the Ming capital. Beijing had served as a capital of the non-Chinese-ruled Jin (1115–1234) and Yuan dynasties (1215–1368) but had been reduced to a regional capital at the beginning of the Ming in 1368 (Naquin 2001, pp. 109–110). Neither buildings for large-scale workshops nor housing and support services for workshop laborers were immediately available. Large numbers of the pieces made during the reign of the Yongle emperor and the following Xuande emperor must have been created in the south and shipped to the palace. However, the foundations of many of the palace workshops were laid during this period.

The Yongle emperor was much more inclined to employ eunuchs at court than his father had been, and the role of eunuchs in the procurement of materials for imperial use, including lacquers, increased dramatically. They were also directly involved with setting up and supervising workshops within the palace itself. The exact nature of the palace lacquer workshops during the Yongle period is a subject of some debate. Records indicate that a workshop was set up at Jade Bridge or Gold Sea-Turtle Jade Bridge in the Imperial City. There artisans employed the carving-and-filling methods (Zhu Jiajin and Xia Gengqi 1995, p. 8). It is likely, however, that these artisans were provided with blanks created in the Jiangnan region and that only the detailed work of carving the fine designs and inlaying them with gold were done at the workshops. The sutra cover (cat. no. 49) might be an example of such a work.

Contemporary information on Ming lacquer comes from the *Xiushi lu,* or Records of Lacquer Décor, written by Huang Cheng, a lacquer artist and author active during the reign of the Longqing emperor (1567–1572). Huang summarized the lacquer craft of the Ming dynasty, classifying lacquerware into different categories and discussing his own experience with these as well as the origins and methods for each (Zhu Jiajin and Xia Gengqi 1995, p. 1). According to Huang Cheng, Zhang Degang at the Work Project Office and Bao Liang were craftsmen from the Jiaxing school. They were summoned to audiences during the reigns of the Yongle and Xuande emperors and were granted titles to work in the imperial workshops (Li Jingze 2007, p. 37). This suggests they were only in the capital for short periods and likely returned to their home workshops after their audience. It also suggests that their service was treated at a higher level than the standard labor service.

More challenging are references to the *Guoyuan chang,* or Orchard Workshop, which first appear during the reign of the Yongle emperor and continue throughout the Ming and Qing dynasties (Li Jingze 2007, p. 35). While existing documents suggest a location for this workshop, its actual function, particularly during the early part of the Ming, is not entirely clear. Although these records indicate that some specialized work in lacquer was carried out at palace workshops in Beijing during the early Ming, the majority of works must have been produced, as before, in local workshops in the Jiangnan area. As mentioned above, it is very likely that most of the work done in Beijing was on blanks shipped there from traditional production centers in the Jiangnan area. The *Guoyuan chang* may have functioned like other imperial warehouses in Beijing, as a storage site for wares shipped from other locations for use, after government inspection and appraisal, by the imperial family (Li Jingze 2007, p. 39).

Like his grandfather the Yongle emperor, the Xuande emperor (1426–1435) was fascinated by lacquer, and production continued at pace during the early years of his reign. He also continued the tradition of adding his reign mark on certain pieces, in particular those with carved red designs. In fact, on numerous examples the Xuande mark has been incised over an existing Yongle mark. In addition to summoning carved lacquer experts from the south, the Xuande emperor had lacquer workmen sent to Japan to learn the craft and imitate the gold lacquer technique unique to Japan. However, the expense of the Yongle emperor's many enterprises and issues with the Ming monetary system led to massive inflation. During the later years of his reign, court coffers were unable to support production at earlier levels. At the advice of his subject Yu Qian, the Xuande emperor ordered a decrease in "vermilion gold appliqué dragon and phoenix lacquerware" (Ch'ien Chai 1992, p. 78).

Following the reign of the Xuande emperor, Ming rulers became less and less involved with the running of the state and other public affairs. The bureaucracy, run by members of the educated elite, governed at the national and local levels. Within the court, eunuchs came to have greater and greater power and proved quite capable in serving the wants and needs—or developing the wants and needs—of the emperors and the ever-growing numbers of the imperial family and hangers-on. Estimates place the number of members of the imperial family in the 1620s as high as sixty thousand, all of whom received stipends from the state. They were obviously a vast drain on financial resources, but were also huge patrons of materials produced at the imperial workshops (*CHC*, vol. 8, pp. 24–25). Objects created at the imperial workshops during these periods, be they ceramics, lacquers, or textiles, often directly reflect the interests and proclivities of the emperor.

The implementation in the late 1500s of the so-called "single whip" taxation system, by which payments in silver could be made in lieu of labor service, also had an impact on imperial workshops. One of the reasons the Ming handicraft industry was able to surpass that of previous dynasties was that artisans of a specific craft could pool their money and hire a long-term substitute to fulfill their labor duties, thereby freeing up other artisans to create craft items to sell on the open market. The most famous of these was Huang Cheng, mentioned above as the author of an important Ming text on lacquer. According to a contemporary account, "His carved red lacquer is comparable to that produced by the *Guoyuan chang*, and his fine carvings of flowers and fruit and figures are rendered with fluid, precise, clear strokes of the knife" (Ch'ien Chai 1992, p. 79).

The city of Beijing changed considerably during the 224 years it served as the Ming capital. As mentioned above, the initial emphasis of the imperial enterprise had been on legitimizing the reign of the Yongle emperor, who had usurped the throne and moved the capital from Nanjing. By necessity, most construction efforts in those early years had focused on creating an imperial capital that appropriately reflected the power and glory of the Ming court. By the 1500s this phase of building was complete, transportation systems and other infrastructures were in place, and the imperial palaces had come to include large numbers of warehouses, work-shops, and even housing for eunuchs and artisans. According to Ray Huang, "together they formed a service and supply center that was undoubtedly the largest of its kind in the world at that time" (*CHC*, vol. 8, p. 115). Many other materials were ordered from places of local manufacture as part of the Ming tax structure. Eunuchs were involved in selecting these materials or inspecting them to ensure that they were fit for imperial consumption. Specialized artisans

Archaeological excavations at the Treasure Fleet Shipyard in Nanjing.

who worked within the imperial compound were registered, and their services considered part of the service levy. Lacquer seems to have been commissioned through both channels. Certainly by the Longqing reign (1567–1572), the *Guoyuan chang* had already been converted into an official workshop where certain types of lacquers were actually produced (Li Jingze 2007, pp. 36–37). However, the exact nature of the work done at this workshop is unclear; there is evidence that materials continued to be imported from the Jiangnan region.

A final burst of imperially commissioned artistic activity occurred during the reign of the Wanli emperor (1573–1619). By the final years of this reign, the Ming court no longer had the financial power to commission works of art in great numbers or of superior quality. Such pieces could demand truly extravagant prices. According to one period source, "in the past, one [lacquer] box cost 3,000 copper cash." This was comparable to the cost of six bolts of superior quality machine-woven cloth or the cost of hiring a basic servant for one and one-half years (Ch'ien Chai 1992, p. 79).

By the end of the dynasty, the major building activities in Beijing were no longer palace or administrative structures but rather temples, many commissioned by eunuchs or imperial family members, and gardens built by the educated elite, often following traditions of the Jiangnan area. (See Naquin 2001, pp. 187–90, on the creation of villas; and pp. 280–83, on the sights and nature of the city in the late Ming.) Members of the imperial household were not immune to these trends; they built gardens reflecting contemporary taste and furnished them in contemporary styles. Hardwood furniture and other items normally associated with the taste of the Jiangnan educated elite were commissioned by members of the court, blurring the lines of distinction between "court" taste and "literati" taste emphasized by studies of Chinese paintings and the writings of late Ming theorists such as Dong Qichang. Even in these materials (see cat. nos. 61–63, 66) there was a greater focus on ostentatious display and images of good fortune, suggesting imperial harmony.

47

明初　剔紅　雉鳥花卉庭院紋八葵瓣形盤　金山亞洲藝術博物館

Plate with long-tailed bird in a garden, approx. 1368–1400
(above, right, and page 90)
Red lacquer with carved designs (*tihong*)
H. 3.8 cm (1.5 in.), D. 32 cm (12.6 in.)
Asian Art Museum, The Avery Brundage Collection, B62M8

Cinnabar, a red crystalline form of mercuric sulfide found in many parts of China, was one of the pigments most frequently used to color the lacquers made at the Ming-dynasty court workshops. There are many reasons for the popularity of cinnabar: for one, the Chinese term for this shade of red is *zhu*, which is the same character as the surname of the ruling family of the Ming dynasty. Red was also the dynastic color for the Ming and a color that represents happiness and good fortune to the Chinese.

A sophisticated understanding of the medium was required before carved lacquers could be created. In order to undergo the chemical change required for curing, lacquer must be applied in thin coats. The thick coverings necessary for carving are achieved by applying multiple coats. The most complex carved lacquers might have a thin wood core reinforced with a layer of lacquer-impregnated cloth; base coats created by adding combinations of ash, rice paste, wood powder, or fine clay to lacquer; and multiple finish coats of refined lacquer. Each coat has special qualities of sealing, filling, leveling, and finishing, and must be applied in the proper conditions and in proper sequence. Since each coat must be cured and mechanically smoothed before another is added, the thickest applications can require as much as a year from the initial coat to the final finish. (The complexity of these applications are well described in Ohba 1988.) These technical challenges had been overcome by the Song dynasty, making possible the elaborately carved works for which the Ming is famous.

This piece presents a long-tailed bird in a garden bordered by flowers of the four seasons. The theme of birds in a garden setting or with a floral background can be traced back to themes for painting at the Southern Song court. The early Ming emperors harked back to this earlier Chinese dynasty and the arts created there to give legitimacy to their own rule. MK

98

detail

48

明初　剔黑　四鳥穿花叢八菱花形盤　金山亞洲藝術博物館

Black lacquer with carved designs (*tihei*) (below and right)
H. 6.43 cm (2.53 in.), D. 38.1 cm (15 in.)
Asian Art Museum, The Avery Brundage Collection, B62M6

Very elaborate lacquer objects such as this plate and the example in red lacquer discussed above had little practical use. They should be seen primarily as either presentation pieces or objects that served some role in court rituals or ceremonies.

In order to create a piece of carved lacquer of this level of complexity, the inner wood core was usually strengthened with lacquer-impregnated cloth. Then several layers of lacquer mixed with very fine clay were applied to form a uniform surface, followed by multiple layers of lacquer. Each layer had to cure fully and then be lightly buffed before the next layer could be applied. In most cases a telltale line in a contrasting color of lacquer was applied in the first several layers. This served as a depth guide for the carver. In this example, alternate layers of black and red served this purpose. The base coat, which appears at the bottom of the most deeply carved areas, is red. An extravagant amount of time and energy was involved before the blank was even ready for carving. MK

49

永樂朝　戧金紅漆　八寶紋　佛寫經文木版蓋面　金山亞洲藝術博物館

Sutra cover (above and opposite above)
Reign of the Yongle emperor (1403–1424)
Red lacquer over white sandalwood core with incised and painted decoration
H. 26.7 cm (10.5 in.), W. 73 cm (28.75 in.)
Asian Art Museum, Gift of the Connoisseurs' Council, 2007.16.a-.b

The Yongle emperor had close associations with the Tibetan Buddhist establishment; during his reign a number of spectacular objects were created at the imperial workshops for consumption in Tibet. The large embroidered thangka (cat. no. 29) is an example of the types of Tibetan Buddhist work created at the imperial workshops, as is this pair of lacquered sutra covers.

The covers are constructed in the traditional shape of wooden covers made to protect Tibetan religious manuscripts. The core is made of closely fitted blocks of costly white sandalwood. Each cover is elaborately decorated with gold-filled incised designs (*qiangjin*) on the top surface and four edges. The surface design consists of four of the Eight Auspicious Buddhist Symbols flanking a central vase with three flaming jewels. Two lotus stems issue from

the central vase, each splitting into two lotus blossoms and forming pedestals for a wheel, victory standard, double fish, and vase on the top cover, and the umbrella, conch, lotus, and endless knot on the bottom cover, all amidst an elaborate floral scroll. The central panels are decorated with two borders, one of single lotus blossoms, and the other of lotus petals. The edges are filled with lotus and leaf scrolls. One end of each cover is decorated with a monster mask, the masks oriented in opposite directions to signal which cover is meant as the top and which as the bottom. The reverse of the top cover is incised with a single lotus petal on top of a lotus base; the area inside the petal is engraved with a bilingual Tibetan and Chinese table of contents, the engraved lettering filled with traces of lapis and turquoise pigments.

This pair of covers once protected volume 14 of the Prajnaparamita Sutra, which is part of the Tibetan canon (Kanjur).

An article in the Chinese archaeology journal *Wenwu* (1985, no. 9, pp. 85–88) describes the discovery in Tibet of two block-print editions of the Kanjur commissioned by the Yongle emperor in 1410, one set in the Potala Palace and another set at Sera Monastery. Ming records note that the emperor presented religious texts to visiting Tibetan religious leaders between 1413 and 1417; sets of the 1410 Kanjur are believed to have been among these texts. The Kanjur set presented by the Yongle emperor in 1413 to Kuntapa, head of the Sakya sect in Tibet, was fitted with sutra covers of this elaborate and sumptuously gilded design. Records show that Kuntapa received sutras on two occasions. TTB

50

永樂朝　剔紅　芍藥花卉紋圓蓋盒　金山亞洲藝術博物館

Covered box (page 102)

Reign of the Yongle emperor (1403–1424)

Red lacquer with carved designs (*tihong*)

H. 8.3 cm (3.25 in.), D. 24.1 cm (9.49 in.)

Asian Art Museum, The Avery Brundage Collection, B60M309

This covered box is representative of a type created in great numbers during the reigns of the Yongle and Xuande emperors. Like many designs of the early Ming dynasty, precedents for the floral décor are to be found in works created at the Southern Song court. Song examples are most often paintings or ceramics; it was in the early Ming that these designs were fully explored in carved lacquer.

In the base of this piece is incised a six-character mark reading *Da Ming Yongle nian zhi*, indicating it was created at the lacquer workshops during the reign of the Yongle emperor. Court records tell us that the Yongle emperor summoned well-known lacquer workers from Jiangnan to the imperial palace workshops, that these workers were granted official titles, and that an official workshop known as the

Guoyuan chang (Orchard Workshop) was established. However, as noted in the introductory essay to this section, there is some question about the actual function of the *Guoyuan chang* in the early years of the dynasty.

In order to make possible the deeply carved designs in lacquers like this box, the object first had to be covered with a large number of thin layers of lacquer—in a piece like this perhaps as many as one hundred layers. Each layer had to cure thoroughly and be lightly polished before the next layer could be applied. In order to cure properly, lacquer must be kept in a stable environment with consistently warm temperatures (21–27°C) and high humidity (75–85 percent). Creating a piece with a hundred layers could require as much as a year or more of this consistent

environment. Climatological studies indicate that Beijing was cold and dry during much of the Ming dynasty, and it is highly unlikely that any building in that city could have maintained the required environment for lacquer to cure. The same studies show that the Jiangnan area along the lower reaches of the Yangzi River, where the lacquer workshops of the Song and Yuan dynasties were located, was humid and temperate. It seems likely that the workshops of the early Ming, where the elaborately carved lacquers were created, remained in the Jiangnan region. The *Guoyuan chang* might have served as a warehouse for storing these lacquers once they were shipped to Beijing. It is also possible that the elaborate blanks were created in the Jiangnan area and shipped to Beijing where the designs were carved. MK

51

明中期　剔犀　長流曲形把葫蘆式執壺　北京故宮

Gourd-shaped, handled ewer with cloud designs, probably 1500–1550

Lacquer on tin alloy (*tixi*)

H. 22.3 cm (8.78 in.), W. 19 cm (7.48 in.)

Palace Museum, Beijing

This vessel takes the shape of a gourd with
an S-shaped handle, curved spout, and bell-
shaped cover with a duck-head-shaped knob.
The gourd shape is an adaptation of an
ancient form of metal and ceramics vessels
popularized during the Tang dynasty
(617–906). The gourd is also the symbol
of one of the Eight Taoist Immortals and
has other auspicious meanings in Chinese
culture. Close obser-vation of the carved
areas reveals that the entire surface was
first coated with layers of black alternating
with red and then carved. The layers were
applied in reverse order from the covered
box discussed above (cat. no. 50), resulting
in a very different feel and appearance.

This elaborate vessel likely functioned
as a ewer for pouring heated liquids, perhaps
wine or tea. While lacquer remains stable
and impervious to liquids at any temperature, the wooden cores commonly employed
can fail if exposed to sudden and extreme
changes in temperature. It would also have
been extremely difficult to create this shape
from wood. This led Ming workshops
to experiments with other materials
for cores—in this case a tin alloy.
MK

52

明中晚期　剔犀　雲頭如意紋蓋盒　金山亞洲藝術博物館

Covered box with cloud-head design, approx. 1500–1600

Black lacquer with red layers

H. 9 cm (3.54 in.), D. 18.8 cm (7.4 in.)

Asian Art Museum purchase, B83M8

Carbon was the primary pigment for black in early lacquers; due to chemical reactions with raw lacquer, however, it often yielded a dull and brownish hue. The desire for a pure and glossy black surface led later lacquer artists to employ pickled iron, often mixed with arsenic. An analysis of the pigments on this box has not been completed, but the contrast between the rich dark brown of the exterior and the shiny black of the base and interior suggests the intentional combination of minerals to create a desired effect.

Lacquers of this sort—with elaborate, multilobed forms and close tolerances between the lid and body—presented

complex challenges for the woodworkers who created the cores. They were faced with issues of making the piece as thin and light as possible while also making it strong and durable. If such a core were carved from a single block of wood, changes in humidity and natural weaknesses in the grain patterns would cause it to warp, check, and break. X-rays of lacquers of this sort reveal that instead of a single block, the cores were made of multiple pieces of wood carefully joined with the grain of each small piece directed to deal with the anticipated stress. These joined

pieces were then covered by a layer of lacquer-impregnated cloth and as many layers of lacquer as required for the carved decoration.

The types of surface designs on this box have been a source of some confusion among specialists outside China. They represent both clouds and the *lingzhi,* a type of fungus. Clouds, or *yun qi,* represent the essential energy, or *qi,* of the universe. The *lingzhi* symbolized longevity. This combination is the signature motif on the *tixi* type of lacquers. MK

53

嘉靖款　戧金彩漆　龍鳳雲頭如意紋方勝式盒
北京故宫

Covered box with dragon and phoenix

Reign of the Jiajing emperor (1522–1566)

Cinnabar lacquer with inlaid gold; six-character reign mark incised in base and filled with gold

H. 11 cm (4.33 in.), L. 31 cm (12.2 in.), W. 21.5 cm (8.46 in.)

Palace Museum, Beijing

On the base of this box, six characters reading *Da Ming Jiajing nian zhi* have been carved and then filled with gold. They indicate that the piece was made during the reign of the Jiajing emperor (1522–1566), a period of high production for all court-related arts, including lacquer. Dynastic power was in decline during the reign of this emperor, who abdicated almost all his authority to court eunuchs. The Jiajing emperor's fascination with Taoism distracted him further from affairs of state, but it exerted a major influence in the arts commissioned by his court.

The unusual shape of this box, which resembles two diamonds overlapped at a corner, was known in the literature of the Yuan dynasty as *fangsheng* (square knot), a type of knitting. The top cover depicts a dragon on one section and a phoenix on the other. In traditional Chinese iconography, the dragon represents the emperor and the *yang*, or male principle, while the phoenix represents the empress and the *yin*, or female principle. Both the dragon and the phoenix are presented on a red field decorated with cloud and *lingzhi* fungus designs. The dragon trails streamers of flames, while the phoenix has very long and elaborate tail feathers. The edge of the lid is adorned with the *lingzhi* fungus interspersed with symbolic treasures. Alternating panels of dragons, phoenix, and cranes decorate the lowest band on the lid. The topmost part of the body is adorned with flower blossoms scattered on ocean waves, while the lower section has dragons, phoenixes, and cranes. Around the foot are stylized triangles, each enclosed with a floral design.

The presence of the dragon and phoenix on this box indicates it was created for the Jiajing emperor and his empress. The inclusion of auspicious motifs and symbols associated with Taoism reflect this emperor's personal interests and beliefs. MK

Inscription on bottom of box, plate 53

54

嘉靖　剔彩　游龍倒海壽石乾坤紋圓帶款蓋盒
金山亞洲藝術博物館

Covered box with a dragon cavorting in the ocean

Reign of the Jiajing emperor (1522–1566)

Multicolor lacquer with carved designs (*ticai*)

H. 8.9 cm (3.5 in.), D. 24.1 cm (9.49 in.)

Asian Art Museum, The Avery Brundage Collection, B60M308

The complex art of carving polychrome lacquer (*ticai*) reached its climax during the Jiajing period. It requires the application of layers of two or more colors at different levels. According to the color scheme and composition planned in advance, the artist carves down to the different sections to expose the appropriate colors.

Decorated with layers of multicolored lacquer, this round box with cover depicts a five-clawed dragon cavorting between heaven, represented by *ruyi*-shaped clouds against a background of air diapers, and earth, represented by the three rocks emerging among the waves, against water

diapers. The hair and beard of the dragon are finely incised, unlike the spiky appearance of dragons of the Wanli period. The body of this dragon does not bear the usual scales; instead, it is decorated with scrolls in the form of clouds. It also has a bushy tail, not unlike that of the mythical beast *qilin*. Above the dragon is a medallion bordered by heads of *ruyi* (wish-granting wands), enclosing the two trigrams of heaven (*qian*, with three solid lines) and earth (*kun*, with three broken lines), representing the *yang* and *yin* bipolar forces of the cosmos. Because of the emperor's interest in Taoism, such symbols abound

in the decorative arts of this era. Around the dragon is a narrow band of florets set in a hexagonal diaper. Four dragons appear in the outer section, enclosed by a narrow diaper border, and finally a band of classic scroll patterns. The same decorative bands, without the large dragon in the center, appear in reverse order on the lower section of the box.

The bottom is coated with dark lacquer and incised with the phrase *Da Ming Jiajing nian zhi*, or "made in the Jiajing reign of the Great Ming." TTB

55

明前期（十五世紀） 填漆 花卉圓蓋盒
Rounded box with lid, approx. 1400–1600
Red lacquer with multicolored lacquered inlays
Asian Art Museum, Gift of the Christensen Fund,
BL77M26 .a-.b

This shallow box with a domed lid is decorated in a technique related to that used for the sutra cover (cat. no. 49). In both examples, the entire body was first covered with thick layers of red lacquer and then designs were carved into it. These designs were then filled with colored lacquer; in the case of the sutra cover lacquer with gold powder, in the case of this box lacquer with yellow, green and dark pigments. The Chinese term for the technique used on the sutra cover is *qiangjin* (lit. inlaid gold) while the technique used on this box is *tianqi* (lit. inlaid lacquer).

The top of the cover of this box is decorated with four branches of flower blossoms, which can be identified as chrysanthemum, lotus, peony, and probably Chinese herbaceous peony, surrounding a central six-petal mallow flower. The same four flowers are repeated on the border with each blossom set in a lobed panel. These panels are separated by a diamond-pattered ground. The body of the box is decorated with six chrysanthemum branches also carved into the red base coat and filled with colored lacquer. Seasonal flowers were

a common theme in the court arts of the Ming dynasty. As a group they represent prosperity through the four seasons.

Providing a precise date for this piece is somewhat problematic. The technique was in use from the beginning of the Ming dynasty and some experts date this piece to the reign of the Xuande emperor (1426–1435). Examples with this color combination are rare, however, and other experts have given a date later in the dynasty. MK

56

明朝　紫檀木嵌百寶　螭龍穿雲紋拜匣　北京故宮

Rectangular box, approx. 1600–1644

"Purple sandalwood" (*zitan*) with inlays and appliqués of coral, mother-of-pearl, amber, agate, and nephrite

H. 16 cm (6.29 in.), W. 26.6 cm (10 .47 in.), D. 16 cm (6.3 in.)

Palace Museum, Beijing

This is an example of a "greeting-card box" (*bai xia* or *baitie xia*). This term appears frequently in Ming poetry and novels to describe a box used by members of the middle and upper classes to hold gift lists (attached to gifts), invitation cards, or introduction (business) cards. The boxes were usually made of wood and were square or rectangular in shape.

Carved in shallow relief on the outer surface of this rectangular box are designs of cloud whirlpools. The top of the cover is adorned with inlays and appliqués of

coral, mother-of-pearl, amber, agate, malachite, and nephrite taking the form of six flying dragonets (*kuilong*). Six additional dragonets are inlaid on outer sides of this box: one at each of the short sides and two at each long side According to traditional Chinese sources, dragonets are the sons of dragons and are identified by a thin body with no scales and a floral, coil tail. Inside the box is a small wooden tray stocked with paper pages, with a shallow wooden cover decorated with lacquered floral scrolls.

This box has an interesting history: during the Qing dynasty (1644–1911) it was used by the Qianlong emperor (1736–1795) to keep his inscription for *Imperially Composed Thirty Verses for Ming Mausoleums* on paper. This fact is recorded in carved characters (gilded intaglio) inside the cover, which also state that the Qianlong emperor wrote the prose in the year *jiyou* (1789). The emperor's calligraphy in clerical script is arranged in seven columns on the right and eight horizontal rows on the left; in between is his seal mark.　MK

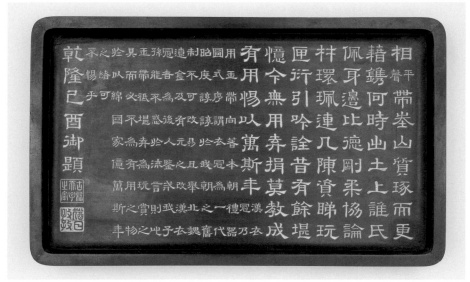

Inside of cover

57

明朝　紫檀木嵌螺鈿　人物花卉紋兩節長方小屜櫃　北京故宮

Rectangular box, approx. 1600–1650

"Purple sandalwood" (*zitan*) with inlays of mother-of-pearl and stone

H. 22 cm (8.66 in.), W. 35 cm (13.78 in.), D. 22 cm (8.66 in.)

Palace Museum, Beijing

This stationery box is related in function to the greeting-card box discussed above (cat. 56). It was used to store works on paper such as letters, writings, notes, books, and albums. It is bigger in size than the greeting-card box, with three levels of storage. The borders between each layer are marked with a meander pattern (*leiwen*) of silver wire inlaid into very fine grooves cut into the wood.

All five visible sides of this box are adorned with pictorial ornament inlaid or appliquéd with mother-of-pearl and different stones. Colors include white, lemon yellow, light blue, dark blue, green, red, brown, purple, and apricot. On the top is a landscape scene with three men standing on the edge of a lake; one turns to his companion while pointing out to the distant mountain, while the third, in a very brightly colored

robe, stands with his hands behind his back. Immediately to their right and farther back is a large pine tree. An elaborate boat with a boatman holding his pole occupies the right part of the scene. In the distance are blue mountains. The sides of the box are decorated with seasonal flowers, each leaf, petal, and branch carefully detailed in dyed mother-of-pearl or stone. MK

58

明朝　紫檀木　荷葉包卷形枕　北京故宮

Pillow in the shape of a lotus, approx. 1567–1644

Purple sandalwood (*zitan*)

H. 10 cm (3.94 in.), W. 24 cm (9.45 in.), D. 16.5 cm (6.5 in.)

Palace Museum, Beijing

This remarkable object, carved out of *zitan*, the most rare and sought-after hardwood during the late Ming dynasty, is a pillow. Collection records suggest it might well have been created for a member of the Ming court living in the Forbidden City. *Zitan*, a tropical hardwood sometimes referred to as "purple sandalwood," was one of the materials impacted by import restrictions; supplies were nonexistent for much of the 1500s. However, with the lifting of these restrictions during the reign of the Longqing emperor (1567–1572), such materials once again entered the Chinese market in considerable quantities. From this it is possible to assign an early date of the late 1500s to this pillow.

China has a long tradition of making pillows in hard materials—the ceramic pillows of the Song dynasty are particularly well known. Such an example in wood is, however, unusual. Carved from a single block of wood, the pillow is quite naturalistic in its lotus form. It is hollow, and all its surfaces, including the inside, are highly finished. Details include long, curved leaves with raised veins on their surfaces, a stem that extends into the interior, and even a wormhole. MK

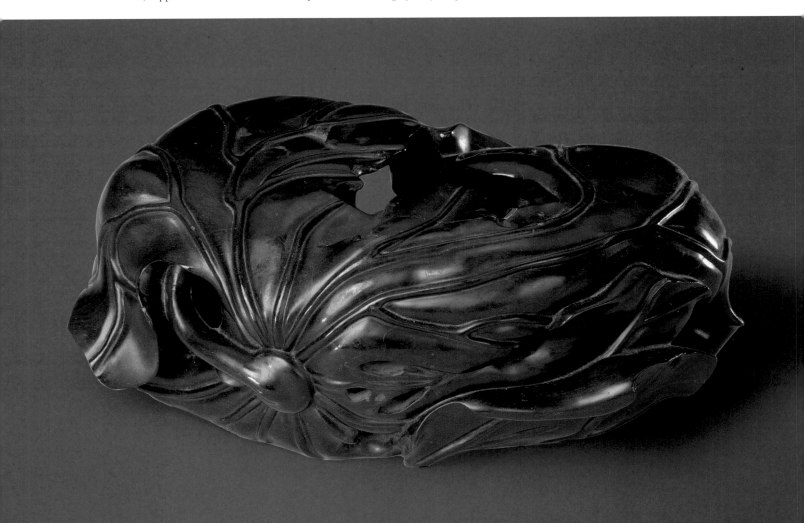

59

明朝　紫漆木洒螺鈿嵌琺瑯　藍黃雙龍戲珠雲頭靈芝紋圓凳一對　北京故宮

Pair of barrel-shaped stools, approx. 1500–1644

Wood with purple lacquer inlaid with mother-of-pearl; cloisonné panel

H. 40.5 cm (15.94 in.), W. 43 cm (16.93 in.)

Palace Museum, Beijing

Barrel-shaped stools were a popular form of informal furniture during the Ming dynasty. Ceramic versions were often used in exterior settings such as gardens, terraces, or open pavilions, while examples in wood were to be found in studies, bedrooms, and other interior spaces. Often made in sets, these stools were smaller and lighter than most chairs and other forms of seating, and they could easily be moved and placed where needed.

Examples of the barrel stool made to reflect the taste of the educated elite most often have little carved decoration and rely on the beauty of the exotic woods from which they were made. This pair is in keeping with the more elaborate taste of the Ming court. The basic material is likely to be a domestic hardwood like elm. It is hidden beneath a layer of dark purple lacquer that has been surfaced with flecks of mother-of-pearl. A round cloisonné panel is inset in the top.

The cloisonné panel features two dragons chasing a pearl on a turquoise green field. The blue dragon represents the *yin,* while the yellow represents the *yang* forces of Chinese cosmology. The field is decorated with auspicious motifs of clouds and *lingzhi,* a fungus associated with longevity. The dragon and these auspicious motifs are further evidence of imperial patronage for these pieces. In all, five colors of enamel are employed: blue, white, yellow, red, and turquoise green. MK

60

明朝　黃花梨木　鳳紋鏤空屏扆梳妝鏡台　北京故宮

Cosmetics cabinet and mirror stand, probably 1570–1644

Rosewood (*huanghuali*)

L. 49.5 cm (19.49 in.), W. 35 cm (13.78 in.), H. 76 cm (29.92 in.)

Palace Museum, Beijing

This combined cosmetics cabinet and mirror stand is an example of a type of furniture made for women; its history as a collected work and the nature of the decoration indicates it was made for an important woman at the court. By the end of the Ming dynasty, it is estimated that nearly sixty thousand members of the Ming imperial family were receiving some form of stipend from the government. Many were women who lived within the Forbidden City. They represented an impressive market for a wide variety of specialized items. (For an imaginative representation of court women at play, see cat. no. 132.)

The piece consists of two main sections: the upper screen, which would have supported a mirror, and the lower cabinet. The screen is made of five removable rectangular panels, each decorated with complex and very finely carved openwork designs. The large central panel features a dragon and a phoenix, symbol of the emperor and empress (see cat. no. 53). Other panels are decorated with dragons, lotuses, and other floral motifs. Dragon heads appear on the ends of the screen's frame, and lions are seated on the posts that support it at the base. The cabinet has two doors with brass mounts; inside are three drawers, two small and one large. MK

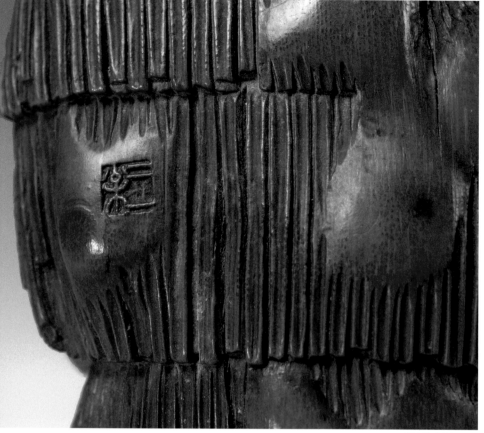

Detail of fisherman

61

晚明　朱三松　竹雕　漁翁　北京故宮

Fisherman

By Zhu Zhizheng (active 1573–1619)

Bamboo

H. 20.5 cm (8.07 in.) (with base)

Palace Museum, Beijing

Carved bamboo figures, like this fisherman, are usually associated with the taste of China's educated elite rather than the imperial court. While the ownership of this piece cannot be traced back to the time of its creation, it is quite possible that it was commissioned or purchased by a member of the Ming court in the final years of the dynasty. By 1600, Beijing had served as a capital for 180 years, and large-scale imperial construction projects had long since been completed. Emperors and other members of the court looked to other projects, one of which was the creation of gardens, which had become a popular pastime among Beijing residents. Some of these gardens were created within the Forbidden City itself, others in the suburbs. These gardens were influenced by the taste

of the educated elite of the Jiangnan area. Such gardens featured rocks, water, certain types of plants, and a variety of buildings—most often an informal studio furnished with the materials appropriate for a scholar's retreat. In this environment, the somewhat artificial boundaries between "court" or "imperial" taste and the taste of the educated elite were broken down, as members of the court became active consumers of the arts normally associated with the educated elite. The buildings in these gardens would have been decorated with the full range of "scholar's objects," including musical instruments like the *qin* discussed below (cat. no. 62), writing implements like the inkstone (cat. no. 63), and objects like this fisherman.

This figure is one of the few surviving works by Zhu Zhizheng, a master from

Jiading in Jiangsu province, one of the leading centers of bamboo carving during the Ming. It is a depiction of a barefoot, long-bearded fisherman wearing a straw rain hat, coat, and cape. His occupation is indicated by the basket he holds, which is filled with fish. On the left back of the figure is carved a two-character seal reading Songsan, taken from his *hao* (sobriquet), Sansong. The base on which the fisherman stands is from a later date.

Documents record that Zhu Sansong was a landscape painter specializing in old trees and donkeys. In bamboo carving, he was known for works with a wide range of subjects, from landscapes to plants, crabs, frogs, figures, and vegetables. MK

62

明朝　木胎黑漆　"漱石寒泉"刻款七絃琴　南京市博物館

Seven-stringed *qin* (zither)

Wood covered with lacquer and carved inscription

H. 12 cm (4.72 in.), L. 108 cm (42.51 in.), W. 21.25 cm (8.37 in.)

Nanjing Municipal Museum

The *qin* and *se* types of zithers were two fundamental string instruments for ritual music during the Bronze Age. The *qin* has survived thousands of years until modern times, while the *se* disappeared after the Han dynasty. From archaeological excavations, the two earliest zither examples were found in the 433 BCE tomb of Marquis Yi of Zeng (Hubei). They featured strings, numbering five and ten, mounted on a hollow soundbox. Three hundred years later in a neighboring state, a seven-stringed zither form was produced for Marquis Dai (*Wenwu* 1974, no. 7, pl. 15-11). What interests yet puzzles archaeologists is that ancient zither remains have been found distributed only in the middle reaches of the Yangzi River, a legendary heartland of ceremonial music of the Chu culture. Not until the Tang dynasty (618–906) did the zither spread quickly nationwide. The Tang zither was introduced to Japan and became the basic model for the Japanese *koto*.

Reflecting different philosophical dimensions of music, three historic books are considered the most important references on Chinese music. *Li ji*, or Records of Rites (compiled approx. 206–100 BCE), traces the growing connection between music, rites, and Confucianism. In *Shengwu aiyue lun*, or Sonance Without Elegy, Ji

Kang (223–262) takes a Taoist viewpoint, explaining how music responded to nature and was increasingly saturated with human spirit. His theory was fully developed by Ming author Xu Shangying (before 1641), whose *Xishan qinkuang*, or The Qin Flavor in Stream Mountains, is a complete study of the instrument's conceptual framework, covering basic knowledge to new interpretations of the zither that developed under the Ming literati aesthetic. Xu's main point was that an expression of personal emotion on the zither should be the primary reason to create a lyric mood, for this was the soul of music, rather than any ceremonial formulation or technical mastery.

Inscription: The four-character inscription in standard script carved inside the soundbox reads vertically *rocks scoured by cold streams*, evoking the zither's fluid, clear sound. HL

63

明朝　石質　抄手歙硯　南京市博物館

Inkstone (above right)

She county, Anhui province

Dark brown stone in three-dimensional form

H. 3.25 cm (1.28 in.), L. 14 cm (5.51 in.), W. 8.5 cm (3.35 in.)

Nanjing Municipal Museum

Along with a writing brush, ink, and paper, an inkstone was one of the four essential materials in a study room. Ink was made by grinding an ink stick against the surface of an inkstone, on which a small amount of water had been placed. Through repeated abrasions, elements in the ink stick such as musk, rosin oil, lacquer, borneol, and Chinese wood oil blend with the water to produce syrupy ink. As recorded in many historical documents, an inkstone's refinement affects the final quality of ink produced. Visible stone veins are a sought-after feature that will determine an inkstone's value among collectors. An inkstone maker would accordingly concentrate his skills on locating the best part of the stone for the rubbing surface, as well as artistically revealing veins for connoisseurship.

This rectangular inkstone forms a beveled surface with a concave indentation on one side to hold ink or water. Standing on the outer edges along three sides, the base has a front opening, which allows the inkstone to be easily moved by grabbing the base with the hand. This practical form is traditionally known as an "inkstone for hand grabbing." The style is noted for its simplicity and the consequent impression of an opened bottom. This stone belongs to the type known as She or Longwei, named after its two sources: She county in Anhui province, and Mount Longwei in Wuyuan county, Jiangxi province. Quarrying for inkstones in Wuyuan began in the 700s and was controlled by the Southern Tang court (937–960). She stone is traditionally regarded as one of the four primary inkstones, along with Duan stone of Guangdong, Tao stone of Gansu, and Chengni stone of Shanxi. The hard texture with delicate veins is known as "human eyebrows." HL

64

萬曆朝　木版刻印書　欣賞篇　南京市博物館

Xinshang bin (**Connoisseurship**)

Reign of the Wanli emperor (1573–1619)

Woodblock-printed book

H. 27.25 cm (10.73 in.), W. 16.75 cm (6.59 in.)

Nanjing Municipal Museum

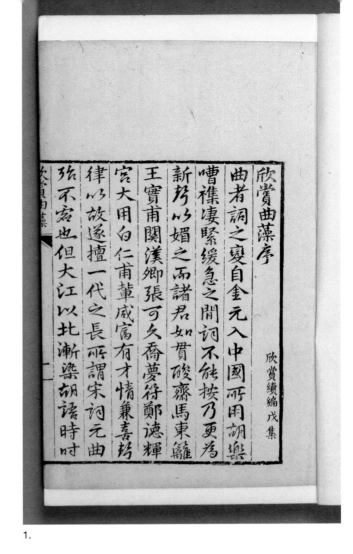

1.

Published as a complement to a 1511 edition, *Xinshang bin* (Connoisseurship), compiled by a Mao Yixiang from 1580 to 1609, is a ten-chapter illustrated encyclopedia on poetic principles, board games, paintings, morphology, classics, symbolic associations, tea, colors, literature, and religion. In the book's preface, Xu Zhongxing, a person of high rank who apparently had forged close ties with outstanding elites of the time, gives an overview of the subjects, which reflect a more personalized approach to classical criticism. Offering an inside view of a highly refined system of cultural connoisseurship, the volume shown here is a lavish evocation of the cultivation of tastes among Ming officials.

Ming woodblock books published through official channels can be divided into five types. The primary "inner palace publications" (*neifu ben*) were produced by the Directorate of Ceremonial, one of twenty-four eunuch-run directorates. Publications by the Directorate of Education (*jian ben*) included those by the northern (Beijing) and southern (Nanjing) branches. The highest number of volumes was published by the Six Ministries (*buyuan ben*) and regional administrators (*fanfu ben*). The last type, to which the *Xinshang bin* belonged, was called

shupa ben, or "book with handkerchief." It was unique in all governmental publications throughout Chinese history, for it was the only time the entire government fell sway to a single fad: that of giving a "book with handkerchief" to each other at business occasions such as meetings, promotions, or retirements.

This volume was printed in movable type, an eleventh-century innovation of Bi Sheng, which during the Ming dynasty was popularized in Anhui, Zhejiang, Jiangsu, Fujian, and Sichuan. In addition to traditional wooden fonts, tin and later brass were used for casting letters in clay or brass molds. Toward the fifteenth century, color prints were made with the use of three- and four-colored blocks, using red, black, green, and purple or yellow (Zhou Xinhui 1998, p. 23).

Following are descriptions of the sample pages from *Xinshang bin* shown here.
1. The "Preface on Appreciation of Dramas" summarizes the history of the musical dramas of western origin that entered China during the Jin (1115–1234) and Yuan (1279–1368) dynasties.
2. The right-hand page lists four of the "Ten Friends" illustrated in the chapter: "Rhythm's friend is a purple bamboo flute"; "An elder's friend is a square bamboo stick"; "Clarity's friend is the jade instrument *qing*"

(see cat. no. 21); and "Speechless's friend is an iridescent inkstone" (see cat. no. 63). The left-hand page shows two rectangular drawings, titled "Friend Duan Stone," illustrating bamboo with inscriptions at the top.
3. The right-hand page notes that the "Friend Duan Stone" drawings were on two sides of a stone slab that Song poet Su Dongpo (1037–1101) erected in his mountain studio. The left-hand page is a drawing of a small-mouthed, elliptical vase painted with flower branches, titled "Friend Ceramic."
4. The right-hand page states that the elliptical vase is a wine jar, a ceramic friend to a mountain studio. The left-hand page, titled "Friend for Conversation," illustrates a long-handled spoon with a bundle of long hair.
5. The right-hand page explains that the spoon is waved by a person during conversation, in order to drive away mosquitoes and insects. The left-hand page shows a bed, titled "Friend for Dreams."
6. The right-hand page describes a jade instrument (*qing*) hanging in a mountain studio, which is named "Clarity" after the sound it makes when being struck. The left-hand page, titled "Friend for Speechless," illustrates a rectangular inkstone. HL

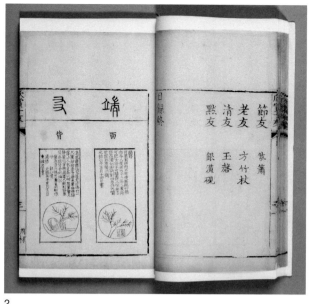

2.

右玉磬股三寸長尺餘古之編磬也
之齋中宏有談及人間事輒之以代清
耳山房呼為清友
贊曰樂造短平夷則中律輕清其塵
貞明其質浮之泗濱應之蓉室輕談
猩事函擊勿失

日錄終

節友
老友　方竹杖
清友　玉磬
黙友　銀漢硯

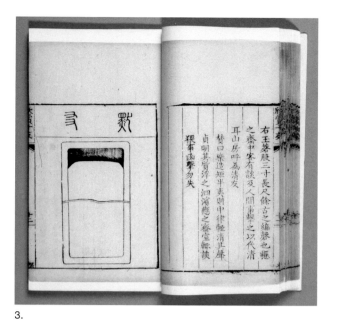

3.

右石屏高二尺有奇廣一尺三寸前後有詩學
竹皆東坡親踏立必端直山房呼為端友
贊曰有石如砥表公之刻竹既瀟瀟詩點
精特乘氣而潤應而而澄清風披拂千古
仰思

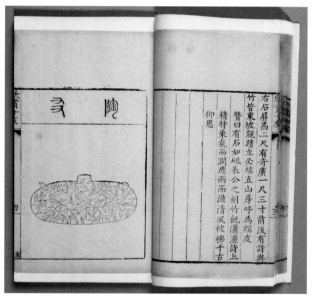

4.

右古陶匜小口圍腹容可二升旁一嘴
寸許如管殊不類人間酒粗山房呼為
陶友
贊曰有古陶匜斟酌隨手瓢區其腹
錢大其口非樽非壺為定為黨醉鄉
日月與爾長怡

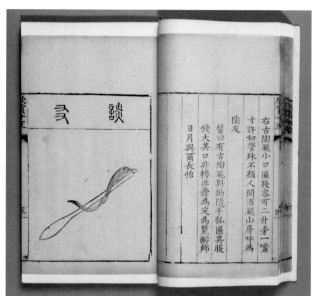

5.

右玉塵柄長尺許上結驄尾著中與客
對談持之致勳不敢近山房呼為談友
贊曰琢玉為柄結尾為拂披風揮月
清真之逸清談欲吐玄簡未窮吾惟
於爾興趣攸同

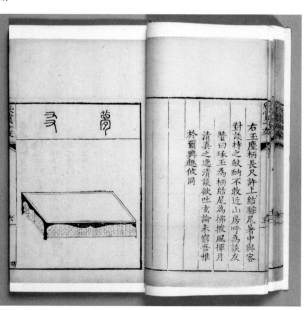

6.

65

永樂朝　南京西北中保村　寶船廠遺址出土　船用木構件3件

Three wooden remnants (pages 118, 119, and 120)

From the Baochuan shipyard site in Zhongbaocun, northwest Nanjing

Reign of the Yongle emperor (1403–1424)

Nanjing Municipal Museum

Between 1405 and 1433, the Ming emperor raised seven extensive naval campaigns "to manifest force on the seas, as well as to demonstrate China's prosperity" (*Mingshi*, chap. 6, p. 7105; chap. 304, p. 7841). Until the 1430s, Ming fleets had come to power in East Asian waters. Under the leadership of Zheng He (1371–1433), the Chinese navy explored places such as Southeast Asia (including Sumatra and Java), Sri Lanka, India, Persia and the Persian Gulf, Arabia, and the eastern coast of Africa, from the Red Sea to the Mozambique Channel. Zheng He commanded the largest fleet the world would see for the next five centuries. The gigantic treasure ship *Baochuan*—with its 138-meter length, 56-meter width, and capacity of 1,000 people—served as the flagship for Zheng He himself and his primary staff, leading some 200 ships and more than 27,000 crew members.

Ming official references to the "Shipyard of Treasure Ships" come mainly from two records, both written during the Jiajing reign (1522–1566). The *Nanshuzhi* (Annals of Southern Hubs) states that the shipyard was located to the northwest of Nanjing and that manufacture of the treasure ships began in 1405. Li Zhaoxiang, Secretary of the Ministry of Works, recorded important events in the shipyard. He writes that treasure ships began to be produced during the reigns of the Hongwu and Yongle emperors in the shipyard on the bank of the "Dragon River," a symbolic name referring to the emperors' rivers. His description also tells us that when exotic treasures were brought back from overseas, they were immediately put into storage within the shipyard, for which the government had to set up security guards. However, the well-administrated shipyard Li describes had already become lax in his time.

Guided by historical records and old maps, Nanjing archaeologists initiated a series of excavations in 1980 in Zhongbaocun, northwest of Nanjing on the south bank of the Jiajiang, a branch of the Yangzi River. The site was cleaned up by 2002, and the local government named the shipyard ruins a theme park. Over 1,500 remnants have been uncovered from the site. Made of either wood or iron, the remnants fall into three general categories: tools such as rulers, rammers, mallets, and knives; equipment and facilities, including pilings, and frameworks of water wagons; and segments and supplies used to build ships. These categories are exemplified by the three pieces selected for this exhibition. These materials have proven to be essential to understanding the shipyard's system of treasure ships. All three pieces are making their debut in the United States.

While many questions remain unresolved, the Library of Congress's symposium on the six hundredth anniversary of Zheng He's voyages, held on May 16, 2005, shed some light on his historic expeditions, exploring topics ranging from the structure of the treasure ships to the navigational maps he used. No doubt, excavations at the Nanjing shipyards will continue to inspire us to look anew at Zheng He. HL

65a

長形條木板

Fragment of floorboard (left)

Wood carved with openings

L.183 cm (72 in.), W. 30.5 cm (12.01 in.), D. 5.75 cm (2.26 in.)

BZ6:272

The unusual black-colored wood was worked into a long floorboard with a slightly convex surface and a flat rear side. Three rows of five openings were formed into a basic rectangle with a curved edge. Thirty-two nail holes pierce through the wood; each of the holes form opposing round and square openings. This piece is one of fifty-six wooden floorboards found, which can be grouped into two types: forty-four single blocks and twelve joined pieces (Nanjing Municipal Museum 2006, pp. 114–127). Only three of them carry carved inscriptions instructing the shipbuilders where to situate them. One statistic from the excavation report reveals that twenty-one of the fifty-six floorboards bear signs of workmanship such as regularly drilled holes for nailing or residues of paints in red, black, or blue. HL

65b

木夯

Rammer (right)

Wood carved with inscription

L. 104 cm (40.94 in.), D. 29 cm (11.42 in.)

BZ6:30

Unique among all the remnants found in the Ming shipyard, this wooden rammer was fixed by iron nails with three wooden ear-shaped handles around the upper cylinder. It was used to ram earth to make a solid foundation for the work station.

   Inscription: Carved vertically on the lower section of the rammer, the inscription indicates its diameter and inventory number: *a diameter of 1.09 feet; no. 2418 on the X*. On the opposite side was branded the character *guan* for "official" or "government," which marked a specific subordinate workshop within the official shipyard where the rammer was used. HL

65c

木錘

Mallet

Wood carved with inscription

Total: L. 68.5 cm (26.97 in.); mallet head: L. 40.3 cm (15.88 in.), D. 10.8 cm (4.24 in.); handle: L. 72.5 cm (28.56 in.)

BZ6:9

This is one of sixteen T-shaped wooden mallets found at the shipyard. The mallet was composed of two parts: a cylindrical head and a long handle fitted through a rectangular indentation in the head and secured with a wedge. Four of eighty-three mallets from the site bear inscriptions, commonly stating a given inventory number (the largest was 8,800), a measurement, and the area where the mallet belonged, which in addition to the mark for "government" shown on this piece, can include the *xian*, or district.

Inscription: On one side of the head are vertically carved inscriptions: one *zhang* and five *chi*. One *zhang* equals 10.9 feet, and one chi equals 1.09 feet, indicating a total length of 15.95 feet, much longer than the mallet itself; thus it is uncertain what was referred to. Near the branded indentations is the character *guan* for "official" or "government," which marked a specific subordinate workshop within the official shipyard where the mallet was used. HL

66

萬曆朝　上海　肇嘉浜路潘惠墓/中山北路嚴姓墓出土　陪葬木製銅鎖家俱14件

Furniture set of twelve pieces (nine shown in the exhibition)

The reign of the Wanli emperor (1573–1619)

From the tomb of the Yan family on North Zhaojiabang Road, Shanghai

Wood with traces of red, black, and/or brown paint; brass hinges and locks

Chairs (2): H. 19 cm (7.48 in.), W. 12 cm (4.72 in.), D. 8.5 cm (3.35 in.)

Benches (2): H. 10.8 cm (4.25 in.), L. 25.4 cm (10 in.), W. 7.68 cm (3.02 in.)

Table: H. 18.4 cm (7.24 in.), L. 24.1 cm (9.49 in.), W. 13 cm (5.12 in.)

Chests (2): H. 26 cm (10.24 in.), W. 19 cm (7.48 in.), D. 14.6 cm (5.75 in.) (on stands)

Basin stand: H. 20.3 cm (7.99 in.), W. 8.9 cm (3.5 in.), D. 8.25 cm (3.25 in.)

Bed: H. 24 cm (9.45 in.), L. 22 cm (8.66 in.), W. 12.7 cm (5 in.)

Cabinet: 23.5 cm (9.25 in.), W. 15.8 cm (6.22 in.), D. 9.5 cm (3.74 in.)

Trunk: 11 cm (4.33 in.), W. 12.7 cm (5 in.), D. 13.6 cm (5.35 in.)

Shanghai Museum

These miniature furniture models were commissioned for burial by a wealthy family who lived in Songjiang, now a suburb of Shanghai (Wang Zhengshu 1993). Similar examples have been found in other tombs in the region. Songjiang was frequently described in Ming texts as a small town densely packed with wealthy officials and court eunuchs; there, even a one-room house would be furnished with gold-painted furniture and antiques (He Jiying 2002). This region was home to many skillful wood carvers and became one of the centers of furniture production during the later years of the Ming dynasty. Burying furniture models was popular during the Ming dynasty because many people believed that these models would allow the dead to maintain the quality of life they left behind.

This set replicates actual furniture of the time. Included are two yoked-back armchairs, a pair of benches and a table, a dome-shaped trunk, a slope-sided cabinet, a clothes rack, a pair of chests on stands (which retain their original brass hinges and locks), a four-post canopy bed, and a four-legged folding basin stand. In addition to the forms, these pieces also replicate the elaborate joinery employed in hardwood furniture of the late Ming dynasty The techniques utilized include mortise-and-tenon frame construction, with exposed tenons on the sides of the frame; complex locking joints, which tie vertical and horizontal members; and tongue-and-groove construction, for floating larger panels in a frame. HL and MK

Ceramics

HE LI

More than any other medium, porcelain played a primary role in ceremonies, daily life, and trade in the Ming court. Its prevalence can be attributed to the efficient and successful revival of porcelain manufacture in Fuliang (Jingdezhen), Raozhou (present-day Jiangxi province), enabled by Zhu Yuanzhang—the future Hongwu emperor—who controlled the region in the early 1360s. Following occupations of the Wu area (Zhejiang and Jiangsu) and the heartlands of Raozhou and Hubei, Zhu Yuanzhang, with the support of his generals, proclaimed himself King of Wu in 1364. This signaled his larger ambition to take over the country.

Zhu built temples in 1364 and 1379 in Nanjing, setting up sacrificial altars dedicated to the dragon and phoenix (*Mingshi,* chap. 1, pp. 12–13; chap. 47, pp. 108–109). This symbolic act invoked an ancient belief in fundamental cosmic forces, representing negative and positive polarities, *yin* and *yang*. The dragon and phoenix, alone or paired, were ancient symbols of dynastic virtue, serving to affirm an emperor's power with blessings. For the new temples, Zhu needed ceremonial vessels with appropriate emblems of power and dynastic legitimacy. His possession of Raozhou, where Yuan dynasty ceramics manufacture in Jingdezhen had flourished for seventy years, enabled him to reorganize and revitalize workshops that had come to a standstill due to the prolonged war between the Chinese and Mongols. An important example of this ceramics revival produced during his reign as the King of Wu (1364–1368) is the vase shown in this exhibition (cat. no. 67).

The rekindling of porcelain production in Jingdezhen by the early 1360s should not be confused with the establishment of Ming imperial manufacture. According to orthodox and unofficial documents compiled from the sixteenth through eighteenth centuries, key administrative decisions pertaining to imperial porcelain manufacture were made in 1369, 1396, 1402, and 1425. At the beginning of the Hongwu emperor's reign, it is not clear whether agents were sent directly by the court to Jingdezhen to oversee production. High-fired porcelain bricks with written inscriptions were found at sites in the Ming palace in Nanjing, providing dates (1371–1377), names of potters, names and titles of officials, governmental agencies, and potters' responsibilities at the Jingdezhen kilns, attesting that porcelain production was overseen and managed by the governors of the prefectures (*Wenwu* 1977, no. 9, pp. 76–79).

The imperial kilns embarked on projects to deliver special orders for diplomatic missions that Zhu Yuanzhang tried to reestablish, both abroad and at home. In 1375, the Ming court presented envoys from the Liuqiu kingdom (a group of islands near present-day Hiroshima in southern Japan) with gifts of textiles, 70,000 ceramics, and 70,000 iron articles for trade with horses. Two years later, Liuqiu envoys returned with forty horses and a message from their rulers: they did not care for the silks; instead, Chinese ceramics and iron utensils were what they most greatly desired (*Mingshi,* chap. 323, p. 825). Other foreign countries apparently felt likewise: in 1384, in return for 200 ivory products from Siam (Thailand), the Hongwu emperor granted generous gifts, including 19,000 ceramic items (*Mingshi,* chap. 324, p. 829). Ming foreign trade was transformed with a new mandate to create mass ceramics. Thus porcelain became the primary product used to fulfill diplomatic missions, whether in the exchange of tribute or in

the bestowal of imperial gifts for the purpose of intimidating or subsidizing foreign states. Porcelain also became a popular commercial good in private trade with foreign states, despite the prohibition of such trade throughout the Ming dynasty.

Customs from the Yuan dynasty continued. An imperial kiln opened whenever an edict was issued from the court requiring porcelain supplies. If no edict was issued, the kiln remained closed or alternatively could make commercial goods for nongovernmental markets. By 1396, the imperial kilns had to submit design samples to the court for approval and for an expense and labor budget. If they exceeded the allowed budget, the court would issue a mandatory order to open additional facilities, and even force Jingdezhen potters to start firing in the capital of Nanjing. Along with the Jingdezhen kilns, those in Nanjing and Chuzhou (Longquan, Zhejiang province—one of Zhu Yuanzhang's early seized zones) seem to have shared imperial production tasks. The factories established in the early 1360s at the foot of Mount Jubao (Assembled Treasures Mountain), on the outskirts of southern Nanjing, were constructed at the behest of imperial orders for building the capital (*Wenwu* 1960, no. 2, pp. 41–48). The architectural tiles from Nanjing (cat. nos. 89–93) exemplify the early Ming productions at Mt. Jubao.

Dragon terminal, main roof ridge of an imperial building, Forbidden City, Beijing.

According to orthodox historical texts from the Yongle period (1403–1424), manufacture in Jingdezhen was managed through the governmental agents appointed by the Ministry of Works. The court began to send eunuchs frequently to supervise porcelain making. Late-sixteenth-century sources record that by 1402 there were twelve kilns under imperial supervision. There were approximately three hundred regular staff, in charge of twenty-three divisions of labor with individual responsibilities. For processes requiring particular skills, a couple hundred laborers would be drafted from seven counties adjacent to Jingdezhen. The workplace, according to a 1597 document, comprised 168 workshops, 70 kilns, 66 storage areas, and 104 firewood storage areas, in addition to two wells, four shrines, nine gates, offices, and dormitories for staff. The required area for these enterprises has been estimated by Jingdezhen archaeologists to have been approximately 54,300 square meters (Liu Xinyuan 1996, pp. 9–49).

The Ming author Song Yingxing recorded a 72-step production process from start to finish (Song Yingxing 1637, vol. 2, "Taoshan"). Every stage of the process, from extracting earth and purifying the clay to potting, glazing, decorating, loading the saggar (a fine clay box), and firing, required considerable care, resulting in a high quality of production. It was impossible for private factories to attain such excellence in manufacture. All porcelain articles for the palace had to follow extremely precise restrictions, from size and shape to design. The dragon and phoenix remained the principal motifs, their use forbidden to common people. For the first time in the history of imperial ceramic manufacture, a reign mark, consisting of four or six characters, was used on porcelains during the Yongle period. The use of reign marks was subsequently standardized in imperial ceramics for the next five hundred years, from the Ming throughout the Qing dynasty (1644–1911).

Arch gate from Bao'en Temple, Nanjing.

The optimum clay source, from four spots on Mount Macang outside Jingdezhen, was monopolized by imperial manufacture and prohibited from private use. Until the Yongle period, the mineral cobalt, used for underglaze blue decoration, was derived from foreign materials originating in the Islamic world, most often said to come from Persia. The suspension of overseas exploration after Zheng He's last voyage (1431–1433) certainly jeopardized the cobalt supply from abroad. The cobalt used on much Xuande-era blue-and-white porcelain was identified as materials from the Pitangqing mine in Jingdezhen (Urban Council et al. 1989, pp. 38–40). By the mid-fifteenth century, advances in extracting cobalt and increased resources from Jiangxi, Zhejiang, and Yunnan helped relieve the shortages in foreign cobalt supply.

The entire system, involving elaborate administration and extraordinary costs requiring the court's subsidization, resulted in mass production of ambitious quantities. Examples of known large orders from the court to Jingdezhen include one for 443,500 items in 1433, and one for over a million items in the Jiajing period (1522–1566). Even during interregnums, production levels remained relatively high. The annual output in 1571, for example, was 120,000 pieces (Zhang Xikong and Tian Jue 1987, p. 575).

Beyond these specific orders were hundreds of forms and decorative styles that characterized imperial manufacture over a period of three hundred years. Among these, appraised by eighteenth-century aesthetic standards, Chenghua-era cups (see cat. no. 82) were considered the most valuable. Such a pair of cups was worth 100,000 coins by the early seventeenth century (Zhu Yan 1774, p. 112). Following in order of importance were wares of the Xuande, Yongle, and Jiajing kilns, while there were also high-quality works made during the Zhengde, Hongzhi, Longqing, and Wanli periods. Selections for this exhibition include an underglaze copper red vase (cat. no. 68), blue-and-white wares (cat. nos. 67, 69–74), a red-glazed plate (cat. no. 75), the elegant cup (cat. no. 82), a "chicken fat" yellow plate (cat. no. 79), polychrome jars (cat. nos. 85–86), and a large hexagonal vase (cat. no. 87), providing a comprehensive view of Ming imperial porcelain as it expanded into many new areas of design, form, and aesthetic exploration.

The Ming's declining years in the early seventeenth century revealed weaknesses in the national treasury, incompetent emperors, and an ineffective and sometimes treacherous bureaucracy. Ironically, the crucial factor in the demise of porcelain making was the exhaustion of fine raw materials in Jingdezhen. At the same time, technology for porcelain manufacture had never been improved under poor imperial administration and management. Imperial porcelain manufacture in Jingdezhen virtually ground to a halt and was not revived again until the Manchu-ruled Qing dynasty (1644–1911).

Sumeruh pedestal, platform of an imperial building, Forbidden City, Beijing(see cat. nos. 94, 95).

67

朱元璋称吴王時期　江西景德鎮　青花　"春壽"龍雲梅瓶　美國金山私人收藏

Meiping (**prunus vase**) **with dragon and characters** (below and page 122)

Jingdezhen, Jiangxi province

Period of the Wu Kingdom (1364–1368)

Porcelain with underglaze blue decoration

H. 39.4 cm (15.5 in.), D. 24.1 cm (9.5 in.)

Lent by Patrick Mounsey

With its small, flat-rimmed mouth, wide, round shoulders, and body that curves inward to the foot, the shape of this piece is that of a *meiping*, or prunus vase, which emerged in central China in the eleventh century and became one of the most popular vessels for wine service, display, and flower arrangement. In comparison to thirteenth- and fifteenth-century blue-and-white vases, it bears production and design features from both the earlier and later periods, reflecting a style that can be described as transitional.

Its relatively unsophisticated finish is observable in its thick, heavy body, bluish clear glaze with bubbles and a few crackles, mostly unglazed interior, and unglazed, unpolished base. The traditional dragon-amid-clouds design is distinctive in its presentation, lacking the conventional secondary friezes that decorate the shoulders and lower body of other vases (see cat. nos. 72, 74). The prominent five-clawed dragon, not in its usual position at the center of the vase, rises expansively to the shoulders. The cloud forms are rendered in ways that do not precisely follow Yuan or Ming blue-and-white models. Appearing from the top downward are two single-fungus-shaped clouds on the shoulder; one cloud connecting double-fungus-shaped clouds between the dragon's tail and front claw; and, on the lower section, two of each of the former motifs, accompanied by a triple-fungus-shaped cloud.

Except for an identical vase in the Shanghai Museum collection, this is the only extant work of this type. The date of the Hongwu reign which was assigned to the Shanghai piece in 1991 should be reconsidered (Ma Chengyuan et al. 1991, p. 34). This vase was one of the early official productions in the years immediately before Zhu Yuanzhang was enthroned as the first Ming emperor. The two characters written in vertical seal script over the dragon's neck represent the phrase "longevity for spring," carrying a message of renewal and a blessing for the newly established era. HL

68

洪武朝　江西景德鎮　釉里紅　龑首雙環耳龍紋瓶　金山亞洲藝術博物館

Vase with a dragon

Jingdezhen, Jiangxi province

Reign of the Hongwu emperor (1368–1398)

Porcelain with underglaze copper decoration

H. 47 cm (18.74 in.), D. 22.2 cm (8.75 in.)

Asian Art Museum, The Avery Brundage Collection, B60P1235

Impressive for its large scale, fine white paste, and vibrant three-clawed dragon in crimson red, this vase is one of only two known examples of this type, along with a similar piece in the Shanghai Museum (Ma Chengyuan et al. 1991, p. 38). On the opposite sides of the two pieces is a corresponding pair of dragons seemingly in dialogue with each other. The pair of vases served as a rare type of ceremonial vessel produced by the Hongwu emperor's official kiln in Jingdezhen. This style of dragon—with short, straight horns, wavy hair, and strong legs with fungus-headed, long-tailed feelers—remained a primary porcelain motif from the thirteenth through fourteenth centuries.

The form of the vase, with a pear-shaped body and two elephant-head handles ending in a loose ring, recalls an ancient form of ritual bronzes. Two white-glazed porcelain vases of similar design have come to light, one from the tomb of General Song Sheng (died 1407) in Nanjing (Nagoya Municipal Government 1989, p. 41, pl. 43), and the other from the Yongle kiln strata in Jingdezhen (Urban Council et al. 1989, p. 125, pl. 21). This particular shape attained new heights in early Ming porcelain. Painted designs, undertaken first on a potted body, were covered with clear glaze for firing. The copper-containing pigment often appears dull, grayish, or diffused. Most surviving early Ming wares with underglaze copper red are dishes and bowls. The uniqueness of the type and the technical achievement in color establish this vase as one of the most important official productions of the time.

Following an essential prescribed step for all new rulers, Zhu Yuanzhang asked *fengshui* masters for guidance in choosing a symbol for his new reign. Since Zhu originated from the south, his astrological fortune was predicted as falling into a movement along the southern cosmic order, controlled by hot, bright power. This prediction in turn related to fire among the five elements (earth, water, fire, metal, and wood). Based on his fate and communal relationship with the cosmic elements, Zhu chose *Hong,* meaning "grand" or "vast," for part of his reign name. *Hong* can also mean "red," a symbol of fire that was associated with passionate will and utter independence. More important, red implies his surname: *zhu* is the Chinese term for cinnabar. The color red therefore came to appear widely in Ming art. HL

69

永樂朝　江西景德鎮　青花　八寶花卉紋淨盆　金山亞洲藝術博物館

Buddhist ablution basin with Eight Treasures (right page)

Jingdezhen, Jiangxi province

Reign of the Yongle emperor (1403–1424)

Porcelain with underglaze cobalt decoration

H. 14 cm (5.51 in.), D. 31.1 cm (12.24 in.)

Asian Art Museum, The Avery Brundage Collection, B60P33+

70

永樂朝　江西景德鎮　青花　花卉紋單把花澆　金山亞洲藝術博物館

Ewer with a handle (page 132 top)

Jingdezhen, Jiangxi province

Reign of the Yongle emperor (1403–1424)

Porcelain with underglaze cobalt decoration

H. 13.6 cm (5.35 in.), D. 15.2 cm (5.98 in.)

Asian Art Museum, Gift of Mr. Roy Leventritt, B69P16L

71

永樂／宣德朝　江西景德鎮　青花　纏枝花卉紋花澆　金山亞洲藝術博物館

Handled ewer with a spout (page 132 bottom)

Jingdezhen, Jiangxi province

Reign of the Yongle (1403–1424) or Xuande (1426–1435) emperor

Porcelain with underglaze cobalt decoration

H. 35.9 cm (14.13 in.), D. 20.3 cm (8 in.)

Asian Art Museum, The Avery Brundage Collection, B60P85

The cultural influences informing the Yongle emperor and his circle were not solely Chinese. There is substantial evidence for the importance of Islamic art at his court. The success of Zheng He's exploration (see cat. no. 65) further encouraged the emperor's hopes of a rapprochement with other parts of the world. Foreign envoys who returned with Zheng He, bearing various tributes, particularly amazed the Yongle emperor. To better fulfill China's diplomatic missions, as well as to reap the benefits of trade, myriad Chinese products were prepared for Zheng He's fleets. The most valuable good that China could produce in mass quantities during this era was porcelain.

A 1988 excavation by archaeologists found ruin strata of early Ming-dynasty official kilns in Jingdezhen. Remains of large porcelain plates, bowls, and jars discovered in the Yongle-period stratum are now known to have been created as exports for Islamic markets. Never in the history of Chinese ceramic manufacture had as many foreign-inspired forms taken shape as in the Yongle emperor's factories. Certain forms among these were even adopted for use in the imperial palaces and temples. One statistic suggests that nine out of twenty-one white-glazed ceremonial types have forms originating in Islamic metalwork (Urban Council et al. 1989, pp. 22–23, pl. 1, 4–6, 8–9, 11, 13, 22).

Three of those nine types are represented by this group of water utensils from the Asian Art Museum collection, demonstrating the Yongle emperor's preference for the Islamic style. They share similarities in their precise potting, refined clay, and smooth glaze without air bubbles. Decorations were rendered in quality materials with precious cobalt imported from the Islamic world, producing distinctive color and luster. Painted on the clay body, the cobalt, with its high iron and low magnesium content, turned to dark blue through glazing and firing, with irregular ferruginous strains where it had curdled. The decorative subjects on these three works combine motifs from different sources: the Chinese traditional meander and flowers, stylized arabesques of Islamic influence, and the Buddhist Eight Treasures and essential lotus. HL

72

宣德朝　江西景德鎮　青花　果枝花卉紋梅瓶　北京故宮

***Meiping* (prunus vase) with flower and fruit designs**

Jingdezhen, Jiangxi province

Reign of the Xuande emperor (1426–1435)

Porcelain with underglaze cobalt decoration

H. 42.7 cm (16.81 in.), D. (at mouth) 6.6 cm (2.6 in.), D. (at base) 14.7 cm (5.79 in.)

Palace Museum, Beijing

With less curiosity about exotic material than the Yongle emperor, the Xuande emperor, while continuing cosmopolitan policies, emphasized internal economic and cultural development. In the visual arts he resurrected more Chinese-rooted, self-contained standards. Thus the ceramic industry in Jingdezhen produced fewer Islamic forms and more traditional Chinese types than it had in the Yongle period. It is well documented that the Xuande emperor and his empress became aficionados of blue-and-white porcelain. The biggest order from the Xuande court to Jingdezhen, in 1433, demanded 443,500 porcelain items, more than half of which were blue-and-white (Li Dongyang et al. 1587, chap. 194, p. 2632). During the Xuande reign, porcelain with underglaze blue decoration reached the highest peak in quantity and form since 1368. It has maintained a reputation through modern times, as "every material [used for Xuande porcelain] was finely processed; its blue-and-white is the most valuable" (Lan Pu 1815, p. 43).

This traditional form of *meiping* was greatly admired at the early Ming court for its multiple functions. Typologically descended from blue-and-white vases of the early fourteenth century, it has a main motif of flower and fruit branches on the central body, set off above and below by a stylized band of lotus petals and banana leaves. As with the Yongle-era basin and ewers (cat. nos. 69–71), the material used for the design is still imported cobalt. The clear glaze in a pale bluish tone, however, has a soft luster, bubbles, and irregular spits known as "orange peel" glaze. Another feature observable on this vase, as well as on large porcelain pieces from this period, is an unglazed wide foot ring and flat base, both polished to a smooth surface marred by ferruginous strains. HL

73

景泰/天順朝　江西景德鎮　青花　官人出行圖紋大罐　金山亞洲藝術博物館

Jar with figures on horseback

Jingdezhen, Jiangxi province

Reign of the Jingtai (1450–1456) or Tianshun (1457–1464) emperor

Porcelain with underglaze cobalt decoration

H. 39.7 cm (15.63 in.), D. 23.8 cm (9.37 in.)

Asian Art Museum, The Avery Brundage Collection, B60P1228

Illustrating a narrative account of a gathering, this large jar provides a glimpse of Ming elite taste and the rigorous standards and skills required of potters. The story unfolds from the right: a gentleman in a two-story pavilion, attended by two servants, prepares for a visit from three official guests who approach on horseback, in fields enshrouded in clouds. Two preceding servants carry a zither instrument and a wrapped sword, which will be used for intellectual cultivation and martial arts respectively at the upcoming gathering. The way the narrative unfolds, the costumes the figures wear, the luxurious trappings, and the graceful movements and poses of the horses all draw from the legacy of seventh-century academicians (see cat. no. 131).

The figure-in-landscape motif that had been popularized in Yuan blue-and-white was sustained in early Ming porcelain. Beginning in the Xuande period, figures were introduced in a very few blue-and-white pieces (Geng Baochang et al. 2002, vol., 2, pl. 144–45). From the mid-fifteenth century, figures in landscapes became increasingly popular in decorations for large-scale pieces. Jingdezhen potters probably executed more orders from wealthy merchants and the educated class, who developed a taste for this material. Such subject matter was a challenge. Potters had to contend not only with common stylized patterns but also with complicated figures, from horses to humans, and compositions comprising architecture and landscape.

Middle Ming porcelain production expressed new fashions and tastes by transferring ink paintings on paper to a hard, three-dimensional medium. One way in which this piece achieves the pictorial effect of brushwork and ink applications is through the use of native Chinese cobalt, which produces a lighter blue, to paint the central scene, and a mix of Chinese and foreign cobalt for the secondary friezes on the shoulder and lower body. HL

74

萬曆朝　江西景德鎮　青花　盤龍啣靈芝紋大梅瓶　金山亞洲藝術博物館

***Meiping* (prunus vase) with a dragon and fungus**

Jingdezhen, Jiangxi province

Reign of the Wanli emperor (1573–1619)

Porcelain with underglaze cobalt decoration

H. 62.8 cm (24.72 in.)

Asian Art Museum, The Avery Brundage Collection, B60P89+

This vase reflects the Ming imperial workshops' method of producing large porcelain pieces. The body, judging by two raised seams circling it, was joined from three individual, prepotted parts. The painted subject is a four-clawed dragon carrying a sacred fungus in its mouth. With a twisted body and a long, tangled tail, the creature stands out against a white sky. A secondary band of lotus petals, each originating in an overturned lotus leaf, appears on both the shoulder and lower body. Although the frieze arrangement clearly follows that of Xuande-period vases, the animated appearance of the dragon, which almost seems to be spitting the fungus from its mouth, differs from more conventional representations on earlier porcelain.

Stylistically, Yongle-era prunus vases with underglaze blue decorations are rather close to those of the Yuan dynasty (1279–1368). Relatively short in height, ranging from twenty to forty-five centimeters, the body of a Yongle vase slightly tapers toward the lower section. The main motifs are limited to lotus scrolls, fruit branches, garden scenes, and the "Three Friends" of plum, bamboo, and pine. The secondary friezes commonly consist of a series of flowering branches framed in lotus petals. In contrast, vases in the Xuande period markedly increased in height, up to fifty-five centimeters or more. With the growth of personalized tastes, more decorative and less serious subjects appeared on porcelain. Even orthodox subjects were sometimes

revamped. A blue-and-white vase reconstructed from shards found in the stratum of the Xuande kiln site in Jingdezhen depicts a new theme never seen before: a single four-clawed dragon presenting a three-whorled fungus from its mouth (Urban Council et al. 1989, p. 259, pl. 88). The vase shown here inherited not only that same theme but also the six-character reign mark, its particular position, and the secondary bands with overturned lotus leaves—all part of a formula that had been passed down for 130 years, from the Xuande to the Wanli period.

Inscription. Above the dragon's head is written a six-character reign mark: *Produced during the Wanli reign of the great Ming* 大明萬曆年製. HL

75

宣德朝　江西景德鎮　紅釉盤　北京故宮

Dish with red glaze

Jingdezhen, Jiangxi province

Reign of the Xuande emperor (1426–1435)

Porcelain with red glaze

H. 4.7 cm (1.85 in.), D. (at mouth) 20 cm (7.87 in.)

Palace Museum, Beijing

In Ming porcelain, copper-containing colorant was popularly employed in three traditional techniques: underglaze and overglaze painting, and monochrome glaze. The first two were associated with the imperial kilns during the Hongwu period. The copper red monochrome glaze was extremely difficult to control. In the early fourteenth century, it was applied only on small items of Jingdezhen production. A new copper red monochrome glaze was used experimentally at the Ming kilns in the better organized system under court-appointed supervisors during the Yongle period. Although some pieces were unsuccessful, the red glaze, usually applied on small and elegant forms, was thin, lustrous, and bright.

The success rate during the Xuande period was much higher. Red-glazed wares became larger, bolder, and more rigorous in form, some with engraved designs. The glaze was thicker and saturated with vibrant deep red with the coloration of congealed fat—described as "ox blood," "holy red," or "ruby red." This desirable glaze color and vessel style were copied by later imperial kilns for over four hundred years.

The shape of the dish illustrated here was one of the standard forms of tableware used in Ming palaces. The lighter, natural tone in the thin glaze around the rim is a conspicuous characteristic of Xuande-era red and blue-glazed plates, which were often imitated in later, inferior copies. These high-fired, red-glazed wares were made only in small quantities. More commonly, tablewares were decorated with polychrome designs and monochrome glazes in white, blue, green, or yellow. From the Jiajing period onward, Jingdezhen's imperial production proved incapable of making the high-fired, copper red glaze, eventually leading to substitution of a low-fired, iron-content red coating. This glaze, lacking the earlier celebrated bright tonality and luster, is known as "date red."

Inscription. A six-character reign mark, in two columns framed in a double circle, is written in underglaze blue at the base: *Produced during the Xuande reign of the great Ming* 大明宣德年製. HL

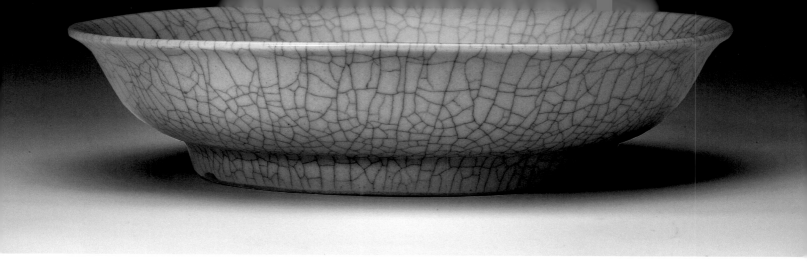

76

宣德朝　江西景德鎮　仿宋代官窯器汝窯釉盤　北京故宮

Dish after Song imperial Ru ware

Jingdezhen, Jiangxi province

Reign of the Xuande emperor (1426–1435)

Porcelain with bluish gray glaze and minor crackles

H. 4.5 cm (1.77 in.), D. (at mouth) 7.75 cm (3.05 in.)

Palace Museum, Beijing

One of the valuable contributions to national culture that the Xuande emperor made was to formalize classical types in official ceramic manufacture. As part of this revival, early celadon became particularly recognized and standardized. Among the most valued celadon was the precious Ru ware with jade-like glaze. Produced in the Ru prefecture (Henan province) for the Northern Song court (960–1126), these celebrated works inspired the potters at the Xuande emperor's workshop to experiment. Due to their limited understanding and knowledge, however, their copies of Song imperial celadon fell short in various ways.

The finishing of this plate suggests that the Ming emphasis on copying Song official wares focused on aspects other than the glaze. The pale bluish gray glaze is relatively thick and smooth, containing minor crackles. On Song Ru wares, these crackles often created an effect referred to as "ash gray" glaze. Nevertheless, on this piece the color tone does not have the Ru's soupy warmth, and the crackles in dark gray lack the subtlety of those in the Ru glaze. Moreover, the glazing does not coat the edges of the foot ring due to the use of a support ring beneath the work during firing. A Ru dish would have been supported by several small spurs at the base, leaving the foot ring fully covered with glaze and tiny "sesame seed" marks embedded in the glaze on the bottom. The shape, with a widely flaring mouth and straight foot ring, also has no resemblance to that of the Song's Ru ware.

Inscription. At the base, a six-character mark, written in underglaze blue and arranged in two vertical rows within a double circle, reads, *Produced during the Xuande reign of the great Ming* 大明宣德年製. HL

77

成化朝　江西景德鎮　仿南宋代官窯青釉開片碗　金山亞洲藝術博物館

Bowl with greenish glaze after the Song imperial style

Jingdezhen, Jiangxi province

Reign of the Chenghua emperor (1465–1487)

Porcelain with greenish glaze featuring brown crackles

H. 5.1 cm (2 in.), D. 12.4 cm (4.88 in.)

Asian Art Museum, The Avery Brundage Collection, B60P1477

Due to the extreme difficulty in technique and the high cost of agate-containing materials in the Song Ru glaze, Ming official kilns did not make a large quantity of Ru-type wares (see cat. no. 76). Most were modeled after official celadon wares of the Southern Song dynasty (1127–1279), from the kilns in the then capital Lin'an (present-day Hangzhou, Zhejiang), where the ceramic programs and technical foundations were built upon the Ru kiln system. A new prosperity that ensured a peaceful realm, coupled with a well-developed taste for ceremonial products, resulted in a greater fashion for jadelike glazes during the Southern Song. The glazes were more varied in tones than ever before. Greenish or bluish glazes became thinner around the mouth rim as they flowed downward during firing, revealing a darker color. The edges of the foot ring, where the glaze had been wiped off before firing, turned a gray color afterward, imparted by the heavy iron oxide content of the regional clay. These two features, known as the "purple-colored mouth and iron-colored foot," were continuously reproduced for the next four hundred years.

This six-foliated bowl shares similarities with official Southern Song celadon ware, especially in its grayish green glaze and crackle patterns. However, its glaze is obviously more vitreous than that of the official Song celadon, and its brown-colored mouth and iron-colored foot are the result of an artificially colored slip deliberately applied around the rim and foot, rather than a more expensive traditional glaze. The absence of high-iron-content clay in Jingdezhen prevented Ming porcelain producers from engaging in greater experimentation with form and glazes. HL

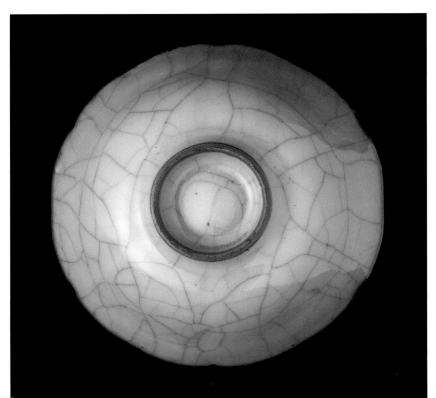

78

宣德朝　江西景德鎮　白釉暗花蓮紋碗　金山亞洲藝術博物館

Bowl with incised lotus scrolls (page 142)

Jingdezhen, Jiangxi province

Reign of the Xuande emperor (1426–1435)

Glazed porcelain with incised decoration

H. 10.5 cm (4.13 in.), D. 20 cm (7.87 in.)

Asian Art Museum, The Avery Brundage Collection, B60P1640

79

弘治朝　江西景德鎮　黃釉盤　金山亞洲藝術博物館

Plate with yellow glaze (page 143 top)

Jingdezhen, Jiangxi province

Reign of the Hongzhi emperor (1488–1505)

Porcelain with yellow glaze

H. 5 cm (1.97 in.) D. 21.5 cm (8.46 in.)

Asian Art Museum, The Avery Brundage Collection, B60P1724

80

嘉靖朝　江西景德鎮　藍釉盤　金山亞洲藝術博物館

Plate with blue glaze (page 143 bottom)

Jingdezhen, Jiangxi province

Reign of the Jiajing emperor (1522–1566)

Porcelain with blue glaze

H. 4.2 cm (1.65 in.), D. 21 cm (8.27 in.)

Asian Art Museum, The Avery Brundage Collection, B60P2087

81

嘉靖朝　江西景德鎮　赭釉碗　金山亞洲藝術博物館

Bowl with brown glaze (page 144 top)

Jingdezhen, Jiangxi province

Reign of the Jiajing emperor (1522–1566)

Porcelain with brown glaze

H. 6.7 cm (2.64 in.), D. 13.5 cm (5.31 in.)

Asian Art Museum, The Avery Brundage Collection, B60P1760

In Ming imperial porcelain, traditional glazes in red, white, blue, celadon green, pale blue, and so on were retained on wares for daily use, ceremonies, or interior display. Certain ancient types among Song official productions (960–1279) were continuously copied. Ming official factories never stopped experimenting with varieties of new glazes, strains, and decorative devices to maintain porcelain's dominance over other ceremonial materials.

A group of tablewares from the Avery Brundage collection illustrates four types of monochrome glazes produced in the Ming imperial factories in Jingdezhen from the early fifteenth through the sixteenth centuries. The Yongle emperor chose the color white and Islamic metalwork–inspired forms to be used at altars and imperial temples. The fifteenth-century white glaze, soupy and smooth, is known as "sweet white."

The dark blue glaze, favored by earlier Mongol rulers, was successfully reproduced during the Xuande period. Blue was often used in ritual celebrations on sacrificial altars. Eloquent names, such as "gemstone blue" and "celestial blue," were documented.

Yellow, viewed as a noble color, became fashionable in the late fifteenth century. This low-fire glaze could cover a previously fired white glaze for refiring, or coat a clay body for only one firing. The yellow wares presented to the Chenghua and Zhengde courts exhibit a delicate body and refined texture with sensitive color tone, winning the admirable description "chicken fat."

The brown glaze resulted from an experiment in the Xuande reign, when official porcelain manufacturers attempted to re-create the brown glaze of a type of ancient Ding ware that had once been presented to the Northern Song court. On Ming imperial porcelain, brown glaze that glimmered on the surface with a shiny metallic luster was called "purple gold," after the description for brown Song Ding ware. Matte brown glaze was referred to as "soybean paste." HL

82

成化朝　江西景德鎮　斗彩　王羲之愛鵝高士圖小杯　北京故宮

Cup with scholars in a landscape (opposite page, bottom and page 145 above)

Jingdezhen, Jiangxi province

Reign of the Chenghua emperor (1465–1487)

Porcelain painted with underglaze and overglaze polychrome decoration

H. 4.4 cm (1.73 in.), D. (at mouth) 6 cm (2.36 in.)

Palace Museum, Beijing

On this small wine cup, a scholar-gathering scene depicts Wang Xizhi (303–361), dressed in an orange-red robe sitting on the ground by his beloved goose. He awaits the visit of a mentor, who walks into the scene opposite Wang, wearing a green robe. Two servants present to their masters a pile of books and a wrapped zither instrument. The background, set by languid willows and cavernous rocks with attenuated foliage, expresses the enchantment of a clear summer day. The subjects, outlined in underglaze blue, are enhanced with dyes and tints of six colorful tones applied over the glaze: orange-red, deep red, dark green, light green, brown, and lavender.

This special type of Ming imperial porcelain is highly treasured for the polychrome decorations. Motifs were outlined in underglaze blue over a formed body, followed by glazing and firing; over the fired glaze, the outlined spaces were filled with color pigments for the second firing at around 800°C. This technique was known during the Ming as *wucai*, "five colors," a term that generally implies polychrome. In an eighteenth-century book titled *Nanyao*

biji (Notes for Southern Kilns), a new term, *doucai*, meaning "joined colors" or "competing colors," was given to this type of production.

Wucai porcelain of this type is believed to have originated in Jingdezhen during the Xuande period, although an incomplete stem bowl decorated with ocean waves in underglaze blue, from the Yongle kiln strata in Jingdezhen, is thought to be finished with overglaze colors. It is known, however, that polychrome did not draw the particular attention of the Yongle court, whose interest focused on monochrome glazes and blue-and-white. During the Xuande reign, polychrome-decorated bowls depicted mandarin ducks swimming in lotus ponds, a rebus for a happy marriage commonly used on imperial art (Urban Council et al. 1989, pl. 33, 89). These works were recognized in Ming texts as "five colors of the Xuande kiln" or "the blue-and-white with additional five colors."

With several new types of *wucai* porcelain, Jingdezhen manufacture received special encouragement from the Chenghua court. Jars, high-stemmed cups, and small cups with five-color decorations won enor-

mous popularity among royal family members. Well-known motifs include grapes, roosters, flying horses in the ocean, floral patterns, and figures. The light blue from Chinese cobalt combined with subtle tonalities of diluted greens, reds, browns, and lavenders on Chenghua cups, which were described by late-Ming writers as "the highest class," "impossible to surpass," "thin as paper," "most delightful," and "producing a pictorial effect."

Inscription. A six-character mark, in two columns framed by a double square, is written in underglaze blue at the base: *Produced during the Chenghua reign of the great Ming* 大明成化年製. HL

83

弘治朝　江西景德鎮　青花釉上黃彩　梔子石榴葡萄荷花盤　印地安納波里斯博物館

Dish with blue plants and yellow background

Jingdezhen, Jiangxi province

Reign of the Hongzhi emperor (1488–1505)

Porcelain with underglaze blue and overglaze yellow enamel

D. 26.2 cm (10.3 in.)

Indianapolis Museum of Art, Gift of Mr. and Mrs. Eli Lilly, 60.87

Variations on this design were popular for about a century after it was introduced during the Xuande period (1426–1435). Here, a spray of gardenia with two buds and flowers fills the center, encircled by cut branches of pomegranates, crabapples, grapes, and a tied bouquet of a lotus flower and pod. Around the exterior is a continuous rose scroll. The plants were painted with cobalt blue under a clear glaze; a yellow enamel glaze was applied to the areas between the plants. Most agree that the best quality of yellow was achieved in the glazes of the Hongzhi reign.

The twisting gardenia leaf continues an earlier pictorial style. However, a departure from the earlier dramatic images is signaled by the highlights created within the plants by the unpainted white porcelain, the lack of texturing details, and the even tones of blue. The yellow enamel indicates a formal, imperial use and perhaps suitably reminds us of the color made from gardenia fruit to dye textiles.

Inscription. A six-character reign mark at the base, in underglaze blue, reads, *Produced during the Hongzhi reign of the great Ming* 大明弘治年製.　Jim Robinson

84

正德朝　江西景德鎮　白釉綠彩暗花　龍雲紋盤　印地安納波里斯博物館

Dish with green dragon design

Jingdezhen, Jiangxi province

Reign of the Zhengde emperor (1506–1521)

Porcelain painted with green enamel

D. 22.2 cm (8.75 in.)

Indianapolis Museum of Art, Gift of Mr. and Mrs. Eli Lilly. 60.86

The exterior has an impressed design of two dragons striding over a background of water above conical mountains. The transparent glaze was left off the bodies and legs, and green enamel was applied to depict the dragons. The green appears in three distinct shades because it covers unglazed areas with deep grooves and some areas that were glazed. On the interior, a single dragon and clouds were created with the same tech-nique. The dragon coiling around the center is like those on glazed roof-tile terminals of early Ming-dynasty imperial buildings.

Imperial patronage and support of the arts were at a low point during the Zhengde reign. The emperor and his predecessor had responded to demands to downsize the number of court artisans, and not much attention was paid to the imperial kilns. Innovations were minimal. The most prolific design during the Zhengde reign was that of a dragon, the symbol of the emperor. The green dragon had long been regarded as the symbol for the direction of east and as the most precious of auspicious animals.

Inscription. A six-character reign mark at the base, in underglaze blue, reads, *Produced during the Zhengde reign of the great Ming* 大明正德年製.　Jim Robinson

85

嘉靖朝　江西景德鎮　青花釉上紅彩　蓮塘魚藻紋大罐　金山亞洲藝術博物館

Large jar with fish in a lotus pond

Jingdezhen, Jiangxi province

Reign of the Jiajing emperor (1522–1566)

Porcelain with underglaze cobalt and overglaze polychrome decoration

H. 29.2 cm (11.5 in.), D. 34.6 cm (13.62 in.)

Asian Art Museum, The Avery Brundage Collection, B60P79+

Fish in a lotus pond, symbolic of eternal prosperity, had been a widespread motif in Yuan porcelain and became repopularized in the Xuande and later periods. With charming naturalism, fish-in-lotus-pond motifs commonly adorned daily wares, particularly blue-and-white and polychrome-decorated porcelain. From the sixteenth century onward, fishpond vessels increased in size, the primary subject varying in composition and components. The round, generous shapes of large jars were an especially suitable format for suggesting

the fluid world of a fishpond. Along with their practical functions as fishbowls, display pieces, warmers, or storage containers, jars with such auspicious motifs satisfied clients' demands for intergenerational symbolism.

The exterior of this large jar is decorated with golden red fish swimming through layers of blue water plants in a deep pond. This vessel is an example of a method developed by the Xuande imperial kiln. On high-stemmed cups, bowls, and plates, potters depicted red dragons or mythic beasts against a blue ocean, or conversely

blue creatures against red seas, by combining two processes: over a prefired blue-and-white piece, red pigment was applied in empty areas drawn by the blue, and then fired again at a temperature of 700 to 800°c. This method was employed for broader subjects from the sixteenth century onward. Attesting to the level of potters' skill during this period, the red color with tints of orange and yellow served to express the glittering scales of the fish. HL

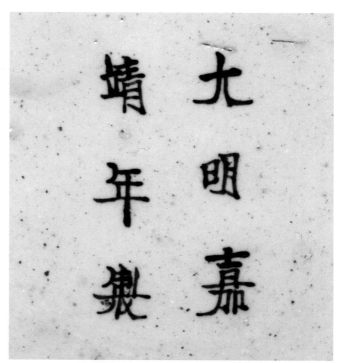

86

嘉靖朝　江西景德鎮　五彩　蓮塘魚藻紋大蓋罐　金山亞洲藝術博物館

Covered jar with fish in a lotus pond (above and page 150)

Jingdezhen, Jiangxi province

Reign of the Jiajing emperor (1522–1566)

Porcelain with underglaze cobalt and overglaze polychrome decoration

H. 49.5 cm (19.49 in.), D. 40 cm (15.75 in.)

Asian Art Museum, The Avery Brundage Collection, B60P78+

87

隆慶朝　江西景德鎮　五彩　鳳穿花紋六方罐　金山亞洲藝術博物館

Hexagonal vase with phoenix (page 151)

Jingdezhen, Jiangxi province

Reign of the Longqing emperor (1567–1572)

Porcelain with underglaze cobalt and overglaze monochrome decoration

H. 25.4 cm (10 in.), D. 21.5 cm (8.46 in.)

Asian Art Museum, The Avery Brundage Collection, B60P2349

As polychrome decoration gained more widespread popularity, advances in the technique were made during the Jiajing period. Potters learned to mix finely ground minerals, such as iron, copper, or cobalt, in order to obtain subdued color hues. Color themes were much more broadened and enriched than those of the fifteenth century.

These two pieces from the Avery Brundage Collection illustrate a method of polychrome decoration in which painting, as well as firing, occurred twice: preceding glaze and over previously fired glaze. Underglaze blue, rather than being used only for outlines as shown on the cup from the Palace Museum (cat. no. 82), was used together with overglaze pigments as color shading to complete the design. The pictorial scene on the covered jar presents an exuberant theme with seven tones in over- all harmony. That the potter sought out new color hues is evident in the attenuated greens and overlapping oranges and reds. The potter's masterly use of tone, clay, and design make this jar especially precious. HL

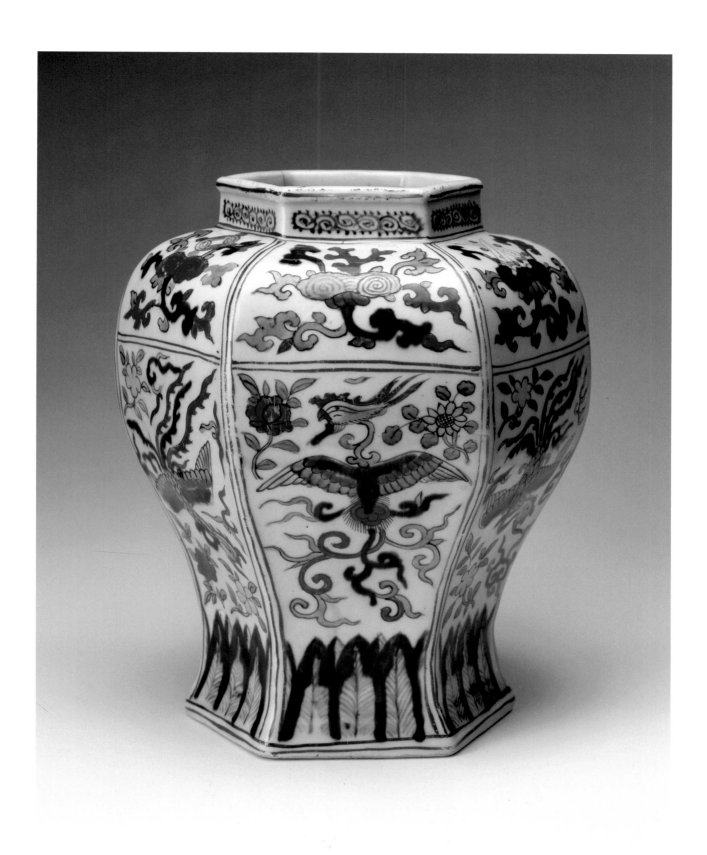

151

88

明洪武七年（1374年）　南京明代城墙遺址發現　紀年款城牆磚

Brick from the capital walls

From the site of the early Ming wall, Nanjing

Reign of the Hongwu emperor (1368–1398)

Earthenware

H. 22 cm (8.66 in.), W. 46 cm (18.11 in.), D. 14.5 cm (5.71 in.)

Nanjing Municipal Museum

This rectangular, solid brick was found in a site of early Ming city walls, Nanjing. In 1378, after years of hesitation, Zhu Yuanzhang announced that Nanjing was to be the capital of the Ming empire. A plan for the new capital was undertaken, including city walls, religious temples, palaces, and cemeteries. Construction of the city's defenses lasted for two decades. New masonry walls were built on an existing foundation and eventually expanded to a 33.7-kilometer perimeter that enclosed an enormous space—even mountains and bodies of water were brought under strategic protection. The wall structure itself was complex, with eighteen gates, defensive blockhouses, and multiple-story barbicans (Ji Shijia 1984).

The foundation of the outer layer of the wall was made of stone slabs, while most parts were built of bricks, affixed with a specially made paste of lime mortar mixed with a syrup of glutinous grain or plants. The majority of bricks were made of regular yellow clay and fired at approximately 600 to 700°c. Lesser numbers that were produced in Jiangxi were of durable beige stone. The need for bricks was considerably demanding. The government had to order inhabitants of the adjacent 118 counties, from 28 prefectures, to make bricks. All workshops, either private or governmental, were under the supervision of civil servants.

Ming brick-wall construction carried on the tradition of the Qin dynasty (221–207 BCE), which had built the Great Wall in 221 BCE. The Ming government, which commissioned the bricks, dictated not only the type and size required but also the identification marks. These inscriptions recorded the names of the brickmaker and his overseers, the date that the piece was produced, and the administrative prefecture or county. With that information, good quality or poor workmanship could be traced to its source.

Inscription. The surface of one side bears stamped inscriptions, reading, *Made by worker Chen Minzhi, under Staff Foreman Liu Weizhong, who was a subordinate of Tang Lijing, Assistant Magistrate to Supervisor at Tongcheng county of Anqing prefecture* [Anhui province], *on X of X month in the seventh year of the reign of Hongwu* 安慶府桐城縣調官主簿唐季靜／司史劉惟中作／臣陳民知／洪武七年月　日. HL

89−90

永樂–宣德朝　南京中華門外大報恩寺遺址發現　琉璃彩釉陶　獅紋飛象紋拱門構件

Two segments of an arched gate, approx. 1412–1431 (above and page 154)

From the site of the Bao'ensi, outside the Central Chinese Gate, Nanjing

Reigns of the Yongle (1403–1424) and Xuande (1426–1435) emperors

Earthenware with low-fired polychrome glazes

Elephant: H. 51 cm (20.08 in.), W. 47.6 cm (18.75 in.), D. 39.5 cm (15.55 in.)

Lion: H. 43.4 cm (17.1 in.), W. 47.7 cm (18.78 in.), D. 42 cm (16.54 in.)

Nanjing Municipal Museum

These two architectural segments were primary sections of an arched gate from the Temple of Gratitude, or Bao'ensi, built by the third Ming ruler, the Yongle emperor. In name, it was dedicated to his father, the Hongwu emperor, and Empress Ma, but in reality it was for his own mother, Lady Qi, who, according to several Ming documents, was a Korean. The Yongle emperor advocated using the temple to commemorate the virtuous deeds of the deceased. Indeed, this proved to be successful in overcoming opposition to his usurpation of the throne, and in winning the moral support of the nation.

It took nineteen years, spanning the reigns of three emperors, to finish the construction, which was completed in 1431. The temple complex included a nine-story octagonal pagoda, surrounded by a total of seventy-two arched gateways. Each arched gate was constructed of twenty-one segments: seven on the arched canopy and seven on each of the rectangular pillars. A monumental quality was conveyed by animated motifs in high relief. On the pillars, motifs on three symmetrical friezes depicted, from bottom to top, a flying elephant, the mount of the Law Protector, Samantabhadra (Puxian); a lion, the mount of Wenshu

(Manjushri); and a flying ram, the deities' companion—all standing out against floral backgrounds. The arched canopy's center showed a crowned, angel-like Garuda—half-bird, half-man, with two opened wings—capturing a snake. The deity was flanked on each side by a flying angel and a four-clawed dragon.

Very possibly, the design took its iconography from Tibetan Buddhism, which the Yongle emperor patronized in part to consolidate the throne. On his invitation, several important Tibetan priests traveled to Nanjing, including Halima, the Fifth Black Hat Karmapa, in 1406, and Sakya Yeshe, the leading disciple of Tsongkhapa, in 1414 (Chen Nan 2005).

The multiple-story pagoda was an ancient style of Buddhist architecture in China, which originated in the Buddhist stupa of India. One of the few remaining early examples is the Songyue Temple in Henan, built in 523. Along with Buddhism from India, the Garuda image traveled through Central Asia to China. An existing sixth-century image of the Garuda inside the Yungang cave temples in Shanxi shows the deity on a frieze standing between a phoenix and Buddhist statues (*ZGMSQJ,* vol. 4, pl. 3). However, not until the Mongols ruled China did the Garuda take a central place on Chinese arches. The famous Cloud Terrace (built 1345) at Juyong Guan, outside Beijing, presents an open-winged Garuda sculpture at the top of the archway (*ZGMSQJ,* vol. 4, pl. 100). That, no doubt, became a direct prototype of early Ming arched gates in religious architecture (*ZGYSYJY* 1999, pl. 100). HL

91

永樂–宣德朝　南京中華門外大報恩寺遺址發現　建築陶構件　五爪龍首形吻

Dragon terminal for the main ridge of a roof, approx. 1412–1431 (below)

From the site of the Bao'ensi, outside the Central Chinese Gate, Nanjing

Earthenware

H. 64.5 cm (25.39 in.), L. 107 cm (42.13 in.), W. 35.5 cm (13.98 in.)

Nanjing Municipal Museum

92

永樂–宣德朝　南京中華門外大報恩寺遺址發現　琉璃彩釉陶　建築構件　四爪龍首形吻

Dragon-head terminal for the main ridge of a roof, approx. 1350–1430 (page 156)

Earthenware with low-fired polychrome glazes

H. 57 cm (22.44 in.), L. 67.25 cm (26.48 in.), W. 26.5 cm (10.43 in.)

From the site of the Bao'ensi, outside the Central Chinese Gate, Nanjing

Nanjing Municipal Museum

Both of these architectural ornaments with dragon images served the purpose of resting on one end of the central tiled ridge of a timber-framed roof; an identical terminal would have rested at the opposite end. Terminals not only reinforced the entire structure, but they also added aesthetic interest to the roofline. The smaller piece, with a four-clawed dragon, is glazed in yellow, brown, and green. The bigger, unglazed piece, with a five-clawed dragon, is unfinished because it was never used. Its unusually large scale reflects the grandeur of Ming imperial architecture. It has a modeled, three-dimensional rectangular form with a hollow interior and relief designs on the exterior. Tile terminals were widely used on the roofs of Chinese buildings, though their depictions varied.

Many of China's most eminent structures were constructed with hip roofs. Such roofs had a finial mounted on the top, rooted in an ancient bird-totem practice that spread widely during the Neolithic period. The high-standing bird was believed to be a powerful protector of the residents under the roof. The earliest known clay house models with a bird-shaped top go as far back as the Neolithic period. During the Bronze Age, the bird acquired a finial form, standing on top of the building (*Wenwu* 1984, no. 1, p. 16). This finial tile was named *chiwei,* or bird tail. The bird was later transformed into an image of the phoenix during the Han dynasty (206 BCE–220 CE). With the influence of Buddhist art, the image began to take the form of exotic creatures such as lions or mythical fish. Excavations undertaken in the late 1980s at the Yaozhou kiln site near the Tang capital, Xi'an (Shaanxi), revealed that large dragon-head tiles in multi-color glazes were produced in mass quantities on court commission (Shaanxi kaogu yanjiusuo 1992, vol. 2, pl. 2). Later the dragon-head terminal tile became standardized on Ming imperial buildings. HL

156

93

明初　南京明代建築遺址發現　綠彩釉琉璃　五爪龍戲珠紋滴水

Tile-end with dragon, approx. 1350–1430 (below)

From an early Ming architectural site, Nanjing

Earthenware with low-fired, lead-containing green glaze

L. 43 cm (16.92 in.), W. 30 cm (11.81 in.)

Nanjing Municipal Museum

Four types of tiles sheathed the roof of a Chinese building: flat tile, curved tile, and two kinds of tile-ends. Rows of curved tile, with raised semicircular ridges, were placed between rows of flat tile. Together they comprised alternating concave and convex surfaces to guide rainwater downward. Each flat-tile row began with a tile-end such as the one shown here, with a lobed, crownlike face, symbolic of an auspicious cloud head. Each curved-tile row began with a round-faced tile-end adorned with relief designs. Horizontally, the two types of tile-ends created a rhythmic modulation between the alternating circles and lobes.

An accomplishment of ancient architecture, this type of roof construction can be seen in excavated individual tiles from the Bronze Age and complete clay house models of the Han dynasty (206 BCE–220 CE). The choice of design or inscription molded on the face of tile-ends indicated the social status of the building's residents. In times of prosperity, when aristocrats sought to show off their wealth and power, massive tile-ends were produced with various motifs, including dragons, phoenixes, mythic beasts, geometric patterns, and literary phrases. With the growth of towns during the golden age of the eighth century, tiles were deco-rated with bright, colorful glazes. After a period when showy architecture fell out of favor under Mongol rule, decorative roof tiles came back in fashion during the Ming dynasty. For the construction of the new capital in Nanjing, millions of low-fired, color-glazed tiles, associated with new standards of Chinese tastes, were manufactured with modeled five-clawed dragons, the emblem of the Hongwu emperor. HL

94

明初　南京明代建築遺址發現　石雕　龍首形建築構件

Dripstone in the shape of a dragon head, approx. 1350–1430

From an early Ming site, Nanjing

Stone carved with relief

L. 92 cm (36.22 in.), W. 30 cm (11.81 in.)

Nanjing Municipal Museum

Like the newel cap (cat. no. 95), this marble dripstone was found in the Ming palace ruins in east Nanjing. Both pieces were from a large rectangular marble platform on which stood an imperial hall or temple. Such platforms consisted of a single-, double- or triple-layered elevation, depending on the building's scale and level of grandeur. Encircling each layer was a balustrade. Dripstones, functioning as downspouts, were set around the upper base of the platform, beneath the balustrade. They had openings at the neck and mouth to channel rainwater off and away from the platform. This piece lacks openings and was left unfinished. It was carved in the shape of a dragon head with detailed hornlike eyebrows, embossed eyes, coiled nostrils, and beard. Simple yet animate, it has a realistic style that was typical of dragons on official Ming stone sculptures.

In profile, these architectural platforms—called Sumeru pedestals (or *xumizuo* in Chinese)—had an inward waist with two symmetrical friezes above and below. Friezes were often carved with shallow-relief flower scrolls or lotus panels, which served as secondary decorations to set off the projecting dragon dripstones. The dripstones were arranged at even intervals around the platform, each one corresponding to the position of a newel post. Larger dragon-head dripstones projected from each corner of the platform. When rainwater poured from the dragon's mouth, it would make marvelous rhythmic tones on the stonework. HL

95

明初　南京明代建築遺址發現　石雕　鳳凰雲紋建築柱頭

Fragment of a rectangular newel with a phoenix-amid-clouds cap, approx. 1350–1430

From an early Ming site, Nanjing

Stone carved with shallow relief

H. 97 cm (38.19 in.), D. 26 cm (10.24 in.)

Nanjing Municipal Museum

This marble newel carved with relief designs was discovered in the ruins of the early Ming palace in east Nanjing, along with the dragon-head dripstone (cat. no. 94). Both pieces were from a large rectangular marble platform that functioned as the foundation of an imperial hall or temple. At the center of each side of the platform were stairs leading up to the main building. Bisecting the stairs was a wide marble ramp, or "sacred way," reserved solely for transport of the emperor's sedan chair. Encircling each layer of the platform was a series of balustrades with rectangular newels, or "watching posts," at regular intervals. The stylized newel posts were decorated with a cylindrical top featuring auspicious symbols such as the dragon, phoenix, lion, or clouds.

Building a main hall on a high platform was an ancient practice. A Bronze Age public meeting place in a state capital was erected on a fourteen-meter-high platform (*ZGYSYJY* 1999, p. 166). During the fourth and fifth centuries, the platform consisted of upper balustrades and a lower base. During the Tang dynasty (618–906), it developed into a two-layered structure in imperial architecture (ibid., pp. 321–365). By the Ming dynasty, a triple-layered platform gave way to a more elaborate type of foundation, with geometrical newels (Liang Sicheng 1984, p. 36). Such newels have been found nationwide in Ming imperial buildings. The white marble was transported from remote mountains. Its whiteness, in distinct contrast to the red walls of the palace, suggested the inviolable pathway leading to the "heavenly" palace. HL

96

正德十二年（1517年）　南京中華門外馬家山吳經墓出土　陶儀仗衛俑63件

Set of 63 figures from a guard of honor, buried 1517 (above and opposite page)

From the tomb of Wu Jing on Mount Majia, outside the Zhonghua Gate, Nanjing

Reign of the Zhengde emperor (1506–1521)

Earthenware with residue of pigments

H. 21.5 cm (8.46 in.)

Nanjing Municipal Museum

These sixty-three handmade clay figures constitute the major part of a guard of honor that was buried with the court eunuch Wu Jing, who served the Zhengde emperor. Arranged in an imperial procession, the figures can be identified by their uniforms, hats, and equipment as representing at least seven types of staff from the inner court. Marching at the head of the procession are musicians from the imperial orchestra, playing percussion, wind, and string instruments. They are followed by imperial cavalry guards, who carry weapons and equipment. A huge staff is mixed with eunuchs, attendants, civil clerks, grooms, and servants. Most worthy of attention is the rear guard on horses, each wearing a six-lobed hat and holding a container, a basin, or a dog (or bird). They served as the "valorous bodyguards," keeping pets and precious animals for the emperor.

From the Yongle reign onward, the corps of imperial bodyguards was largely controlled by eunuchs, who came to dominate governmental administration. Reversing the rules established by the Hongwu emperor that prohibited eunuchs from interfering in state affairs, the Yongle emperor gave high authority to his trusted eunuch advisors. The eunuchs' power increased even further after the eunuch system was made hereditary (by brothers or nephews) in 1446. Their domination of Ming government eventually paralyzed the Ming court toward the end of the dynasty.

Wu Jing (active 1505–1517), chief of the imperial household staff, was one of those eunuchs who, at the height of his power, imposed brutal measures and committed horrible crimes. Given the opportunity to lead a vanguard to the south for the Zhengde emperor, he kidnapped female hostages to extort money from peasants. For that, Wu Jing was banished from the court to the southern capital of Nanjing, where he died serving in a garrison stationed at the imperial graves (*Mingshi,* chap. 304, p. 757). One can imagine, after his glory days in the palace, how Wu Jing suffered bitterly at being reduced to patrolling graves in the hinterlands. His ambitions might have been fulfilled only in the afterlife, manipulating these clay figures he was buried with. HL

A civil official

Blowing a trumpet

Holding a wrapped sword

A groom leading his horse

Metal and Cloisonné

HE LI

In 1534, an imperial academician named Wen Peng (1489–1573) published a confidential edict issued by the Xuande emperor in 1428. This edict had been handed down through a prominent family, who originally had obtained it from the Xuande emperor's herald, eunuch Wu Cheng (see cat. no. 113). This edict had had profound implications for art production of the Xuande period (1426–1435).

The document stated that, after receiving envoys from thirty foreign countries in his court, the Xuande emperor felt deep uneasiness. Seeing the superb tribute bronze presented by envoys from Siam (Thailand), he was concerned about the shoddy and inadequate display of ceremonial vessels in the Imperial Ancestral Temple (*Taimiao*). The emperor thus ordered his administration to begin casting new vessels with first-rate bronze obtained from Siam. Because of his personal fascination with the traditions of the Song dynasty (960–1279), the Xuande emperor decided that Song official wares should be collectively viewed as a national style to be imitated in this new imperial production. Specifically, the newly cast pieces would be modeled after ritual vessels from the Song court of the Xuanhe emperor (1119–1125), and after Song ceramics from the Ming imperial household.

In response, the Ministry of Rites proposed a project of 3,365 items in 117 designs to assimilate Song origins, with the goal of achieving an organized system of classical ritual art. This number was eventually finalized at over ten thousand items. The Ministry of Works was responsible for the cast execution and the necessary financing. The foundry was apparently located in Beijing. New vessels would be distributed to the imperial temples, palaces, governments of Beijing and Nanjing, and mansions of royal merit (Wen Peng 1534; *Mingshi,* chap. 52, pp. 118–119).

To achieve this ambitious production program, the court had set aside fifty stores of materials and 108 staff from six professions, which the Ministry of Works confirmed with Wu Cheng. The inventory of materials included 39,600 *jin* (43,651.5 pounds) of Thai copper, 1,000 *jin* (1,102.3 pounds) of Japanese copper, 800 *liang* (1,410.96 ounces) of gold, 2,600 *liang* (4,585.6 ounces) of silver, imported lead, iron, and a variety of imported and indigenous mineral substances, fuels, and furnace equipment. The allocation and composition of the new vessels would be in accordance with social rank. For instance, among the eight imperial temples, the Imperial Ancestral Temple would receive fourteen rectangular, legged incense burners made of gold with silver inlays, and the Imperial Merit Temple would receive six vessels cast in gold and inscribed with the names of honorable Ming military leaders, including Xu Da (see cat. nos. 2, 134) and Mu Ying (see cat. nos. 100–101).

In general, diverse materials were blended in various alloys and compositions. Several vessels in this exhibition illustrate this diversity of physical properties (see cat. nos. 97, 100–101, 104, 110–111). Far more complex than those of the Bronze Age (approx. 2000–220 BCE), Ming metals were made of complicated formulas. Archaeology and scientific analysis have focused on ancient bronzes in recent decades. However, a systematic survey has not yet been done on the elements of Ming metals. Lacking physical and chemical data, scholars have paid more

attention to Ming metal forms and styles than to their composition. The common term "copper alloy" is often used loosely to define the constituent elements of many Ming metals, aside from the more specific types such as brass, pewter, and platina (cupronickel).

The Xuande emperor's goal was to achieve the full propaganda potential of the classical Chinese visual vocabulary, adapted to ceremonial use. The new ritual vessels sparked a frenzied passion among aristocratic circles for sumptuous objects. As stated in Wen Peng's text, the primary form of vessel to be cast was incense burners. At least in the early Ming, eight staff members—four inside the palace and four at the Imperial Ancestral Temple—were devoted to incense rituals and vessels (*Mingshi,* chaps. 1–2, pp. 12–14; and chap. 74, p. 165).

In practices established as early as the third century, burning incense was an essential component of Buddhist ritual that the Chinese had learned from India. Among the aristocracy, incense was used also in Taoist rituals, women's makeup, medical treatments, and the cultivated life of scholars, and as an air and textile freshener. Burning incense enhanced a civilized lifestyle. Since the sixth century, collections of incense and incense burners were among the prized possessions of people of high social rank. Along with this popularity came the increasing importance of incense materials and recipes, methods of mixing and burning incense, and incense utensils.

By the eleventh century, imports of Chinese incense to governments in Southeast and Western Asia earned highly profitable revenues. The Book of Incense, published in the early twelfth century, describes in full detail twenty-two incense formulas, containing mixtures of woods (such as white sandalwood), diverse flowers, and organic materials such as musk. Incense intended for burning was made in the shape of balls, cones, elliptical lumps, sticks, or patterned threads, or as powder. The vessels in this exhibition (cat. nos. 102, 109–11) represent typical types of Ming incense burners designed to accommodate these varieties of incense.

Surviving cast-metal vessels from this era, now preserved mainly in the Palace Museum, Beijing and National Palace Museum, Taipei, attest to the glory of the Xuande reign and its ambitious material production. Immediately upon the Xuande emperor's death in 1435, the casting stopped. Widespread floods, failure to collect taxes, and anti-Ming rebellions from the frontiers made the new emperor's position extremely difficult. The first measure adopted to solve financial problems was to shrink administrative budgets, from the inner palace to government bureaus. The imperial agencies for gold and silver mining in Qian (Guizhou) in southern China, and those overseeing textile mills in the northwest were shut down in 1436 (Zhang Xikong and Tian Jue 1987, pp. 384–86). Metal casting was inactive for decades.

Subsequently, from the sixteenth century onward, the court tried to have works cast in interesting shapes to please the emperors. The Zhengde emperor was one of those who desired new metalwork production. For displays in his entertainment complex known as Leopard House (built 1508–1512 at a cost of 265 pounds of silver), he collected numerous artworks (see cat. no. 110). The Jiajing and Wanli emperors, both deeply immersed in Taoism, admired utensils with symbolic motifs. But never again would the court return to the level of casting achieved in the Xuande period. Their intimates and favored eunuchs engaged in substantial bribery, using much of the revenue to purchase art directly from regional markets. Thus, many fine works by the best metal makers from the southeast, like Zhang Mingqi and Hu Wenming, still entered the Forbidden City (cat. nos. 111–12).

Apart from traditional casting, another type of artisanal metalwork enjoyed popularity during the Ming dynasty. Cloisonné, a colorful and decorative craft of western origin, was brought to fruition in Ming China. Many thirteenth-century cloisonné works that the Ming court obtained from the Yuan palace influenced new currents among the noble class. Cloisonné combines inlay crafting and goldsmithing. The process of making cloisonné begins with grinding quartz, porcelain clay, feldspar, sodium borate, and metallic minerals into cloisonné powder, which is then smelted and painted onto a roughcast, baked, and cooled. Some items then need to be polished or plated with gold. The cost for the gold and imported enamels used in cloisonné was great, and the complex technique was not popularized among Chinese artisans. It has been speculated that cloisonné was among a few crafts (such as glass) that were produced exclusively in the imperial workshops near or inside the Forbidden City. These luxury items were created to fulfill the extensive needs of the imperial family, especially court ladies who wanted to make their residence grander.

Cloisonné pieces with reign marks are found only from the Xuande (1426–1435), Jingtai (1450–1456), Jiajing (1522–1566), and Wanli (1573–1619) reigns, while a large quantity of cloisonné from various periods is unmarked. Good production techniques became fully established during the Xuande period. However, many court members and artisans regarded the wares of the Jingtai reign as representing the highest level of cloisonné. To benefit from this pedigree, imperial workshops of later periods would engrave a Jingtai reign mark on their own cloisonné or on undated wares brought in for embellishment or repair, regardless of when they were made. Even dated pieces sometimes had a Jingtai mark engraved over an originally inscribed reign. This deceptive practice was widespread until the nineteenth century (see cat. nos. 106–07).

Cloisonné ware possesses both the sturdiness and luster of gold, as well as resistance to corrosion of the enamels, making it both practical and beautiful. Extant examples from the Ming dynasty include incense burners (cat. no. 109), cups, vases (cat. no. 106), boxes, board games (cat. no. 105), scroll knobs, candle holders (cat. no. 108), and ceremonial vessels (cat. no. 107), with a wide variety of uses. Judging by the standards applied to conventional court art, fine wire work, a densely arranged composition, and slightly opaque enamels with a muted elegance distinguish Ming cloisonné of the "imperial class." This benchmark for quality and luxury remained established through modern times.

97

明洪武六年（1373年）　銅製　嘉定府造紀年款權　南京市博物館

Weight, 1373

Reign of the Hongwu emperor (1368–1398)

Copper alloy

H. 8.5 cm (3.35 in.), W. 6 cm (2.36 in.), Wt. 578.25 g (20.4 oz.)

Nanjing Municipal Museum

This solid metal weight from a steelyard has a high iron content and cast-on inscriptions. The loop knob on top, which allowed the weight to be hung from a cord, indicates its function as a sliding weight, the most common type of scale used in China. Located at one end of a steelyard, the scale would have consisted of a hanging tray in which to place an object for measuring; by sliding the weight on a beam until it was balanced with the tray, the object's weight could be read at a gradation marked on the beam.

The earliest known weights were made of iron or bronze in the Qin dynasty (221–207 BCE), when China became unified under the first emperor, Qin Shihuang. The standardization of weights and measures was part of Qin Shihuang's unification program. Two Qin weights found in Hebei, dome

shaped with a loop knob on top, weighing 32.85 and 32.6 kilograms, are inscribed with long decrees relating to the standardization (*Wenwu* 1979, no. 12, p. 92). In later periods, metal weights and the standards they represented were subject to change. For instance, a bronze weight representing the 621 official standard for one *jin* (today equal to 1.1 pounds, or .5 kilogram) weighs 59.7 kilograms, while a 1077 *jin* weight from Zhejiang weighs 62.5 kilograms. The 1077 weight has the longest inscription ever found on weights from all periods, comprising 168 characters that state where, when, how, and by whom it was produced, in addition to its actual weight (*Wenwu* 1975, no. 8, pp. 93–94). On thirteenth-century weights, bilingual inscriptions in Chinese and Mongolian were commonly shortened, usually mentioning

only the regional government and the date it was made (*Wenwu* 1972, no. 2, p. 78; 1979, no. 12, p. 12; and 1985, no. 3, p. 31).

For more than five hundred years before 1280, the Director of the Bureau of General Accounts at the Ministry of Revenue controlled weight making and guided every aspect of the regional manufacturing. From 1280 through the Ming period, these tasks were taken over by prefectures under the supervision of the Ministry of Works.

Inscription. The inscriptions read at one side, *In the sixth year of the Hongwu reign* [1373] 洪武六年; and at the other, *Produced by the Jiading prefecture* [present-day Suzhou] 嘉定府造. The two characters placed on two sides of the lower section read *Ministry of Works* 工部. HL

98

明洪武十年（1377年）　銅製　洪武十年鳳陽行府造火銃
南京市博物館

Gun (bombard), 1377
Reign of the Hongwu emperor (1368–1398)
Copper alloy
L. 44.5 cm (17.52 in.), D. (at mouth) 4.75 cm (1.87 in.)
Nanjing Municipal Museum

Detail

This gun, hitherto unpublished and unseen outside China, is one of the earliest barreled weapons that used gunpowder. Behind its long barrel is the usual bulbous, walled explosion chamber, followed by a conical, hollow socket that can hold a wooden handle. The gun was made in a foundry in Fengyang, Anhui province, the hometown of the Hongwu emperor and a center of metal weapons manufacture during the early Ming dynasty. Inscriptions on excavated metal guns or bombards of the early Ming dynasty commonly claimed the manufacture was executed by a training officer and military artisan under the supervision of a battalion officer; here, the supervisor was Liu Ju, who was responsible for a similar gun found in Heicheng, Inner Mongolia (*Wenwu* 1973, no. 11, p. 55).

Thirty-eight metal artillery weapons of the fourteenth century, including guns, cannons, and bombards, have survived, most made of bronze but four of cast iron. Depending on their size and weight, they were matched with various supports such as wheeled carriages, benches, posts, or other framework (*Mingshi,* chap. 92). On them are either cast-on or engraved inscriptions recording where, when, and/or who made them, along with their weight and uses. One weapon designated for use while afloat was relatively heavy, at 15.75 kilograms (L. 36.5 cm, D. at muzzle 11 cm). A gun designated for assaults, dating to 1351, was lighter (4.75 kilograms) but longer and thinner (L. 43.5 cm, D. at muzzle 3 cm). The latter was referred to as a "hand-firing gun" according to a description by military general Qi Jiguang (1528–1587). The gun shown here is almost identical to that in dimension and weight (*Wenwu* 1962, no. 3, pp. 41–44; Needham 1986, pp. 290–324).

Even before the introduction of metal artillery in the late thirteenth century, the use of gunpowder-propelled incendiary arrows can be traced back to the Song dynasty (Needham 1986, pp. 154–59). In Ming texts, "artillery" referred to fire-tubes or fire-barrels (some with a large, bowl-shaped muzzle), cannons, or guns. These weapons shot lead, iron, stone, and other projectiles. A triggered musket on a wooden support was employed to shoot heavy lead projectiles at a distance of three hundred steps (Mao Yuanyi, chap. 126).

Inscription. *The Fengyang prefecture government made [this] to weigh three* jin *and ten* liang; *manufactured under supervision of Judge [in Battalions] Liu Ju, Training [Officer] Zhu Guanbao, and Military [Artisan] Xiao Yang, on the X day of the X month, the tenth year of the Hongwu reign* 鳳陽行府造/重三斤十兩/監造鎮[撫]劉聚/教[匠]朱官保. 軍[匠]小陽/洪武　年　月　日造. HL

99

明初期　銅製　廚子通行腰牌　南京市博物館

Personal ID plaque for an imperial chef, approx. 1368–1400

Nanjing, Jiangsu province

Copper alloy

H. 11.7 cm (4.6 in.), W. 9.5 cm (3.74 in.), D. 0.6 cm (0.23 in.)

Nanjing Municipal Museum

Known as a "passing-through-the-palace plaque" or "waist plaque," this two-part plaque served as a proof of personal identification for a cook in the imperial kitchen. It is an adaptation of a Bronze Age "tiger tally," used to ensure the secure transmission of military orders. These tallies consisted of two identical tiger-shaped pieces that fit together by mating their respective convex and concave interior edges. The plaque shown here, with inscriptions cast on the outer faces and a food symbol of two fish on the interior, could be tied onto a belt through the round opening on top. A cook would give one half to the security staff, and hold onto the other half for passing through the palace.

Mandatory kitchen service was one type of labor dues levied by the Ming government. Those who were recruited as cooks had to prepare daily meals and imperial banquets in the inner palace. Normally they worked under the supervision of the Court of Imperial Entertainment, a subordinate office in charge of catering for the imperial household, headed by the Minister of Rites. When passing through the inner palace or staying overnight, cooks had to carry the plaque as a type of ID card. Although they earned their family an exemption of two other labor dues, the kitchen recruits suffered from an imprisoned life and frequently escaped from the palace (*Mingshi,* chap. 77). To prevent their running away, as well as to secure the palace, plaques were often inscribed with certain determinative regulations.

Made of wood, copper alloy, or a silver- or iron-containing metal, Ming waist plaques had officially registered license numbers and specific motifs and inscriptions that indicated users' occupations. For instance, one extant plaque reads, "Warrior of the official defense in the imperial guard for keeping leopards" on one face, and has a leopard motif on the other face (*Wenwu* 1984, no. 10, p. 17; Gao Shouxian 2006). By the Yuan dynasty, the ID had become a round plaque with a lotus-leaf canopy on top and inscriptions in Mongolian and Chinese on two faces. Horse-riding messengers had to carry a waist plaque and a metal bell, which served as a resounding siren (*Yuanshi,* chap. 5; *Wenwu* 1962, no. 11, p. 65). Retaining the Yuan form, Ming plaques dropped the Mongolian inscriptions. Plaques were further transformed into decorative variations by the Qing dynasty court in the seventeenth century.

Inscription. *For a cook who has to carry this plaque with him when staying overnight [within the inner palace]. Invalid at the four gates of the Imperial City* 凡遇直宿者懸帶此牌/出皇城四門不用/廚子. HL

100–101

明洪武二十五年（1392年）　南京將軍山沐英墓出土　銅製　喇叭，號

Horn and trumpet, buried 1392 (horn: below left; trumpet: right)

From the tomb of Mu Ying at Mount General, Nanjing

Reign of the Hongwu emperor (1368–1398)

Copper alloy

Trumpet: L. 115.5 cm (45.47 in.), D. (at mouth) 21 cm (8.27 in.)

Horn: L. 109.25 cm (43.01 in.), D. (at mouth) 23.5 cm (9.25 in.)

Nanjing Municipal Museum

The trumpet and the horn are two principal instruments in a Chinese orchestra. They are often played together in ensemble. The largest size of their kind from Ming excavations, these two instruments were recovered from the tomb of Mu Ying (1345–1392), an adopted son of the Hongwu emperor and Empress Ma. Having achieved political prominence and a knowledge of literati traditions in his early years, Mu Ying rose to fame as a skilled military general by his thirties. The death in 1392 of Empress Ma, to whom he felt great sentimental attachment, threw him into deep despair and led to his sudden death that same year.

Carrying on an ancient tradition, Ming imperial music was performed by an orchestra, sometimes accompanied by singing and dancing. The Hongwu emperor appointed professional musicians in 1368, boys who could be trained in the different instruments under government musicians. Ming court music generally fell into two categories: music for performance at religious ceremonies, and music to commemorate the glorious history of Chinese imperial power. In the latter category, the music played at the 1382 court banquet celebrating Mu Ying's military victories on the frontiers consisted of nine variations on a theme. The sixth variation, titled *Music of Jinling* (Nanjing), was dedicated to the Ming conquest of the Nanjing area (*Mingshi*, chap. 63, p. 7228).

It was during those tumultuous years of the Hongwu reign that this trumpet and horn were made. Rarely were such large instruments made in the middle and later years of the Ming dynasty. The inclusion of musical instruments as funeral articles symbolized fruitfulness and endless renewal, serving as a means to live and die with the Ming forever. HL

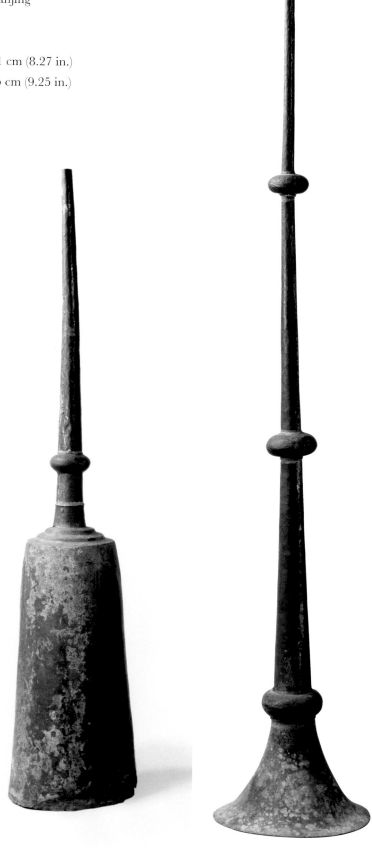

102

明永乐二十二年（1424年）　南京太平門外板倉徐欽墓出土　銅製　香爐

Covered incense burner, buried 1424 (below and opposite page below)

From the tomb of Xu Qin, Duke of Wei, at Bancang, Nanjing

Reign of the Yongle emperor (1403–1424)

Copper alloy

H. 13.13 cm (5.24 in.), D. (at mouth) 11.4 cm (4.49 in.)

Nanjing Municipal Museum

This drumlike incense burner represents a traditional form produced in ceramics and metals beginning in the twelfth century. The cylindrical work consists of three individual parts: a hollow chamber, a cover, and a small tray beneath the cover. A front ash-dump is reinforced by two narrow bands encircling the upper opening and lower body, with four vertical straps affixed between them. A ladle hangs from a loose-chain handle suspended from opposite sides of the body. Both the hat-shaped cover and the tray are pierced with air vents. The flat base was soldered with three Z-shaped lath lugs. Unlike the incense burners that functioned as receptacles for directly burned incense (cat. nos. 109, 111), this one was designed to heat incense indirectly from charcoal burning in a prefilled bed of ash at the bottom of the chamber. A lump of incense, placed on the pierced tray above the charcoal, would eventually begin to smolder and release its fragrant smoke through the holes in the cover.

This fine example of a daily utensil was buried with Xu Qin (died 1424) to serve him in the afterlife. The tomb also contained a considerable variety of tin, brass, iron, and ceramic items, including cooking vessels, tableware, candle holders, teaware, ritual objects, flower vases, locks, and boxes. A few gold ornaments attest to a social status equivalent to that of a duke or marquis (*Wenwu* 1993, no. 2, p. 76). The number and type of burial articles are in accordance with restrictions issued in 1369 on a prince's funeral (*Mingshi,* chap. 14). Despite the high rank that they reflect, Xu Qin's reputation in life had been tarnished when his involvement in a political scandal was exposed. He was subsequently discharged from the court and had no influence in state affairs until his death. However, due to his lineage—he was the oldest grandson of Xu Da (1332–1385), the famed Ming general whose son-in-law was the Yongle emperor—Xu Qin was allowed to keep the family title, Duke of Wei, and to have a funeral on a scale befitting a duke. HL

103

明正统四年（1439年）　南京將軍山沐晟墓出土　鐵製　刀，木套

Iron sword, buried 1439 (above)

From the tomb of Mu Sheng at Mount Jiangjun, Nanjing

Reign of the Zhengtong emperor (1436–1449)

Iron in a reconstructed wood case

L. 84 cm (33.07 in.), W. 2 cm (0.79 in.)

Nanjing Municipal Museum

This sword's high-iron-content metal and original wooden case have been largely corroded from being long buried. Along with two halberds, the sword was unearthed in 1959 from the tomb of Mu Sheng (1368–1439), who must have used them during his lifetime (*Kaogu* 1960, no. 9, p. 31, pl. 8). The second son of Mu Ying, Sheng displayed great military prowess while campaigning in the south. His abilities were recognized by the Yongle emperor, who sought to bring Annam (now northern Vietnam) under Ming control. Mu Sheng's brigade succeeded in quelling the minority tribes in Qian, which he would later govern, and in seizing large parts of the southern borders, including Annam. After his death, the Mu family continued its governorship of Qian (Yunnan and Guizhou) until the end of the dynasty.

The sword and halberd were the common equipment of Ming foot soldiers, symbolizing the idea of *wu,* or military force. The two weapons together convey the best representation of *Hongwu,* or "vast armed force," which Zhu Yuanzhang took as the name for his reign. Evidence of military equipment made during the early Ming period has been found in a few military officers' tombs, including that of Kang Maocai (1313–1369; *Kaogu* 1999, no. 10, p. 15).Mu Sheng's descendants, Mu Changzuo (see cat. nos. 11, 13–14) and Mu Rui (see cat. nos. 15–18), did not bring any weapons with them into the afterlife. Instead, they furnished their tombs with more ornaments and jewelry, which became a fashion from the middle Ming onward. HL

104

明銅製 "百歲團圓"鏡 南京市博物館

Mirror with designs celebrating longevity, 1475–1644

Copper alloy with molded relief

D. 22.5 cm (8.86 in.)

Nanjing Municipal Museum

This large mirror is unique among known metal mirrors of the time for its complete union of literati pursuits and Taoist icons. The mirror is decorated on the rear face with relief motifs. At the center, a character for "king" is surrounded by sacred beasts—a dragon and a pair of tigers, symbolizing the holy Dragon and Tiger Mountain, headquarters of the Orthodox Unity sect of Taoism, in Jiangxi province. There, according to a Taoist legend, the first Celestial Master, Zhang Daoling (second century CE), refined the elixir of immortality. He and his hereditary Celestial Masters have been traditionally portrayed in Taoist art as long-bearded

figures holding a sword, accompanied by a dragon and a tiger. Here, the two beasts serve as incarnations of the master.

In the background, four gentlemen present a traditional statement of literati identity. Each holds an object—a wrapped zither (*qin*), a chessboard, a volume of books, and a painting scroll—representing the four pursuits that were universally studied and practiced by educated elites. Mastering the four was the lifetime goal of a true gentleman. More interesting, each of the four is marked with a character, which together make up the phrase "Reunion for a Hundred Years."

Multiple functions and symbolic adornments made the mirror an appealing utensil or thousands of years. Dating back to the Bronze Age, a metal mirror was thought to contain magical power that could exorcise evil spirits. According to the philosopher Ge Hong (283–343) in his two-volume *Baopuzi* (The Master Who Embraces Simplicity), a Taoist priest would carry a metal mirror on his back for protection while strolling in the mountains. The brightness of the mirror would prevent him from being attacked by ghosts and evil spirits (Xu Dishan 1999, p. 136). HL

105

宣德朝　掐絲琺瑯　戲獅紋雙陸棋盤　北京故宮

Backgammon board with lions

Reign of the Xuande emperor (1426–1435)

Copper alloy with gold gilding and polychrome enamel inlays (cloisonné)

H. 15.5 cm (6.1 in.), L. 57.5 cm (22.64 in.), W. 37.5 cm (14.76 in.)

Palace Museum, Beijing

This backgammon board was made for the royal family by the imperial shop under the Directorate for Imperial Accoutrements, Beijing. It is in the form of a rectangular tray enclosed by short sidewalls. The board surface is framed by narrow borders. Each of the two longer borders is lined with twelve round points for the checkers. The board's center is adorned with five lions playing with flaming balls on a stylized diamond background. The inner sidewalls are filled with floral scrolls; the outer with ten lotus-shaped designs, presenting seasonal flowers. The separate pedestal has a rim for the board and narrow sidewalls with lobed aprons. Terminating in fungus-shaped feet, eight corner and central legs rest on a flat frame. The metal body is gilded throughout and inlaid with colorful enamels in red, white, yellow, lapis blue, and dark green on a turquoise background.

Backgammon was introduced to China during the third century; its Chinese name was "two-land chess." The earliest known Chinese documents on backgammon (approx. 1040) state that it originated in India and took hold at the Chinese imperial courts. Stories and poems describe how members of the court were drawn to the game and that royal ladies and concubines knew best how to beat the emperors. The game eventually became widespread among all classes. Reflecting different ways to play, backgammon boards varied in formation. Each player played with twelve, fifteen, or sixteen checker pieces, which could be round or cubic, in black or yellow. HL

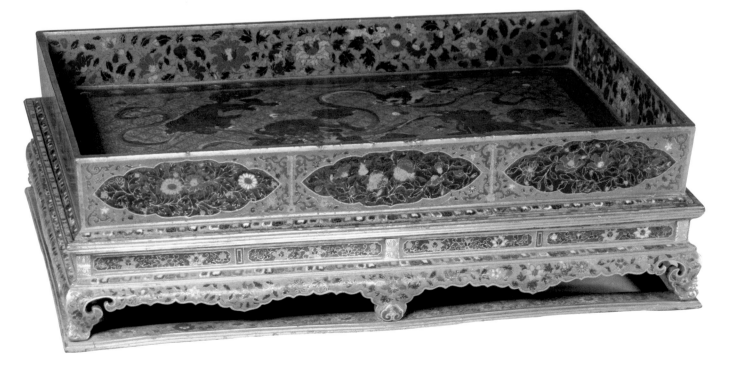

106

宣德朝　掐絲琺瑯　纏枝蓮紋尊　北京故宮

Vessel with lotus scrolls in an ancient bronze shape (below)

Reign of the Xuande emperor (1426–1435)

Copper alloy with gold gilding and polychrome enamel inlays (cloisonné)

H. 18.25 cm (7.19 in.), D. (at mouth) 14.5 cm (5.71 in.)

Palace Museum, Beijing

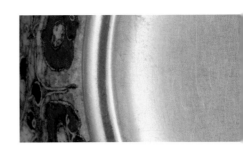

Displayed on an altar table of the inner palace or a shelf in an imperial temple, this vessel served many functions: as ritual ware, a flower vase, or just a decorative receptacle. A hollow, high foot with a turned-out rim supports a drum-shaped body with sides flaring to a trumpet-shaped mouth. The sides of the stand, body, and mouth are interspersed with four lugs, giving an imposing effect. The entire exterior and inside mouth are rendered with a Buddhist emblem, lotus scrolls. The lotus blossom—showing petals in red, yellow, white, and lapis blue amid green-leaved scrolls against a turquoise background—is a stylized design on Ming cloisonné works.

This vessel exemplifies a longstanding form, *gu,* based on a type of pottery cookware that emerged in the Neolithic period (approx. 5000 BCE) from southeast China to the central lands. Retained by the rulers of the Bronze Age (approx. 1600–1100 BCE), the form was produced as large-scale bronzes and used as ceremonial wine vessels. For its qualities of stability and solemnity, the form was used alongside other ritual wares, usually incense burners and tripod vessels, for thousands of years. In the eleventh century the imperial shops began reproducing the shape in different mediums, from ceramics to metals and jades, to satisfy emperors' passion for archaism. Not until the Xuande reign, however, was the *gu* form adopted in metal cloisonné. Before that time, only three forms—bottles, boxes, and incense burners—had been produced in metal cloisonné. At the imperial workshop, new forms, more than ten in number, largely expanded cloisonné's functions.

Inscription. On the gold-gilded bottom, a Buddhist symbol, two crossed thunderbolts, is carved in the center, indicating the piece functioned on Buddhist occasions. Beside the symbol is a six-character reign mark (大明景泰年製) for the later Jingtai period (1450–1456), carved at a later time. HL

Bottom of Tibetan-style vessel, plate 107

107

明中晚期　掐絲琺瑯　纏枝蓮紋藏草瓶　北京故宮

Tibetan-style vessel with lotus scrolls, approx. 1500–1600 (above right and above left)

Copper alloy with gold gilding and polychrome enamel inlays (cloisonné)

H. 13.7 cm (6.97 in.), D. (at base) 15 cm (5.9 in.)

Palace Museum, Beijing

Unlike common Chinese vessels, this one has a high, flared mouth in the form of a cup, resembling a Tibetan butter lamp. Again the decorative theme is a Buddhist symbol, the lotus. As in the typical style of adorning porcelain pieces, the entire body bears lotus blossoms, accented by narrow floral friezes that encircle the rims of the mouth and foot. The gold gilding covers the outer mouth and stops at the inside shoulder. Two mythical single-horned beasts, also in gold, stand on two sides of the shoulders; those shown are later replacements for the original missing ones. In addition to

commonly used red, white, yellow, green, lapis blue, and turquoise enamels, brown was included in the color scheme.

The influence of Tibetan Buddhism in Chinese art was already underway before the Ming dynasty. But no Ming emperors had been personally involved in adopting elements from Tibetan Buddhism for artwork designs until the Yongle emperor in the early fifteenth century. Art supplied to his palace from imperial manufacturers reproduced various shapes and motifs that harkened back exactly to the original Tibetan Buddhist models. The Yongle emperor's

Tibetan taste remained a strong influence in court art throughout the Ming period. Among all of the Ming Tibetan-styled wares, this form is rare.

Inscription. On the gold-gilded bottom is an inscription carved in a later period. Framed by double lines, the six-character reign mark reads, *Produced during the reign of the Jingtai emperor of the great Ming* 大明景泰年製. A Jingtai-period mark was often added to later cloisonné works as a reminder of the best cloisonné, produced during the Jingtai reign (1450–1456). HL

108

萬曆朝　掐絲琺瑯　梔子花卉枝葉紋蠟臺　北京故宮

Candle stand with flowers

Reign of the Wanli emperor (1573–1619)

Copper alloy with gold gilding and polychrome enamel inlays (cloisonné)

H. 14 cm (5.51 in.), D. 18.5 cm (7.28 in.)

Palace Museum, Beijing

Another cloisonné work by the imperial workshop, this candle stand has a shallow basin supported by three lugs shaped like cloud heads, a popular symbol associated with heaven. In the center of the basin is a tall, three-tiered, pointed candleholder, resembling a stupa. Different designs distinguish the bottom and wide sides. The bottom is decorated with stylized flowers, with red blossoms surrounded by malachite-green stalks, dark green calyxes, and yellow leaves against a lapis blue background. In contrast, white gardenias on a green background adorn the flared sides. The central candleholder, lugs, and entire exterior have been gilded in shiny gold. Simplicity, as seen in its well-balanced proportions and distinct color scheme, gives this candle stand a dignified quality.

The imperial workshop first began to make cloisonné candle stands of this kind and to employ native Chinese flowers on metal cloisonné during the Xuande reign (1426–1435). On this later work, the five- or six-petaled gardenia is of Chinese origin. It appeared in flower paintings not later than the eleventh century. The fruits of the gardenia plant were a primary ingredient for yellow dye, considered an imperial color. The stylized red flowers were an alteration of the lotus, introduced to China along with Buddhism and known from the fourth century as the "flower with treasured aspects."

Inscription. Engraved vertically in a single line on the base, a six-character reign mark reads, *Produced during the reign of Wanli of the great Ming* 大明萬曆年製. HL

109

萬曆朝　掐絲琺瑯　異獸(角端)踏蛇香薰　北京故宮

Pair of incense burners in the shape of mythical beasts (below and page 162)

Reign of the Wanli emperor (1573–1619)

Copper alloy with gold gilding and polychrome enamel inlays (cloisonné)

H. 37.5 cm (14.76 in.), L. 25.5 cm (10.04 in.), W. 19 cm (7.48 in.)

Palace Museum, Beijing

This pair of hollow incense burners depicts two single-horned creatures sitting firmly on their haunches, their forelegs stretched straight. The head, joined to the body by a hinge under the neck, can be opened; when closed, the incense smoke can escape from the opened mouth. Under the chest of both creatures, between the forelegs, is a docile snake, one with its head facing upward and the other facing downward. The fur on the chest lies in three bands of lotus-petal-shaped patterns. Two wings curling over the shoulders bear a red floral embellishment consisting of a pair of scrolls branching left and right. A stretched floral tail is fully attached to the haunch. Both the outer and inner surfaces are gilded with gold. Classic enamels of red, yellow, white, and lapis blue fill the designs against a turquoise background.

The fearsome beasts are descendants of an ancient mythological icon used for exorcising evil spirits. A composite creature—sometimes shown as a human or a beast on the upper half of the body, with a snake's body below—it frequently appeared in texts of the fourth to third centuries BCE. Adapted from bronze images, single-horned beasts were sculpted in earthenware and buried in pairs in tombs beginning in the first century. Sitting on their haunches with intimidating features, they functioned as tomb guardians, meant to protect the dead from attacks by evil spirits. For hundreds of years, the formula of representing tomb guardians as single-horned beasts did not vary much in configuration or gesture. What is interesting about these mythical icons is how they evolved to serve different purposes. Rather than simply filling the role of protecting the dead, in the Ming period they appeared increasingly in decorative art and on items used in daily life or religious worship.

Inscription. On the back of its neck, engraved horizontally in double lines, a six-character reign mark reads, *Produced during the reign of Wanli of the great Ming* 大明萬曆年製, which verifies the craftsmanship of the imperial workshop. HL

110

正德朝　銅製　阿拉伯文長方形帶座香爐　北京故宮

Rectangular incense burner with Arabic letters

Reign of the Zhengde emperor (1506–1521)

Copper alloy

H. 12 cm (4.72 in.), W. 10.5 cm (4.13 in.), D. 9.25 cm (3.64 in.)

Palace Museum, Beijing

This rectangular vessel from Ming imperial households—probably made in a Ming imperial shop—is an example of a new type used for smoking incense. In parallel with traditional work adopting archaic types, new forms of incense burners were developed from the fifteenth century on. One side of the outer walls of this example was cast with a fungus-head panel with Arabic letters in shallow relief. Compared to the Hu Wenming vessel (cat. no. 111), this smaller piece with thinner walls is better suited to smoking than to burning incense. Smoking incense is a complicated process. Burned charcoal is placed in a thick layer of ash to absorb some of the heat. The top portion of the charcoal is covered with another layer of ash. Over this layer a silver or metal sheet is placed—this will hold the lump of incense. Smoked by the transmitted heat, the incense releases a moderate fragrance.

When the Zhengde emperor was enthroned in 1506, he was fifteen years old. Frivolous and light-hearted, the Zhengde emperor surrounded himself with eunuchs and young companions from the elite class. He preferred entertaining in the "Leopard House" he built in the west part of Forbidden City, or in hunting fields, social wine shops, and brothels, rather than in the court. He was enamored of material luxury, and his reign was characterized by opulent display and corruption, as the eunuchs embezzled from the national treasury to buy exotic pets, jade belts, gold jewelry, crafts. and textiles from every part of the country.

In 1510, the Zhengde emperor proclaimed himself Great Garrison Enlightened Buddha. With this high-sounded formal title in mind, he cultivated a taste for unusual artwork with religious-oriented statements in foreign languages. As a result, many mental and porcelain incense burners made during his reign carry Tibetan, Islamic, Taoist, Arabic, or Mongolian inscriptions. To make these objects suitable for elegant settings in a scholar's office or personal room, the vessels were made in smaller sizes than in the past.

Inscription. At the center of the base, within a rectangular frame, a cast reign mark of six characters reads vertically produced during the reign of Zhengde of the great Ming. 大明正德年製　HL

111

晚明　銅鎏金　胡文明款塹刻鳳凰異獸紋簋式爐　北京故宮

Incense burner in the shape of an ancient bronze vessel, approx. 1550–1600

By Hu Wenming

Copper alloy with gold gilding

H. 11.2 cm (4.41 in.), D. 17.6 cm (6.93 in.)

Palace Museum, Beijing

A production of Hu Wenming takes inspiration from a ritual vessel of the Bronze Age in its rendering of a squat, rounded shape with two animal-head handles, resting on a high foot ring. The primary decorative band presents dancing phoenixes, flying beasts, and running mythical creatures in chased relief. Corresponding bands at the neck and foot are adorned with inlaid silver threads in the form of flower medallions and meanders. Gold gilding accents the raised relief and covers the rim and foot ring.

As frequently illustrated in artworks and paintings (see cat. nos. 46b, 141), an incense burner of this type was often set on an altar table outdoors. Filled with sand or ash, these common, wide-mouthed vessels were used to contain directly burned incense. The technique is demonstrated in paintings from the eleventh to thirteenth centuries: a person would pick up an incense lump from a box with his or her thumb and forefinger, and press it directly into an ash- or sand-filled vessel. Another documented method was to ignite incense powder that had been sprinkled directly onto the sand to form a particular character or pattern. Once the powder was burning, the rising smoke would take the shape of the incense-formed pattern.

Fascination with archaism remained an ongoing theme throughout the Ming dynasty. Ming literary sources mention a metalworker named Hu Wenming, who lived and worked in Yunjian (present-day Shanghai). Hu's vessels—particularly the classical bronze forms with gold gilding and elaborate inlays of gold and silver—attracted high market value and were sought after by the upper classes. Even the court commissioned him to make incense burners, as confirmed by pieces bearing his name that are now preserved in the Palace Museum, Beijing, and the National Palace Museum, Taipei.

Inscription. An intaglio inscription, *Produced by Hu Wenming from Yunjian* 雲間 胡文明, appears in the center of the base. HL

112

晚明　銅製　張鳴岐款鏤空花手(香)爐　金山亞洲藝術博物館

Hand warmer

By Zhang Mingqi (active approx. 1580–1630)

Copper alloy with openwork

H. 10.1 cm (3.98 in.), W. 12.2 cm (4.72 in.)

Asian Art Museum, Gift of the Yeh Family, R2002.49.42.A-B

Warming utensils made of various mediums and heated by wood or charcoal have been used in China for centuries. These vessels, made mainly of brass, can be round, spherical, square, rectangular, elliptical, or polygonal in shape. They were used to warm one's hands, feet, or bed, or to burn incense.

A hand warmer is usually composed of an openwork lid—with or without a handle—and a fuel container. This octagonal hand warmer has vertical walls that curve gently toward the shoulder. The slightly domed lid, edged by a solid hoop, shows an openwork design of flowers. The exterior surface is smooth and lustrous, with a warm patina due to years of handling. The rough interior shows remnants of corrosion.

A native of Jiaxing, Zhejiang province, Zhang Mingqi was recognized by his contemporaries as one of the Four Distinguished Craftsmen for his excellent skills in making hand warmers and incense burners. The other three were bamboo carver Pu Cheng, inlaid-lacquerware maker Jiang Qianli, and Yixing potter Shi Dabin. Zhang's warmers were described as being well made, of a refined quality of brass, with elaborate openwork and perfectly matching at the rim—all features that can be seen in this piece.

Inscription. At the center of the base is a square seal mark in two columns: *Produced by Zhang Mingqi* 張鳴岐製. HL

Brightness and Shadows
The Politics of Painting at the Ming Court

RICHARD VINOGRAD

Art Against History

Liu Jun's painting *The First Song Emperor Visiting Zhao Pu on a Snowy Night* (cat. no. 121) offered a pictorial history lesson to its Ming dynasty audiences just as it does to modern viewers. The founding emperor of the Song dynasty, Taizu (927–976), is shown on a mission of statecraft, braving the physical discomforts of the snowy cold and the social unease of seeking help from one of his subordinates, all for the greater good of his regime. The trusted minister Zhao Pu was in the habit of remaining dressed in his official robes after returning home, in anticipation of late-night visits from the emperor (see Sung 1999). On this stormy evening, thinking such an imperial visit unlikely, he had changed into his informal clothes. Despite the surprise visit, Zhao Pu shows himself ready to host the emperor and offer his advice. Although the painting shows a human side of court life, the ancient emperor's status is clearly marked. The open reception hall frames his substantial and frontally displayed figure, dressed in a dragon robe with strong white highlights. The more drably dressed minister, shown in profile, occupies a lower level, and both figures are attended by the minister's wife entering from the side. Outside the gate, the emperor's retinue is left to shiver in the cold.

Liu Jun, a court painter with the honorary title Commander of the Embroidered Uniform Guard, probably executed this work after 1485, around the midpoint of the Ming dynasty (1368–1644). The Ming regime that sponsored this painting often sought to align itself with prestigious eras and episodes from the past, as a kind of sanction for their current rule. The Ming founder had been the survivor among several rebel claimants to power following some decades of disorder in the mid-fourteenth century Mongol, or Yuan, period. It was tempting to see the Ming as a political and ethnic reestablishment of native rule and cultural traditions after a century of foreign domination and a still longer period of alienation of northern China. Claiming affinities with the Song dynasty (960–1279) implied a distinguished genealogy, historical continuity, and legitimacy for the Ming regime.

The visual treatment of Liu Jun's painting implies qualities in keeping with the subject. The scene is spacious and legible, with an orderly progression from foreground gate, to reception hall, to rear hall that is a more modestly domestic version of the axial order of the imperial palace complex. The buildings and furnishings are solidly described, craftsmanlike in their careful observation and rendering of foundations, structural elements, joinery of roof supports, and ornament. Solid foundations and clear structure could be political virtues as much as architectural ones, and something of the sort is no doubt implied here. A specifically artistic connection with the Song court is suggested as well, because this kind of precise, descriptive, and technically polished style, embellished with patches of decorative color in the costumes and carpets, had been normative for Song court painting. The painted landscape screen that frames the emperor and his minister, with its diagonally oriented composition and misty mountain reaches, sketches a further link evocative of later Song court painting.

Constructing affinities with the famous painting traditions of the Song reflected luster on Ming court painting, but the Song also cast a long art-historical shadow on the Ming court, from which it has only recently emerged.* Ming court painting has often been seen as a lesser imitation of Song painting rather than being evaluated for its own considerable interests. Indeed many Ming court paintings virtually disappeared into the shadows cast by famous Song artists, acquiring spurious Song signatures to increase their prestige or market value. Zhou Wenjing's *Celebration of the New Year* (cat. no. 120) is such an example in the present exhibition, bearing a false signature of the twelfth-century court painter Ma Yuan that was accepted by an imperial collector, the Qianlong emperor in the eighteenth century. The art-historical obscurity of Ming court painters was deepened by their usual status as professional artists rather than scholars with a literary education; for the most part they wrote little, and little was recorded about them.

Because the first emperor of the Song had been a military leader and a conqueror, some specific parallel with the equally martial Hongwu emperor, founder of the Ming in the later fourteenth century, might readily come to mind for a viewer of this painting. The stern, active virtues of the ruler are suggested by his retinue and by the wintry environment, but it is primarily his civil and administrative skills that are endorsed here, in his concern with good governance, which might apply to the Chenghua (reigned 1465–1487) or Hongzhi (reigned 1488–1505) emperors, who ruled China during Liu Jun's later career. The other symbolic elements of the painting—the bare tree, snow-covered bamboo plants, and eroded garden stone—all evoke an array of personal virtues, of strength of character and persistence through adversity, that were often associated with scholars and officials. In that way, Liu Jun's painting embodies a lesson about social virtues as well as history.

The visual qualities of spaciousness, orderliness, and legibility in Liu Jun's painting create an effect of narrative transparency, as if setting a stage for the clear telling of a story. Like most paintings from the Ming court, it would be more accurately seen as a construct, a pictorial device for making certain claims and meanings. The implications of historical and cultural continuity, wise administration, physical fortitude, strength of character, and good order conveyed in this painting were common currency in the Ming as in many other court environments, which sought to maintain their legitimacy against competing claimants. Even the most carefully fashioned pictorial constructions, however, can reveal fissures indicative of deeper contradictions. In the case of Liu Jun's painting, we might discern a certain underlying anxiety about the relationship between the emperor and his officials, shadowed by the threat of coercive force or violence as embodied in the retinue of bodyguards outside the gate.

Indeed, most of the ideals embodied in Liu Jun's painting could be called at best hopeful fictions. Recruitment of able officials was indeed a matter of great moment at the Ming court, but the Ming rulers were anything but deferential toward them. Ming court history was an often bloody affair, marked by frequent floggings and executions of officials who dared to criticize imperial decisions or of generals who failed in military campaigns. The founding Hongwu emperor (reigned 1368–1398), who came from a peasant background, was particularly suspicious of the scholarly elite, and one of his purges counted prominent artists among his thousands of victims, who were variously banished, imprisoned, or killed.

Continuity and legitimacy were also elusive values in the Ming. The founding emperor set great store by regular procedures of succession, but formal succession to the throne was abnegated almost from the outset of the dynasty by the founder's son, the future Yongle emperor (reigned 1403–1424; see fig. 1). He usurped the throne from his nephew at the beginning of the fifteenth century, essentially refounding the dynasty by moving the capital from Nanjing in the southeast to Beijing in the northeast (*CHC,* vol. 7, pp. 192–205). Beijing was strategically more advantageous from the viewpoint of defense against the ongoing Mongol threat from the north, and closer to the Yongle emperor's power base, established when he was a prince in the region. However the relocation of the capital involved shifts in governmental institutions and architectural symbols of authority.

Fig. 1. Seated portrait of the Yongle emperor (r. 1403–1424), approx. 1403–1425. Hanging scroll, colors on silk, 86.6 x 59 in (220 x 150 cm). *The National Palace Museum, Taipei*

* See especially the many path-breaking studies of Ming court painting by Dr. Houmei Sung (Ishida), whom I cite abundantly throughout; I am especially indebted to her research and to the insights she offered in personal conversation. For other pioneering studies, see Barnhart 1993; Suzuki Kei 1968; and Vanderstappen 1956–1957.

Another continuity crisis emerged within a few decades, when Zhu Qizhen, who reigned as the Zhengtong emperor (1436–1449), was captured and held for ransom by Mongol forces following a misbegotten military expedition in 1449. His younger brother was installed as the Jingtai emperor to lessen the diplomatic value of the imperial hostage and to protect the state. Even after a long-delayed return of the captured emperor, he forswore the throne and lived in obscurity until he was restored to rule as the Tianshun emperor (reigned 1457–1464) through palace intrigue after a six-year hiatus. Yet another succession-related crisis preoccupied the mid-sixteenth-century court of the Jiajing emperor (reigned 1522–1566), descended from an uncle of the reigning emperor, who died without a male heir. The Jiajing emperor insisted on performing filial rites for his biological father rather than to his uncle, the former emperor, precipitating a bloody struggle over ritual propriety that lasted decades and occasioned the violent deaths of many officials. Toward the end of the Ming, the Wanli emperor (reigned 1573–1619) resisted officially designating his eldest son heir apparent and beginning his educational preparation for emperorship for some fifteen years, before finally bowing to official pressure. The Wanli emperor's misgivings are supposed to have extended to suspicions about the legitimacy of his eventual heir, who in any case lasted on the throne barely a month before dying, it is suspected, from poisoning engineered by the consort mother of his chief rival for the throne (*CHC*, vol. 7, pp. 337–39, 440–50, 516, 547–50).

That so-called Red Pill Case surrounding the death of the ill-fated Taichang emperor was only one of several suspected poisonings that affected the Ming rulers (*CHC*, vol. 7, p. 593). Some may have been murders, others the unfortunate side effects of ingesting supposed long-life elixirs or aphrodisiacs by emperors who subscribed to Taoist religious regimens. Usurpations, assassination plots, intrigues by eunuchs, consorts, and empress dowagers, forced abortions of potential rival heirs, bloody repressions, and executions were at any rate frequent subplots within the glorious official Ming history. These are the shadowy regions of the Bright Dynasty (as the name Ming implies), sometimes criminal and violent, often factually obscure and subject to speculation and rumor. At times the details are quite well recorded. The Jiajing emperor, who had precipitated the ritual and succession controversy involving his biological parents, antagonized many factions at court with his violence and short temper, including some court officials, imperial relatives, and even his own concubines. In 1539 he survived several fires while traveling that may have been arson attempts on his life, and in November 1542 a group of concubines attempted to strangle him in his sleep using silk cords from the bed curtains of his favorite concubine's chambers (*CHC*, vol. 7, p. 464). One of the most intriguing aspects of the Ming world is the way in which the cultural realm—popular lore, drama, fiction, private historical notes, rumors and scandals—became an active force in public and political life. Without giving credence to legends and fabrications, we can still recognize the potency of popular speculations about court life and the many channels through which information about life in the Forbidden City flowed out into the wider empire.

Life in the Palace

That curiosity was a two-way street. The Zhengde emperor (reigned 1506–1521) was fond of roaming the streets of Beijing in disguise to taste real life and, it is said, large quantities of wine, unencumbered by the trappings of status and ritual propriety. In 1517 he left the Forbidden City, again in disguise, to pursue military adventures against the Mongol forces on the northern frontier. A few years earlier, his love of military games had led to the destruction of the residential palaces of the Forbidden City when novel fireworks installed for the Lantern Festival celebrations of the New Year season ignited stored gunpowder and caused a great conflagration (*CHC*, vol. 7, pp. 404–05, 416, 420). The world of painting seldom conveys the full richness and occasional violence of Ming court life, but there are some exceptions. A handscroll in this exhibition (cat. no. 115) depicts an array of leisure pastimes at the palace of Emperor Xuanzong (the Xuande emperor, personal name Zhu Zhanji, reigned 1426–1435). Mostly sports and recreations, they are in part games of martial skill—archery and equestrian target practice—as well as a soccer-like game of kickball, pitch-pot (a darts-like game of tossing arrows into a vase), and a croquet- or golf-like game employing clubs and flagged targets in a bounded field. The emperor is shown mostly as an interested spectator, seated on the porches of pavilions or beneath outdoor canopies, but he descends from his elevated position to participate actively in the pitch-pot and golf-like games, a stocky figure dressed in formal court robes. While some of these pastimes were of great antiquity, recommended as far back as Confucius's time as beneficial recreations for the worthy gentleman, the rarely depicted golf-like game appears in two fifteenth-century scrolls in this exhibition (see also cat. no. 132), suggesting its contemporary fashionability.

Most of the early Ming emperors were interested and active hunters and military leaders, even if some of their military adventures ended disastrously. Emperor Xuanzong had attracted the notice of his grandfather, the very martial Yongle emperor, while still a child for his precocious hunting and military interests (*CHC,* vol. 7, p. 285). Soon after his accession to the throne, Xuanzong sought to improve diplomatic relations with Korea, in part to secure Korean-bred war horses as diplomatic gifts, or tribute. The Korean court also presented falcons, hunting dogs, and leopards, indicating the direction of the Chinese emperor's interests (*CHC,* vol. 7, p. 301). A huge mural-size painting known as *Emperor Xuanzong's Amusements,* attributed to the Xuande-period court painter Shang Xi, shows the emperor and a large retinue of eunuch companions and servants on a hunting outing near the Forbidden City (fig. 2). All of the nearly two dozen principal figures are shown on horseback, resplendent in court costumes, with paired auspicious animals scattered around the hunting park (Yang Xin et al. 1994, cat. no. 2, p. 134; Wang Chenghua 1998, pp. 226–52).

Fig. 2. Emperor Xuanzong's amusements, approx. 1400–1500, attributed to Shang Xi (active. 1426–1435). Hanging scroll, colors on paper, H. 83.1 in (211 cm) W. 139 in (353 cm). *The Palace Museum, Beijing*

Emperor Xuanzong was more than a military leader and hunter. Besides his substantial political and diplomatic accomplishments, he is known as one of China's foremost artist-emperors. In this arena as in many others, the Ming stood in the considerable shadow cast by the Song, whose Emperor Huizong (reigned 1100–1125) had been a painter, calligrapher, collector, and tastemaker of wide renown. Surviving paintings attributed to Xuanzong are often depictions of aristocratic pets or hunting dogs like salukis in garden settings, with accompanying symbolic plants of bamboo, orchids, or lilies. His paintings are documented with prominent imperial inscriptions and seals, sometimes precisely dated or with the notation "playfully painted by the imperial brush." Styles range from ink monochrome works, to some ink with light colors, and others heavily colored. The detailed and closely observed renderings of animals and plants suggests an affinity to Song dynasty court painting modes, while the symbolic plants done in ink monochrome, the prominent inscriptions, and the inscribed suggestion of playfully dabbling in art evoke the scholar-amateur artists of his own and earlier times.

Xuanzong's paintings in this exhibition include several versions of the subject of a rat gnawing on bitter gourds, melons, and lychees (cat. no. 113). Paintings of this sort may embody a witty message of warning about the consequences of greed, since the rat may be unaware that the gourds he is about to eat are bitter (Wang Chenghua 1998, p. 244). The dedication of one of the versions to a eunuch Directorate-level official named Wu Cheng at least suggests such a purpose, although the gift of a dedicated painting from the imperial hand would have conveyed tremendous prestige regardless of the symbolic message. The emperor's dedication is also symptomatic of a larger shift in court politics and art patronage during his Xuande reign

(1426–1435), which saw eunuchs replacing the Grand Secretaries as the major wielders of power and influence (Sung 1990, pp. 46–47). This shift in patronage widened the split between scholar-artists serving at court as drafters and calligraphers on the one hand, and professional court painters on the other, and it encouraged the denigration of court painters by writers of art history. The two modes still coexisted, if somewhat awkwardly, in Xuanzong's own art. The version dedicated to the eunuch Wu Cheng, dated to the sixth year of Xuanzong's reign (1431), and another in fan-shaped album-leaf format are brightly colored, with meticulously described animal and plant forms and textures, features that suggest an indebtedness to Southern Song court styles. An earlier version of the subject from 1427 is in ink monochrome only, with fluctuating "calligraphic" brushwork in the rock outlines and deeply shaded ink patches used for the leaves and plants. The imperial inscription also is slightly less formal in style than the 1431 version, and describes the painting as "playfully sketched." The treatment here suggests an affinity with the scholar-official painters in approach and style. This mixture of scholarly and courtly devices suggests a syncretic artistic program at the early Ming courts that goes beyond the stereotyped image of court artists as unliterary but highly skilled craftsmen. Another of Xuanzong's paintings in the exhibition, a short handscroll of lotus in the shade of a pine tree (cat. no. 114), also suggests affinities with scholarly tastes. The simple monochrome treatment is combined with a series of favorite scholarly motifs of landscapes with pines, symbolizing long life and persistence through adversity, eroded Taihu stones, and lotus, the "gentleman among flowers," incorruptible and also associated with the birth of sons (Bartholomew 2006, pp. 47, 72).

The commingling of polished, colorful academic styles with scholarly monochrome brush performances in Emperor Xuanzong's paintings is symptomatic of a larger trend in Ming culture: the widespread crossing of class and cultural boundaries, and the confusion of formerly distinct categories. Elite and popular forms, courtly and urban environments often intersected in unpredictable ways. One result of this lively cultural stew was a reaction in art-historical writing during the Ming, which is often interested in establishing distinct lineages and clear regional schools, suggesting anxieties about the blurring of formerly comfortably distinct categories (Cahill 1978, p. 77; Cahill 1982, pp. 6–27). Another by-product of this cultural interaction was the appearance of hybrid artistic types. The educated, urban professional artist is one such type well represented among some of the most prominent mid-Ming painters, such as Du Jin (active mid- to late fifteenth century) and Tang Yin (1470–1524). These were classically educated men who aimed at passing the elite civil service examinations and achieving the wealth and fame that accompanied appointment to high official position, but who were frustrated in their ambitions by bad timing or unfortunate personal associations. Forced to live by their wits, and specifically by their talents in literary composition, fine calligraphic writing, and painting, they most often lived and worked in the prosperous urban centers of commerce and craft production in the southeast, such as Suzhou and Nanjing, or in the capital city of Beijing (Cahill 1978, pp. 154–66, 193–200).

Du Jin, for example, came from an official's family, received a classical education, and passed the national exams at the highest (*jinshi*) level in the late fifteenth century. He was not offered an appealing post, however, and so made a living from his painting, calligraphy, and literary talents in Nanjing and Beijing (ibid., p. 154). Du Jin thus had the social background of a court scholar-official, probably worked for some of the same kinds of patrons as did court artists such as Liu Jun (see cat. no. 121), and painted related historical subjects, but for an urban art market (Barnhart 1993, p. 280). As a professional painter he specialized in historical figure subjects such as paragons of learning and poetry, which he painted in a descriptive, colorful mode that evoked both the atmosphere of past eras and contemporary manners. His *Court Ladies in the Inner Palace* handscroll in this exhibition (cat. no. 132) seems to offer an intimate glimpse of life in the inner palace quarters of the imperial concubines and palace ladies, the most forbidden sectors of the Forbidden City. This might be a counterpart to the handscroll of Emperor Xuanzong's palace amusements (cat. no. 115), except that Du Jin's painting is based on historical imagination rather than documentary observation. Various counterpart images of palace women's activities from earlier times survived in private collections as originals, copies, or sketches, and Du Jin's tableau was no doubt based on one of these. His painting shares some specific features with a composition attributed to the tenth-century painter Zhou Wenju called *In the Palace,* of which fragments are preserved in various museums (Ho et al. 1980, pp. 27–29). Some compositional arrangements of figures into complementary pairs, furniture types, and specific vignettes, such as that of an artist sketching a portrait of one of the women, are shared by the Zhou Wenju and Du Jin paintings. The stylized lead-white cosmetics are also found in old court paintings. Other details of costume and garden furnishings, however, suggest the contemporary Ming world of urban gardens of wealthy officials or merchants, and perhaps their courtesan visitors, while the scene of women playing a golf-like putting game seems to reflect contemporary palace recreations, as seen in the Xuande-era scroll in this exhibition (cat. no. 115).

Du Jin's images of palace women thus seem aimed at responding to the curiosities and fantasies of contemporary urban audiences about life in the inner court—an ongoing topic of popular speculation and rumor in Ming society, when the court was often embroiled in scandal, violence, and intrigue. This represents another kind of boundary crossing and engagement between courtly and urban cultures, in which paintings for urban markets and patrons offer glimpses of the innermost domestic spaces of the palace, rendered in imitations of courtly styles. Another of the vignettes in Du Jin's painting, showing a palace lady being offered a basin to wash her hands, has a counterpart in the anonymous *Scooping the Moon from a Golden Basin* hanging scroll (cat. no. 141), which might be a similarly themed painting from the Ming court. Two palace ladies and three serving girls are shown at leisure in an ornate garden setting, with red painted balustrades, a black lacquered table inlaid with mother-of-pearl, elaborate jeweled necklaces and ribbons, and a wary cat perched on an embroidered cushion. The paired cranes in the foreground, flowering peonies, and fruit add auspicious messages of long life, wealth, and nobility to this luxurious scene.

Scenes of palace women's lives proved a successful genre for professional artists later in the Ming as well. The most famous example is a handscroll by the Suzhou professional Qiu Ying called *Spring Dawn at the Han Palace* (fig. 3), which offers an opulent fantasy of marble terraces, painted pavilions, and peacock strolling the palace grounds, interspersed with vignettes extracted and copied from famous old court paintings. Qiu Ying's son-in-law, You Qiu (active approx. 1540–1590), was also a professional artist in Suzhou, and his version of a similar subject in *Spring at the Han Court* (cat. no. 133) offers some of the same voyeuristic satisfactions, although transposed into the subtler register of plain outline monochromatic drawing. The scenes

Fig. 3. Spring dawn at the Han palace (selected panels), possibly 1500–1530, by Qiu Ying (active 2nd half of the 15th century). Handscroll, colors on silk, 13.5 x 186.8 in (34.2 x 474.5 cm), *The National Palace Museum, Taipei*

include an emperor and one of his consorts embracing on a couch behind drawn-back curtains that suggest an imperial bedchamber; other scenes appeal to curiosity about the opulence of palace life, including images of furniture, serving dishes, and palace delicacies. The plain outline (*baimiao*) style of precise drawing was You Qiu's specialty, but it may also reflect the sources of some of the compositional set pieces seen here in monochrome sketches of old paintings. The precise outline manner may have also appealed to viewers who were increasingly familiar with woodblock print–illustrated books with similar visual qualities, due to an explosion in book publishing that accompanied the increasing prosperity and urbanization of the later Ming economy.

Mapping the Ming Court: Patrons, Artists, and Institutions

Imaginary reconstructions of court life by urban professional artists such as Du Jin and You Qiu fall outside any strict definition of court painting, although they reflect a widespread consciousness of the court in Ming culture at large. It would be equally misleading to follow an overly narrow conception of court art, restricted to direct commissions by the emperor or imperial family within the Forbidden City. The Ming court was a complex and far-reaching social and institutional system, with correspondingly diverse forms of art production and patronage.

Historians of the Ming distinguish between the inner and outer courts. The inner court included the emperor, empress, consorts, and concubines but also a substantial administrative bureaucracy with two main factions: the Hanlin scholars and the eunuchs. The founding Hongwu emperor had in 1380 abolished the post of Prime Minister as head of the outer court bureaucracy and its ministries. In place of a Prime Ministership, the Ming system emphasized the role of the Grand Secretariat (*neige*), trusted senior advisors to the emperor drawn from the ranks of scholar-officials in the Hanlin Academy. At times a senior Grand Secretary dominated this institution, while in other periods a group shared authority more or less equally (*CHC,* vol. 8, pp. 72–87). The Grand Secretaries included some of the most able statesmen in the Ming government. They shared the background and many of the values of the scholar-bureaucrats of the outer court ministries, but their position in the inner court and access to the emperor and to the flow of information and documents gave them privileged influence.

The major rivals to the Hanlin scholars and the Grand Secretariat were the eunuchs. Eunuchs were servants of the inner court, castrated to ensure that their access to palace women would not result in corruption of the imperial genetic line, whose formal institutional role lay in the day-to-day management of palace life. They staffed some twenty-four offices under an overarching Directorate of Ceremonial (*CHC,* vol. 7, pp. 362–63). Eunuchs could be highly educated and many were extremely able. Their roles could extend far beyond palace management. Many led military campaigns, and the famous early-fifteenth-century admiral and explorer Zheng He (1371–1433), who led naval expeditions to southeast Asia, India, the Arabian peninsula, and as far as the East African coast, was himself a eunuch (*CHC,* vol. 7, pp. 232–36).

Eunuchs benefited especially from their close proximity and access to the emperor and to palace women and their relatives, and they were often involved in palace intrigues, plots, and the factionalism and politics of Ming court life. Some eunuchs became trusted confidants of youthful, weak, or indifferent emperors, amassing tremendous wealth and power, and at times virtually running the empire. These were the notoriously corrupt, often violently vengeful eunuchs of Ming history. They were the natural rivals of the Hanlin scholars who staffed the Grand Secretariat, since both groups competed for influence with the emperor and for policy-making roles (*CHC,* vol. 7, pp. 286–8; 364–70). But it was the scholars who wrote the official histories, and their frequent vilifications of eunuchs in the historical record, however much deserved, was doubtless sharpened by the institutional rivalry as well as by a certain cultural contempt for those who had willingly suffered mutilation and emasculation of their bodies in pursuit of power. A pervasive Chinese ethic, sometimes identified with Confucian filial piety, held that one's physical body was a gift from one's ancestors and should be maintained whole, even to the point of growing one's hair long and leaving it uncut as was the style in the Ming. Even eunuchs are said to have shared this value, to the extent that they preserved their castrated parts in jars for eventual burial together with the rest of the body. In any event there was no shortage of candidates, or of eunuchs: some ten thousand were in imperial service in the late fifteenth century, already as many as the total ranked civil service in the empire, and by the end of the dynasty in 1644, their number may have grown to as many as seventy thousand in the capital alone, with others posted elsewhere (*CHC,* vol. 7, p. 365).

Each of these groups, power centers, or institutions participated in art production. To these inner court constituencies, we could add the outer court ministries, headed by powerful officials who might commission paintings personally or for architectural decoration, or receive paintings as gifts. In addition the imperial family was not limited to the Forbidden City. It included princes who were awarded regional estates, sometimes ruling regions as virtual fiefdoms at the beginning of the dynasty. Some of the Ming princes were notable art collectors and patrons of artists. Imperial in-laws, relatives, and clans of empresses and favored consorts could also be awarded special ranks and privileges outside the normal bureaucratic process, and likewise take on roles as patrons or consumers of art. As with the eunuchs, the sheer numbers of imperial relatives and in-laws grew massively over the nearly three centuries of the Ming, becoming a fiscal drain on the imperial treasury. Imperial clansmen were awarded financial stipends, but by the later sixteenth century this had become such an insupportable burden that some of them were reduced to the status of commoners by fiat (*CHC,* vol. 7, p. 489).

Meritorious generals and officials could also be awarded estates, such as the Eastern Garden in the initial Ming capital, Nanjing, bestowed on the early Ming general Xu Da (1332–1385), who helped the founding Ming emperor consolidate his rule by pursuing aggressive campaigns against the Mongols. After Xu Da's death, the Eastern Garden passed to his descendants, including one Xu Taishi, who in 1527 used the garden to host a farewell gathering for Chen Yi, attended by famous officials. In the following year Chen asked Wen Zhengming (1470–1559) to compose a literary record of the event, and in 1530 Wen supplemented that with the commemorative *Eastern Garden* handscroll painting (cat. no. 134) in the present exhibition (*ZGHHQJ,* vol. 13, no. 23, p. 7; Laing 1997, p. 688). The artist Wen Zhengming's involvement with the event was thus at a considerable distance, and his relationships with the host and honored guests could have ranged from friendship to social or merely functional acquaintance. Wen had a brief and unsatisfying career as a scholar-official in the Hanlin Academy in Beijing from 1523 to 1526, but by the time of the *Eastern Garden* commission, he had returned home to Suzhou to a life of cultural production of calligraphy and painting. Wen's social affinities were largely with the so-called literati, or scholar-amateur painters, who professed disdain of the technical skill and representational accuracy of the court and professional artists. Wen's *Eastern Garden* seems to fall in between those camps. The painting is attentive to the layout of the garden and to the appearance of its buildings, rocks, and inhabitants. The lavishness of the precinct is signaled by a half-dozen pavilions, three by the side of an artificial pond, and an equal number of large, distinctively eroded Taihu garden stones framing the pavilions or half-submerged in the pond. Four men peruse a scroll in one of the pavilions, while in another, two men play chess by the pond. The garden buildings and stones are meant to convey natural simplicity and rusticity, but garden compounds such as this embodied a considerable investment in land and labor. The bright colors of the painting also suggest a relatively lavish commission that increased the stature of the current owners of the garden, and so in that sense it was a functional object. At the same time, the painting could be read as the casual record of a spontaneous literary and social gathering, with Wen Zhengming's characteristic brushwork and stylized trees adding value as emblems of the artist's temperament. Recent research on Wen and his associates has illuminated the ways in which such artists negotiated the slippery ground between the cultural prestige of the amateur scholar-artist's role and the practical rewards of professional practice through various subterfuges and euphemisms, like the accumulation of "elegant debts" (Clunas 2004, pp. 75–81, 105–10).

The emperors remained the central figures in court painting production, whether as producers, sponsors, or subjects of painting. We have already encountered Emperor Xuanzong (the Xuande emperor, reigned 1426–1435) as a painter and calligrapher (cat. nos. 113–14). The emperors were also frequent subjects of depiction, including their amusements and many formal imperial portraits. As with most formal portraiture, these imperial images are heavily conventionalized. The emperors are shown enthroned, dressed in court robes decorated with imperial symbols, in somewhat abstracted settings that might be furnished with elaborate carpets and freestanding screens as signs of status and symbolic authority. How much resemblance such portraits held to their imperial sitters cannot be known with any certainty, but we can say that the imperial portraits are distinguishable one from another by facial features, indications of age and body type, and sometimes by a vivid sense of personal temperament. Even those individuating features might partly be conventions, utilizing coded references to physiognomic lore about reading character and fate from facial structure, or emphasizing qualities that suggested heroism, forcefulness, or sagacity (see Fong 1995). The extremes of expressive purpose to which such combinations of convention and observation could be put appear in surviving portraits of the Yongle and Hongzhi emperors. The Yongle emperor (reigned 1403–1424), military conqueror and usurper of the throne, is shown as a robust, ruddy-faced figure with dynamically flaring mustaches and a long beard (fig. 1). He sits enthroned but in a pose of incipient action or command, his feet and knees spread wide apart, his left arm pressed force-fully on his thigh, his right elbow thrust out to further accentuate the already massive breadth of his torso, and his right hand grasping his belt and its insignia of authority. The three-quarter pose both accentuates his physicality and suggests a specific direction or object of attention to his intense gaze.

The Hongzhi emperor, who reigned from 1488 to 1505, was born to a concubine who came from one of the southwestern aboriginal tribes that had rebelled against the Ming, so he may represent a different ethnic type than the Yongle emperor (*CHC*, vol. 7, p. 347). Posthumously designated the "Filial Ancestor," he seems to have been a relative paragon of propriety, deeply, and apparently exclusively, devoted to his empress, the former Lady Zhang, and standing as a model of Confucian virtue in his adherence to classical teachings and their ethical values, as well as in the punctilious performance of his governing duties (ibid., p. 352). Something of those qualities, though very little of his personality, is conveyed in the frontal portrait made of him, enthroned before a three-panel dragon screen (fig. 4). The frontal position of the emperor allows him to confront the viewer with his gaze, but the effect is of a blank stare rather than one of penetrating command. Frontality also flattens the imperial figure, which appears to be almost bodiless or indiscernible beneath the heavy court robes that are lavishly decorated with the insignia of emperorship. The effect is of the individual swallowed up by his status and symbols of rank, but also by the obligations of ritual and administrative performance, and all the heavy weight of ethical standards and historical precedent that this emperor particularly valued, and that all emperors were expected to observe.

The emperors as artists and subjects for painting were involved with many other themes than these, which could include symbolic representations of court society, auspicious wishes, or exemplary virtues, but we will leave those for a later discussion of genres and meanings of court painting. The emperors were also primary sponsors of painting, through their appoint-ment and employment of court artists and commissioning of specific projects. The complex history of imperial and other court patronage and of artistic careers at the Ming court has been illuminated by the pioneering research of Dr. Hou-mei Sung, and I have drawn heavily on her work in the discussion that follows.

The two emperors whose portraits are discussed above played pivotal roles in the history of imperial patronage. The Yongle emperor tried to revive a painting academy in the Ming, although it seems that court painters of this period only rarely had the kind of systematic training, standardized examination and selection, or regular institutional affiliations that they

Fig. 4. Seated portrait of the Hongzhi emperor (r. 1488–1505), approx. 1488–1506. Hanging scroll, colors on silk, 82.6 x 45.3 in (209.8 x 115 cm). *The National Palace Museum, Taipei* .

had enjoyed in the late Northern Song (eleventh to early twelfth centuries) in particular. The founding Hongwu emperor, coming from a peasant background, had little sympathy for art and employed painters primarily on temporary appointments for functional projects of palace decoration or portrait painting. Some eminent scholar-artists who had been associated with the Prime Ministership before the abolition of the office in 1380 fell afoul of the Hongwu emperor's demands and suffered the penalty of banishment, imprisonment, or execution as a result. The Yongle emperor's efforts at reviving a court painting academy were interrupted by his frequent military campaigns, but during his reign, painters were at first closely linked to the scholar-officials and directly under the supervision of the Grand Secretary Huang Huai, who personally selected painters for court appointments. When Huang left the court under a cloud in 1413, painters fell under the supervision of eunuch-controlled bureaus, the Directorate of Imperial Accoutrements (*Yuyongjian*) and the *Wensiyuan* (Crafts Institute), which were associated with artisanal production, including jewelry, metalware, and fine brocade textiles for imperial use (Sung 1990; Sung 1995, p. 56). Eunuchs were active patrons of art in their own right. The expanding purview of the eunuch bureaucracy throughout the fifteenth century meant that eunuchs were put in control of the imperial silk and porcelain factories as well as supervising major palace, imperial tomb, and temple building projects (*CHC,* vol. 7, p. 366). One notable surviving example of such eunuch patronage is the construction and decoration of the Fahaisi, or Temple of the Dharma Sea, in the western hills of Beijing. Pious eunuch patrons sponsored the construction, and muralists borrowed from the Forbidden City executed the temple murals of processions of Buddhist deities (fig. 5; Weidner 1994, pp. 55–57). Thus, almost from the outset of the Ming, court painters were embroiled in the rivalry between the major power factions of the inner court, the Hanlin scholar–dominated Grand Secretariat, and the eunuch palace administrators.

The Yongle emperor's grandson, the painter-emperor Xuanzong (reigned 1426–1435) was another key figure in the evolution of court painting institutions. A Ming version of a painting academy took shape with the emperor's personal involvement in the interviewing and examination of painter candidates for appointment to the court. Its main institutional centers during this era were the Hall of Benevolence and Wisdom (*Renzhi dian*) and Hall of Military Valor (*Wuying dian*). Both halls signified bureaucratic attachment and titles of appointment, often recorded in artists' signatures, and the Hall of Benevolence and Wisdom at least served as a place for the emperor to view paintings and to interview and examine artist candidates (Sung 1990, pp. 43–47).

While the eunuch-supervised artisan agencies were in charge of most court painting institutions by the time of Xuanzong's reign, the backgrounds and affiliations of court artists remained very diverse. This was in keeping with Xuanzong's own dual connections as a painter to descriptive academic styles on the one hand and to scholarly themes and calligraphic qualities on the other. Xuanzong's favorite painter, Xie Huan (approx. 1360s–after 1452) was classically educated and came from a scholarly family. Xie was closely connected to the scholars of the Grand Secretariat, to the point that he included his own self-portrait in one version of a group portrait of the Grand Secretaries, *Elegant Gathering in the Apricot Garden,* commemorating an event hosted by Yang Rong on April 6, 1437 (fig. 6). This would have been an extraordinary presumption in other circumstances, but it indicates the esteem in which Xie was held by the most powerful scholar officials of his time. Xie amassed a major collection of painting and calligraphy. The emperor personally awarded him high military titles with accompanying honors and salary, along with gifts of gold, silks, and poem scrolls (Sung 1989).

Fig. 5. Depictions of Buddhist deities, 1439–1443. Fresco, color pigments on plaster. *Temple of the Dharma Sea (Fahai Si), Beijing.*

In the present exhibition, *Elegant Gathering in the Bamboo Garden* (cat. no. 124), painted collaboratively by Lu Ji and Lu Wenying in 1499, closely parallels Xie Huan's earlier *Apricot*

Garden scroll (fig. 6). According to the preface written by the famous literatus and official Wu Kuan (1436–1504), the painting commemorates the sixtieth birthdays of three notable officials: Zhou Jing (1440–1510), Minister of Revenue and the owner of the Bamboo Garden in Beijing; Tu Yong, Minister of Personnel; and associate Censor-in-Chief Si Zhong (1440–1511). On June 12, 1499, they gathered with seven of their friends, all high or rising officials (Yang Xin et al. 1994, cat. no. 5, p. 135; *DMB,* vol. 1, p. 268). As in *Elegant Gathering in the Apricot Garden*, the participants show themselves to be men of culture as well as political acumen: some are writing calligraphy at a stone table or evaluating a hanging scroll painting, while Tu Yong inscribes a stalk of bamboo. Each of the fourteen principal figures depicted in the scroll is identified by an adjacent name cartouche, and is further distinguished by costume, activity, and demeanor. Despite the air of casual sociability, this work, like most of its counterpart images, was an elaborate cultural and social production, meant to certify the status of its participants. In addition to the preface by Wu Kuan, the ten principal guests each added poems to the scroll, and the host added a colophon. The painters Lu Ji and Lu Wenying were both major artists at the Hongzhi (1488–1505) court, awarded sinecure appointments as Commanders in the Embroidered Uniform Guard, at a relatively high rank. Lu Wenying was responsible for the figures and portraits, while Lu Ji, better known as a flower and bird specialist, painted the rocks and trees, auspicious plants, and birds.

Fig. 6. Elegant gathering in the apricot garden,1437, by Xie Huan (active. 1426–1440). Handscroll, colors on silk, 14.5 x 465 in (37 x 1181 cm). *The Zhenjiang Museum, Zhenjiang.*

Both the *Apricot Garden* and *Bamboo Garden* literary gathering paintings in turn followed earlier idealized templates such as *Eighteen Scholars of the Tang*, represented in this exhibition by Du Jin's four screen paintings (cat. no. 131), more or less contemporary with the *Bamboo Garden* scroll. The subject is most often linked to the Southern Song court painter Liu Songnian (approx. 1150–after 1225), and Du Jin follows that precedent in showing groups of scholar-officials practicing gentlemanly cultural skills—appreciating the music of the *qin* (zither), playing *weiqi* positional chess, examining old books and paintings—while seated in front of imposing, freestanding painted screens. Servant boys bustle about attending to their needs in a garden setting decorated with Taihu stones and miniature trees, and furnished with antique vessels and polychrome enameled porcelain stools. As an educated professional painter active in Nanjing and Beijing, Du Jin's clientele likely included wealthy retired officials who would have been flattered by the implied comparison with ancient paragons of culture and refinement.

Other painters at Xuanzong's court were linked more to artisanal painting traditions of palace and temple decorations, murals, and portraits. One such was Shang Xi, who is reported to have painted murals in a temple dedicated to Guan Yu south of the capital, and who produced a nearly mural-scale painting in his *Guan Yu Capturing General Pang De* (fig. 7), a heroic tableau of martial valor, loyalty, and violence drawn from the history and literature of the turbulent Three Kingdoms era of the third and fourth centuries (*ZGMSQJ, huihua bian,* vol. 6, no. 81, p. 32). Guan Yu, a historical figure but also a literary hero and popular god of war and commerce, is portrayed as a powerful, dynamic presence, strikingly reminiscent of the surviving portrait of the Yongle emperor (fig. 1). Shang Xi and his patron may have intended the visual association as a way of saluting the Yongle emperor's martial successes, or as a more general promotion of values of martial valor and loyalty.

Court painters could be distinguished by their social and educational backgrounds, by their networks of patronage, and by their institutional affiliations or bureaucratic rank, as well as by their favorite painting subjects and thematic or symbolic implications. Style alone was not necessarily a primary marker of categorical distinctions among artists, since both the scholarly Xie Huan and the muralist Shang Xi worked in versions of heavily descriptive, decorative, and technically proficient painting. In other circumstances, both scholarly and artisan-academic painters might work in a sketchy monochrome style.

Some court painters, such as Liu Jun, came from military families that performed with artisan functions, as might be expected in an era when military affairs were an ongoing preoccupation, closely supervised by the emperors and with substantial bureaucracies attached to the outer court (Sung 1999, pp. 65–66; Sung 1998, p. 92). Many Ming court artists, whether or not they had military connections, were awarded titles in the Embroidered Uniform Guard (*Jinyi wei*), an imperial bodyguard corps that also was given investigatory powers and functioned in part like a trusted secret service (*CHC*, vol. 7, pp. 213–14). These titles were a way of inserting artists within an established and finally calibrated bureaucratic ranking system and need not have implied any actual military or surveillance duties. The Embroidered Uniform Guard could accommodate quite high ranks and salaries, however, and some artists who did come from military families utilized the possibility of passing inherited ranks from father to son to further accelerate their status and perquisites (Sung 1998, pp. 95, 105). Moreover, some emperors utilized a procedure of special promotions outside the standard civil service channels (called *quanfeng*) to reward favorite painters and artisans as well as imperial in-laws. This irregular system operated within the inner court, from the emperor, to the eunuchs, to the Grand Secretariat particularly prevalent during the Chenghua emperor's era (1465–1487), and it stimulated reactions of protest on the part of regular administrative officials, resulting in the rescinding of many such promotions and appointments from 1485 onward (Sung 1999, p. 65). This reassertion of scholar-bureaucratic prerogatives against the steady accumulation of power by eunuchs continued in the Hongzhi era (1488–1505), with a resulting curtailment of the career prospects for court artists. Finally in the following Zhengde era (1506–1521), many court painters had their ranks and salaries substantially reduced, and many others were dismissed outright (Sung 1998, p. 105). This marked the end of a flourishing court painting academy in the Ming, although artists continued to affiliate with the court in various contexts through the remainder of the regime.

Fig. 7. Guan Yu capturing general Pang De, possibly 1426–1435, by Shang Xi (active. 1426–1435). Hanging scroll, colors on silk, H. 78 in (198 cm) W. 93 in (236cm). The Palace Museum, Beijing

Making Meanings: The World in the Court

The emperors of the Ming dynasty, as in other periods, embodied long-established conceptions of world order. As the Son of Heaven, the emperor served as intermediary between heaven and earth. He was also identified with the Pole Star and the north as a position of power, and his ritual performances at imperial temples and other sites were meant to ensure the continuing harmonious operation of the cosmic order. In the earthly realm, the emperor's ritual plowing of the first furrow at planting time symbolically called forth the continuing bounty of the harvest, and in the human sphere, the imperial performance of ancestral rites set a model for proper familial and social relationships throughout the empire.

The emperor's position was unique, but parallel conceptions of world order and systems of classification were widely disseminated through encyclopedic publications that ranged from basic almanacs to multi-volume compendia. These were often accompanied by woodblock illustrations, such as the *Sancai tuhui,* or Pictorial Compendium of the Three Realms, compiled by the Shanghai natives Wang Qi and Wang Siyi and published in 1609. Such encyclopedias were ways of classifying the world under macrocosmic headings like Heaven, Earth, and Humankind (Clunas 1997, pp. 77–101). These cosmological categories could then be subcategorized into topics like astronomy, calendars, and ceremonies for Heaven; geography, geomancy, maps, buildings, utensils, birds and animals, and plants and trees for Earth; and famous people, bodies, anatomy, medicine, physiology and physiognomy, costumes, and human affairs (which included

194

the arts of music, chess and other games, calligraphy, painting, archery, martial arts, and physical exercise for Humankind). Whether imperially or privately sponsored, such encyclopedias reflect a concern with making the world legible amid the profusion of new objects, products, and indeed new arenas of knowledge.

The painting subjects practiced and patronized at the Ming court were inflected by political and rhetorical purposes and by the traditional spectrum of painting genres. Still the Heaven-Earth-Humankind triad accommodates most of the major genres at the Ming court: religious painting and seasonal themes and festivals for the category of Heaven; landscapes, architectural monuments, and natural subjects like birds, plants, fish, and animals for Earth; and historical, exemplary, and portrait figure subjects for Humankind.

The significance of such paintings could emerge from multiple aspects. Religious paintings, primarily Buddhist and Taoist, but including various popular deities and mythologies, carried with them their own well-established iconographies and narratives from scriptural sources and legends. Many plant and animal subjects had well-established symbolic meanings, such as the wealth and opulence of the peony blossom or the heroism of the eagle. Those meanings sometimes emerged from the natural characteristics of the plant or animal, or from prominent literary or historical associations. In many cases there was a linguistic dimension to the significance of paintings. The pronunciation of the name of the motif was often a homophone for another word or phrase that conveyed a specific, usually auspicious meaning. Thus one of the names for the peony could be read as the "flower of wealth and honor," and the term for eagle was homophonous with the term for 'hero" (Bartholomew 2006, pp. 125–26, 155). In this way, pictorial motifs could be understood as visual puns, and combinations of such motifs could be combined as a rebus to form an extended message.

Lū Ji's painting of a pair of pheasants in winter (cat. no. 126) embodies some of these meaning-making devices. Pheasants were associated with the "five virtues": literary talent (from the resemblance of their head combs to officials' cap tassels), martial spirit, bravery, benevolence, and trustworthiness. Of these meanings, the link between the literary talent of the scholar and the beauty of the pheasant's feathers was most firmly established (Sung 1993, pp. 8, 9). In this painting, the combination of pheasants with the wintry bamboo and plum plants and paired white-headed birds suggests an appropriate presentation piece for a senior scholar official, combining literary talent, white-haired age, and endurance through hard times (ibid., pp. 12, 13).

The significance of court paintings was also affected by the circumstances of their production and reception. The general environment of court paintings implied purposes of reinforcing the hierarchies and ideologies of the imperial system, glorifying the emperor, or reinforcing values of loyal service. The specifics of production and sponsorship—which could range from works personally painted by the emperor, to paintings commissioned by officials for their associates, to functional works for particular ceremonies produced by imperial workshops—could modify the implications of a work. Many paintings acquired textual inscriptions, or colophons, after they were painted, recounting circumstances of viewing, the status of their owners or audiences, or perhaps recording a more generally evocative literary response to the painting or its subject. In many such cases, it is more useful to think of the meaning of the painting as being actively construed by the recipient or viewer rather than being simply inserted by the artist or patron to be extracted passively.

Heaven

For the category of heavenly things, we can point to court patronage of Buddhist and Taoist religious institutions and images. Relatively few paintings in this exhibition belong to the religious sphere, but emperors and empresses, officials, and eunuchs were often active devotees of Buddhism or Taoism, or of a religious syncretism that encompassed Confucianism as well (*CHC,* vol. 7, pp. 146–47). The Chenghua, Hongzhi, and Jiajing emperors were particularly devoted to Taoist beliefs, and in the cases of the Chenghua and Jiajing emperors, to Taoist medicinal and sexual aphrodisiac regimens (ibid., pp. 350, 355–56, 479–84). Buddhist clerics were trusted advisors to some of the early Ming rulers, including the founding Hongwu emperor, who had once been a monk himself, and Buddhist institutions also received the favor of eunuchs (Weidner 1994, pp. 52, 55–57). The Fahaisi (Dharma Sea Temple) in the western suburbs of Beijing, for example, still preserves extraordinary murals of Buddhist deities from the early 1440s that were probably produced by court artists on loan from the palace, due to the patronage of the eunuch Li Tong (died 1453), who had been Director of Imperial Accoutrements under Emperor Xuanzong. Other powerful eunuch patrons of Buddhism in the 1440s and 1450s founded temples, sometimes as personal memorials, and encouraged the entry of laypeople into Buddhist monastic life. We recall that the court was not limited to the Forbidden City palace complex, but could be extended outward through the patronage of court members, from the emperor down to high officials and eunuchs (see Li and Naquin 1988). Just as the wider world was symbolically embodied at the court, so the court extended out into the wider world.

The Buddhist paintings in this exhibition are from much later in the Ming era, during a period of religious syncretism and engagements between lay believers intrigued by Buddhist philosophy and members of religious communities (Cahill 1982, p. 221). Many late-Ming Buddhist and Taoist paintings seem imbued with a "this-worldly" orientation. Wu Bin's striking 1602 image of the bodhisattva Samantabhadra seated on the back of an elephant (cat. no. 140) is a traditional iconography, but the deity is modestly scaled, equal in size to the five monks or *luohans* who attend him. The dominant motifs are the giant branches of blossoming blue and white peonies that overshadow all the figures in the gardenlike setting. Wu Bin's monks or *luohans* are outlandish looking figures, with misshapen heads and wizened or swarthy features, but in other contexts they might be compared to foreigners residing in the current and former capital cities of Beijing and Nanjing. The bodhisattva Samantabhadra is portrayed as a very human-looking being, more wistful than hieratic, and his closest, white-robed, attendant gazes out at the viewer with a familiar directness. Chen Hongshou's painting *Boys Worshipping the Buddha* (cat. no. 144) seems even worldlier in its combination of court painting traditions with what seems a parody of religious devotion. The children make offerings to a miniature image of the Buddha—or is it an imaginary vision?—but the attention of two of them is focused more on the bare buttocks of their companion than on the Buddha image. Both Wu Bin (active approx. 1591–1626) and Chen Hongshou (1598–1652) had episodic appointments to the court as artists, but much of their Buddhist painting may have been made directly for monasteries or to satisfy their own religious inclinations (Cahill 1982, p. 255).

The Xuande-era court painter Zhou Wenjing references another aspect of the heavenly realm in a painting of a New Year's celebration (cat. no. 120). This painting, like many others from the Ming court environment, has clear antecedents in Southern Song court painting, and even a specific model in the *Banquet by Lantern Light* scroll by Ma Yuan, whose spurious signature adorns this painting, overshadowing the proper artist's seal of Zhou Wenjing (*ZGHHQJ,* vol. 10, no. 117, pp. 30–31). Zhou's painting is richer in incident and detail than its Southern Song model, with crisper architectural drawing and clearly depicted figures engaged in seasonal visits and greetings.

The Earthly Realm

Court paintings of subjects from the earthly realm included birds, flowers, and symbolic plants, as in Lū Ji's painting of pheasants (cat. no. 126), discussed above, as well as animals, fish, and insects. The huge carp swimming amid water plants and smaller fish in a work by the Xuande-period court painter Miu Fu (cat. no. 117) is a motif often associated with success in the civil service examinations; and large fish surrounded by smaller ones could represent the hope that sons would follow their father's official career path (Bartholomew 2006, pp. 92, 112, 151). The term for large carp could also be read as a homophone for the generally auspicious term "great profit." Still other meanings attach to fish, including concepts of abundance and a free and contented life. Each of these potential meanings is appropriate for a presentation picture for court officials or aristocrats.

Horses were almost the quintessential court animals, since each imperial court maintained stables of prized steeds, and horses were associated with hunting and warfare. Horses also were symbolically linked with the loyal service of human officials (see Silbergeld 1985). Those in *Two Horses under a Willow and Plum Tree* (cat. no. 136), by a court painting master of uncertain date named Hu Cong, seem clearly to be imperial steeds. They are elaborately groomed with cinched tails, combed manes, and red nosepiece decorations. The accompanying bamboo and blossoming apricot plants are often associated with scholars, suggesting these self-consciously posed and tethered steeds might stand in symbolically for loyal courtiers.

Along with plants and animals, the other great painting theme of the earthly realm was landscape. The subjects could be specific imperial domains, such as the hunting park depicted in Shang Xi's *Emperor Xuanzong's Amusements* (fig. 2), probably the Western Park near the Forbidden City (Wang Chenghua 1998, p. 233). Other particular landscapes embodied historical and literary associations, such as the Lake Dongting surroundings of the Yueyang Tower in An Zhengwen's painting (cat. no. 138). The tower was a major landmark with rich historical and literary associations, including a commemorative poem by the Northern Song minister Fan Zhongyan written on the occasion of the tower's renovation in 1045. Fan's poem is concerned with statecraft and the primacy of concern for the state over personal enjoyment. Such associated sentiments would have made a painting of the tower an appropriate subject for presentation to court officials. The artist An Zhengwen was a Battalion Commander in the Embroidered Uniform Guard, but otherwise little known. This painting and a companion piece depicting the Yellow Crane Pavilion on the Yangzi River are both detailed and proficient "ruled-line" paintings, measured and legible renderings of carpentered objects like the buildings, gateways, and boats seen here. An's rendering adds a bit of visual drama to the scene, with the roiled waves of the lake and windblown trees providing a setting for the tricky docking of a boat at the gated landing. Visitors sightseeing or writing poetry in the tower above overlook the scene below, emphasizing the tower's status as a historically resonant travel destination.

Most landscape paintings produced at the Ming court were generic in the sense of lacking place-names, but they could embody a wide range of meanings, depending on their titles or inscriptional content, circumstances of commissioning or presentation, or thematic inflections such as seasonal landscapes or landscapes of reclusion. *Searching for Plum Blossoms in the Snow* (cat. no. 127) by Wang E (active 1488–1521) had a well-established association with the annual quest of Tang poet Meng Haoran (689–740), departing from his mountainside reclusive dwelling to catch sight of the first plum blossoms of the new year in the capital. The painting subject was specifically linked to the Ming court by the composition of a play of the same title by a playwright grandson of the founding Ming emperor named Zhu Youdun (1379–1439) (Park 1995, pp. 136–37). As with flower-and-bird paintings, most Ming court landscapes were couched in versions of Northern or Southern Song court painting styles. These offered a ready-made vocabulary of texture-stroke and tree types, templates for themes and compositions, and an overarching implication of continuity with the imperial past. Old paintings in the Ming court collections could provide tangible sources for reference and models for imitation.

Court-affiliated artists belonged to diverse social milieus, however, and their stylistic and expressive choices could range far from the standard manner. Yao Shou's *Fishing in Seclusion on an Autumn River* (cat. no. 122) harbors a theme of reclusion that is, somewhat paradoxically, tied to sociability. Yao Shou (1423–1495) was a Censorate official in the early Chenghua period who retired to his hometown of Jiaxing in the southeast following a demotion. *Fishing in Seclusion* was painted in 1476 for a calligrapher friend named Zhang Bi (*ZGHHQJ,* vol. 11, no. 60, pp. 15–16). The style references Yuan dynasty scholar-amateur sources rather than Song dynasty court modes. The modest skiff under the trees alludes to a long tradition of images of fisherman as carefree rustics, free of social pressures and constraints. In the year after he dedicated this painting, Yao Shou built for himself a rather more luxurious craft, to convey him on excursions among the waterways of southeast China while he composed poems and paintings to add to his onboard collection (*DMB,* vol. 2, p. 1560).

Broad River and Clear Peaks (cat. no. 118) by the Xuande-period painter-in-attendance Li Zai (died 1431) is an altogether more imposing mountainscape, accompanied by rich narrative detail. The central peak that twists diagonally back and forth into the distance, culminating in a sharp profiled summit, is reminiscent of the Northern Song court painter Guo Xi (active late eleventh century). At the foreground, riverbank figures listen to a flute player in two boats moored by the shore, while other figures, in a series of pavilions and cottages in the river valley and mountains above, gaze out over the water or welcome guests.

Traveling in Snowy Mountains (cat. no. 119) by Li Zai's fellow Xuande-period painter-in-attendance Dai Jin (1388–1462) carries the dynamic zigzag rhythms of leaning cliffs to a further level of sketchy exuberance. A party of travelers crossing the foreground bridge and entering an imposing gateway head toward pavilions high up in the mountains. Looming over the valley are jagged cliffs whose deeply shadowed forms at times dissolve into looping cursive outlines. The sketchy manner seen here and in some other Ming court paintings is in a different register than the casual, placid ink sketches of scholar-amateur artists. It answers a taste for visual excitement and energy that has a counterpart in the angular facets of rocks and stark profiles of branches in more polished court landscape and figure paintings, such as *Misty River at Dusk* (cat. no. 137) by the early-sixteenth-century court painter Zhu Duan. At the same time, the aesthetic of sketchiness in general makes claims to values that bridge the social divides among scholar-officials, court painters, and urban professionals: freedom from convention, personal expression, and eccentricity, even a kind of inspired genius.

Humankind

Some aura of genius and eccentricity certainly attached to Wu Wei (1459–1508), nicknamed the "Little Immortal" by a Ming prince. Wu possessed the biographical marks of genius, noted as a child prodigy who composed poetry and painted by the age of seven. He entered the Chenghua-period court as a painter in attendance and served through the Hongzhi period when he was awarded the rank of Company Commander in the Embroidered Uniform Guards by the emperor, who also bestowed upon him a seal calling him the Principal Graduate among Painters, with an implied equivalence to the most outstanding scholar among the palace civil service examinees. Wu had a classical literary education, wrote poems and songs, and engaged with scholars and officials as an equal, winning the admiration of many of the literary-minded painters of his day. Unlike most court painters, about whom we know very little, there are many recorded anecdotes about Wu Wei, whose talent and idiosyncrasies made him famous— or notorious. Wu's eccentricities extended to his scandalous behavior at court, where he was reported to have appeared drunk and disheveled in the presence of the emperor, only to win forgiveness through his astonishing displays of painterly skill. Wu Wei painted landscapes, but he is better known for figure paintings, as he is represented in this exhibition, often bravura performances directly painted on silk without any underdrawing (Barnhart 1993, pp. 223–41). His image of the Chan (Zen) Buddhist eccentric and poet Hanshan holding a scroll (cat. no. 128) is marked by bold, dynamic brushstrokes for the angular pine branches and windblown, tattered robe of Hanshan, who peers at the painted full moon with an exaggerated smile that suggests a combination of beatific wisdom and simplemindedness. Wu Wei's educated background, indulgence in the urban pleasures of drinking, theatrical entertainment, and courtesans, and his participation in an expressive performance aesthetic link him to other educated professional artists of his era, mostly out of court, such as Tang Yin and Du Jin.

Qiu Ying was another brilliantly talented professional painter, whose gifts won him the admiration of the literary and artistic elites in Suzhou. Wen Zhengming sometimes collaborated with Qiu and frequently wrote admiring colophons for his paintings (Little 1985, pp. 9–13, 41–70). One of Qiu's most admired skills was in painting excellent copies of technically refined Song dynasty court paintings, some of which had found their way into local private collections. Qiu Ying was thus in way a kind of court painter at a distance, never personally serving at court but working often in old court styles and subjects. His career exemplifies another way in which court culture was disseminated into the world at large, through dispersal, emulation, and imitation of objects and styles from the prestigious imperial realm out into the increasingly prosperous private society of Chinese cities. Since Ming sumptuary laws severely regulated the ways in which the contemporary court and its symbols could be imitated or displayed, a safer strategy involved the acquisition or imitation of works from the precursor native dynasty of the Song (960–1279).

Qiu Ying's *Tribute Bearers* handscroll (cat. no. 135) is just such a work, a free copy of a monochrome handscroll by the early Southern Song court painter Wu Kewen (active approx. 1130–1160), painted for Qiu's patron Chen Guan, who owned the Song model, and inscribed by Wen Zhengming, among other elite gentlemen (Little 1985, pp. 61–63). Using rich color and intricate details of costume and ethnic appearance, the painting depicts emissaries from thirteen foreign states bringing tribute gifts to the Tang emperor. The general subject of tribute bearers was the perfect embodiment of the Chinese imperial ideology, of the Son of Heaven as a universal ruler who deserved subservience from all other states, expressed ritually through the offering of tribute gifts. The subject had been a theme for Chinese court painting in every period since the Tang, and Qiu Ying's version, with its rich palette of mineral blue and green pigments and lavish ornamental detail, belongs fully to that tradition.

Wu Wei, Dai Jin, and other court artists occasionally painted rustic fisherman or nicknack peddlers to acknowledge the existence of lower and laboring classes, but most court figure paintings depicted contemporary elites or cultural paragons from former times. Ding Yunpeng's *Yuchuan Brewing Tea* of 1612 (cat. no. 142) portrays the Tang dynasty poet Lu Tong (died 835), a devotee of tea culture, preparing to enjoy his favorite drink while relaxing in a garden amid bamboo, banana palms, and a deeply eroded Taihu garden rock (Yang Xin et al. 1994, cat. no. 61, p. 155). Ding Yunpeng served at court for about ten years, but this painting was dedicated to the collector and painter Wang Shimin (1592–1680), who was just twenty years old at the time. Since Lu Tong was a poet and tea connoisseur who never sought office, presentation of such a painting may have been a flattering way of praising the recipient's connoisseurship as well as his high-minded lack of worldly ambition.

The Ming Court in Dissolution

Ding Yunpeng, Wu Bin, and somewhat later Chen Hongshou were among the very few painters of note who served at the Ming court after the first decades of the 1500s, and they seem to have done so only briefly and with a sense of dissatisfaction. The Wanli emperor, who reigned from 1573 until 1619, was so beset by factional conflict at court that he largely withdrew from active supervision of the bureaucracy for much of the last three decades of his reign (*CHC,* vol. 7, pp. 514–17, 550–57). Paralysis at court, with large numbers of official positions lying vacant for years on end and the national treasury drained by the emperor's avarice and extravagant expenditures, was counterbalanced by a burgeoning of the market economy and urban culture in general. The pronounced distortions and seeming eccentricity in figure paintings by Ding, Wu, and Chen were aimed in part at winning notice in the crowded and competitive urban art markets in which they primarily operated. The art world of the late Ming had greatly expanded in its commercial and intercultural dimensions since the early Ming: both Ding Yunpeng and Chen Hongshou were deeply engaged in woodblock-print publishing, and Wu Bin probably appropriated pictorial elements from European engravings brought to China by Jesuit missionaries (Cahill 1982, pp. 179, 219, 246–59).

The dynamic changes in late Ming visual culture that are signaled by the inventive distortions, patterned colorism, and visual wit of such figure paintings had no discernible impact on the genre of formal court portraiture, represented in this exhibition by the princely portrait of Zhu Youyuan (cat. no. 147), father of Emperor Shizong (reigned as the Jiajing emperor, 1522–1566), and the portrait of Zhu Youjiao (cat. no. 149), or Emperor Xizong (reigned as the Tianqi emperor, 1621–1627). Both portraits are frontal, static images that emphasize the symmetrically paired symbolic insignia of rank more than the body or visage of the aristocratic personage. The portrait of the Tianqi emperor Zhu Youjiao offers a particularly rich display of textiles, gilded lacquer furniture, porcelain, and bronze objects, which along with other imperial objects are so abundantly represented elsewhere in this exhibition. It was not that formal court portraiture was necessarily static; the energetic and individuated portrait of the Yongle emperor discussed above (see fig. 1) testifies to the potential for visual distinctions within the genre. Rather, these late Ming court portraits embody a general lethargy that affected court painting ateliers and the conduct of state affairs alike. The Tianqi emperor's brief reign was disastrously afflicted by factional struggles between the corrupt eunuch Wei Zhongxian (1568–1627) and his allies, and the reformers associated with the Donglin Academy, who suffered bloody repressions and purges at Wei's hands; as well as by military defeats to the Manchus in the northeastern frontier regions. The Tianqi emperor, who has been described as "physically weak, poorly educated, and perhaps mentally deficient," was of no help to these situations, which were resolved only with his early death at age twenty-one and the purge of Wei Zhongxian and his faction by the succeeding Chongzhen emperor (reigned 1628–1643) (*CHC,* vol. 7, pp. 595–614).

Dong Qichang (1555–1636), the leading painter and art theorist of his era, lived through this unhappy era mostly in retirement, cultivating safe, if not good, relationships with members of both factions through the cultural work of dedicating, inscribing, or authenticating paintings (Riely 1992, pp. 430–31). Dong's writings cast a long art-historical shadow back on the court art of the first half of the Ming. Dong Qichang's dichotomously structured Northern- and Southern-school theory of earlier Chinese painting history may echo the factional polarities that affected political life during much of his own career, but it oversimplifies the contrast between a pejoratively evaluated Northern school of academic and professional painters and the Southern-school painters who were marked by literary accomplishment and gentlemanly amateur status. Dong mostly avoided discussions of early Ming court painting, but he cast aspersions on the Zhejiang, or Zhe school, of Ming painting which produced many court artists (Cahill 1982, pp. 13–14, 27). It was a short step for other critics to extend the lineage of Northern-school court academy painters and professionals into the Ming court, and they often did so in ways that seriously distorted the nature of artistic relationships that had obtained there, which included often appreciative and collaborative associations of literary-minded scholar officials and skilled court painters.

Dong Qichang's *Misty Aspects of Mountains and Rivers* hanging scroll (cat. no. 143) was dedicated in 1628, just a year after the death of the Tianqi emperor and the subsequent disgrace and suicide of the eunuch Wei Zhongxian and many of his close allies. Dong mentions in his inscription the family of a certain Censorate official named Wu, so the painting was likely executed in full awareness of contemporary court politics. Dong's inscription focuses primarily on art collecting and art commerce, with a nod toward some of the paragons of his Southern school:

> *The family of the Censor Wu of Liangxi has passed down this picture by Shen Qinan [Shen Zhou].*
> *It can be put against the Four Masters of the Yuan period. As soon as I had set eyes on it, some meddle-*
> *some art lover bought it. So I did this in trying to recall it. . . .* (quoted in Ho 1992, vol. 2, p. 77;
> I have slightly modified John Hay's translation.)

The painting and its inscription suggest an active effort of protection and recovery against the threat of loss—of the Shen Zhou painting to an avaricious collector, and of its memory image to the ravages of time. Dong further asserts a historical continuity between Shen Zhou and the Four Yuan Masters of his favored Southern School lineage. But the painting itself is full of ambiguities, instabilities, dynamic tensions, and raw structural contradictions, more akin perhaps to the breakdown of governing structure at the Ming court and the stresses of factionalism there than to an imagined smooth continuity with the past. We might be reading too much into the painting to see it as an image of historical disruption and of discontinuities in the world order, but that disruption did occur with great finality with the fall of Beijing, the suicide of the Chongzhen emperor, and the dissolution of the Ming court some sixteen years later.

113

宣德朝　宣宗朱瞻基繪　苦瓜鼠圖卷　紙本設色

Rats after bitter melons and fruits, 1427 and 1431 (below, page 203)

By Zhu Zhanji (1398–1435)

Reign of the Xuande emperor (1426–1435)

Handscroll, ink and colors on paper

H. 28.2 cm (11.1 in.), W. 38.5 cm (15.12 in.)

Palace Museum, Beijing

These three individual works from different years were painted by Zhu Zhanji, the fifth Ming emperor (reign title: Xuande), whose significant role in art has not been justly acknowledged. Mounted onto a single handscroll at a later time, the works all share the same subject: a rat after many-seeded fruits. An undated round painting depicts a rat biting into the small red fruits of the *yangmei*, or Chinese bayberry (*Myrica rubra*). A rectangular work, dated 1431, shows a rat eating a lychee (*Litchi chinensis*). The third, dated 1427, depicts a rat greedily eyeing ripe bitter melons (*Momordica charantia*).

The rat is traditionally associated with qualities of intelligence and fertility. Many-seeded fruits, such as the three types illustrated here, are also symbolic of fertility. Together, the rat and fruit represent the Chinese popular saying "May you have sons and grandsons for ten thousand generations," expressing the Xuande emperor's wish for everlasting dynastic succession. Giving the rats different poses, minute details, and surface textures on the body, the emperor demonstrates his skill with delicate strokes, dry-ink jabbing, and ink washing. His vital portrayal of eating fruit, with exquisite coloring in a clear-cut composition, was among the early manifestations of interest in decorative, still-life depictions, which many Ming artists would specialize in.

Documents describe Zhu Zhanji as a gifted poet and artist, stealing moments away from countless tasks to compose poetry and paint. His paintings had the quality of improvisation, involving a degree of free-style brushwork (Mu Yiqin 1988). Eager to interact with literati, the Xuande emperor often gave away his own paintings as rewards to favored subjects and servants. The majority of the fifteen surviving paintings by him were executed from 1426 to 1431 (*GGSHTL*, vol. 6, pl. 141–59; *ZGMSQJ, huihua bian*, vol. 6, pl. 74–77). The Xuande emperor's chosen subjects were usually cute images of pets and animals, or motifs with implied metaphorical meanings: a celebration of long life and health, blessings of prosperity and good luck, or admiration for nobility and emolument.

Signatures. The painting of the rat on the rock is signed, *Playfully painted by me, the sovereign, in the year Ding-Wei of the Xuande reign* [1427] 宣德丁未／御筆戲寫. The painting of the rat biting the lychee is signed, *Bestowing to my eunuch Wu Cheng, brushwork by me, the sovereign, in the sixth year of the Xuande reign* [1431] 宣德六年／御筆／賜太監吳誠.

Seals. *Treasure of Vast Fortune* 廣運之寶. Seals of the Qing imperial household: *For the thorough appreciation of the three-rarity court* 三希堂精鑑璽; *The treasures for the examination of His Majesty Qianlong* 乾隆御覽之寶; *Appreciation of Qianlong* 乾隆鑑賞; *Blessed posterity* 宜子孫; *Treasures* 重華宮鑑藏寶; *The treasures for the examination of His Majesty Jiaqing* 嘉慶御覽之寶; *The treasures for the examination of His Majesty Xuantong* 宣統御覽之寶; *Valuable treasures on the stone channel* 石渠寶笈; *Discernment and appraisal by stone channel* 石渠定鑑; *Valuable treasures reregistered* 寶笈重編; *Examined by Song Luo* 宋犖審定 [minister at the Ministry of Personnel during the Kangxi reign]. HL

114

宣德朝　宣宗朱瞻基繪　蓮蒲松陰圖卷　紙本設色

Lotus pond shaded by a pine tree (above, page 205)

By Zhu Zhanji (1398–1435)

Reign of the Xuande emperor (1426–1435)

Handscroll, ink and light colors on paper

H. 31 cm (12.2 in.), W. 53.8 cm (21.2 in.)

Palace Museum, Beijing

The two river scenes by Zhu Zhanji, the Xuande emperor, are typical examples of his "painting an idea." Such paintings represent an imaginary nature in the artist's heart rather than sketched nature. Both scenes capture the tranquility of an ordinary summer day through their lively rendering of textures. A lone pine tree stretches from a riverbank in the upper composition, forming a canopy over the water. Far away across the river are cloudy mountain peaks, with subdued touches of light blue. A bird grasps the stem of a lotus seedpod, as if pondering how best to get a sip of water below. Opposite, a large lotus leaf curves downward into a soft gathered skirt with flounces. The two scenes were mounted in a typical imperial format, with a preface written on a piece of apricot-colored paper painted with gold dragons by the royal workshop.

The Xuande emperor espoused a loose style, tempering it with a type of expressive brushwork known as "boneless," in which a picture is rendered directly, not over any previous outlining or drawing. The "boneless" technique was a relaxed method developed in the tenth century to endow painting with personal sensibilities. A twelfth-century work by Emperor Huizong of the Song dynasty (reigned 1100–1125), *A Pond at Evening in Fall*, now in the National Palace Museum, Taipei (Xu Guohuang 2003, p. 64), was energized by crusts of ink spots. Huizong's "boneless" depiction of a lotus pond might have served as a model for the Xuande emperor, who greatly admired Song culture.

His enthusiasm for cultural pursuits set him apart from all his Ming predecessors, who were more obsessed with politics and military affairs. Because of his personal involvement, the imperial academy flourished more than it had during the previous four reigns, institutionally and functionally.

Signature. *Brushwork by me, the sovereign* 御筆.

Seals. Treasures for the Palace of Peace and Happiness 安喜宮寶. Seals of the Qing imperial household: For the thorough appreciation of the three-rarity court 三希堂精鑑璽; Blessed posterity 宜子孫; Appreciation of Jiaqing 嘉慶鑑賞. HL

205

115

宣德/成化　明人繪　宣宗朱瞻基宮中行乐圖卷　絹本設色

Amusements in the Xuande emperor's palace, approx. 1426–1487 (pages 207, 208)

(pages 217 and 218)

Handscroll, ink and colors on silk

H. 36.6 cm (14.41 in.), W. 687 cm (270.47 in.)

Palace Museum, Beijing

A rare painting by an anonymous Ming artist draws on the Xuande emperor's fascination with martial arts to offer us a series of scenes from early-fifteenth-century sports. The emperor is depicted in this handscroll as an avid sportsman who is thoroughly engaged in the outdoor amusements, which he either inspects or plays himself. He is dressed in sporty attire: a mandarin cap and loose-fitting robes with tight sleeves and pleated skirts. The scenes are presented from a bird's-eye view in a narrative style, divided by painted walls or curtains into four grounds.

Beginning from the top right, the first sport is archery (a), one of the Six Arts—along with rites, music, chariot riding, literature, and mathematics—established by ancient aristocrats and later endorsed by Confucianism. Archery was practiced either on horseback or on foot; the latter is shown here, with a revolving, upright target.

The second game, a type of soccer (b) or kickball, had been played for centuries by all classes in the north. The ball was made of leather stuffed with animal fur (*Qian Hanshu*, pp. 146–49). By the eighth century, air-inflated balls emerged; their light weight was loved by new women players. The game could be played with or without a goal area. The first professional soccer teams—probably the first in the world—were organized during the eleventh century. Playing soccer became a habit for most Ming emperors, except the first. For fear of exhausting the limited strength of the Ming army, he prohibited soccer among the troops. However, this ban did not last longer than the reign of the Xuande emperor, who was completely addicted to the sport.

Next is the emperor's inspection of polo players (c). What is unique about this scene is its depiction of polo being played around a goal hoop on a vaulted wooden backboard. Known by the third century as "hitting a ball" (Cao Zhi, p. 166), polo became widespread, and its enthusiasts ranged from emperors to cavalrymen.

To celebrate the imperial civil examinations, a court in the seventh century held a yearly polo contest for both military and civil officials. Even women played polo on donkeys, though at a slower pace for the sake of safety. During the Ming period, the sport was maintained as a form of supplemental cavalry training.

After participating as a judge in the first three sports, the emperor becomes a competitor in a game similar to golf or croquet (d). As in modern golf, the goal was to hit the ball into a hole in the ground using spoonlike sticks resembling golf clubs. Later it developed into a game played on multiple-hole grounds. Players could number from one to ten. In 1282 the earliest known book on golf history was published. This long-standing sport, however, was abandoned by the Manchu rulers after 1644.

Next, the emperor and his subjects engage in a traditional sport now known as pitch-pot (e), which involved throwing a javelin into a vase. This game could also be staged indoors on rainy days. Classical texts describe it as part of a drinking game used to entertain guests (Zheng Xuan, p. 1665). The loser, who missed the target, had to drink wine as punishment. The Xuande and Wanli emperors were remembered as great patrons of the game.

In the final episode, the emperor leaves the grounds (f) with recharged spirit. HL

a

b

c

d

e

f

116

明中期　明人繪　湖畔射猎圖軸　絹本設色

Regal hunting scene, approx. 1450–1550

Hanging scroll, ink and colors on silk

H. 106.7 cm (42 in.), W. 124.8 cm (49.13 in.)

Palace Museum, Beijing

This work depicts five hunters in the field, all on horseback. Each of the hunters indicates his noble identity by riding a handsome horse with a spotted roan or chestnut coat; such mounts were regarded by the Chinese as "the superior red horses." The figures, all carrying quivers of arrows, are loosely arranged on a riverbank. The background seems somewhat atypical of wilderness due to the pinkish lotus blooms lying across green leaves and cranes flying above reeds waving gently in the late summer. As was custom for royal portraits such as this, the artist does not leave his name or seal. The attention given to the definite lines and

colors of the horses follows the fundamental approach for horse painting established by fourteenth-century masters. Using a technique of quick, fluid textural strokes to give a more natural representation, the artist absorbed elements of style from classical landscape for the backdrop. The riders convey the excitement of the hunt through their gestures and movements. They proceed toward the center in a triangular configuration, evoking dramatic tension with their strategic hunting plan.

It was during the Xuande reign that depictions of regal hunting were first produced as a new theme among the primary

subjects of Ming academic painting. Surpassing earlier Ming emperors who were good horsemen, the Xuande emperor was enamored of riding and especially hunting, displaying an almost fanatical devotion to the sport. Not satisfied with the hunting ground near the palace, Son of Southern Sea, he insisted on exploring wild fields, placing a heavy burden on regional agencies. The hunting theme permitted court painters to appeal to dynastic virtues, but its popularity fell once the monarch's fascination for hunting waned. HL

117

宣德朝　繆輔繪　魚藻圖軸　綾本設色

Fish and water plants (right)

By Miu Fu (active 1426–1435)

Reign of the Xuande emperor (1426–1435)

Hanging scroll, ink and colors on silk

H. 171.3 cm (67.44 in.), W. 99.1 cm (39.02 in.)

Palace Museum, Beijing

An underwater world of aquatic plants and fish, representing phallic symbols, sets the scene for an old Chinese proverb, "May you be as harmonious as fish and water." At the center is a big carp with an open, bossy eye and alert feelers that proclaim its tyranny of the underwater world. Other species, akin to grass carp and catfish, seem to be chased away by the big carp. Slender aquatic branches drift in waves, giving the picture the flowing movement of water. The composition displays a subtlety of balance, particularly in the diagonal duet of two aquatic plants: the triangular, long-stemmed arrowroots,

deeply rooted into the bottom in the left foreground, and the rounded water lilies floating at top right.

The fifteenth-century court painter Miu Fu found metaphors in fish and aquatic plants, and selected certain motifs with auspicious meanings for inclusion in one pictorial presentation. Because in the Chinese language, the word for "fish" sounds like the word for "abundance" or "profit," the fish is always an emblem of wealth. The arrowroots imply compassion, as well as benevolence. The water lily symbolizes peace and safety, according to popular beliefs.

Such politically optimistic productions easily gained acceptance or favor of the monarch. The specific theme, delicate coloring, and sensually painted aquatics characterize his academic training in the classical realism established by Huang Quan (903–965).

Signature. *Painted by Embroidered Uniform Judge, the Hall of Military Valor, Miu Fu from the Su region* 武英殿直錦衣鎮撫蘇郡繆輔寫.

Seals. *Liangzuo* 良佐; *Rijin qingguang* [When daytime comes, the light gets clear] 日近清光. HL

118

宣德朝　李在繪　闊渚晴峰圖軸　絹本水墨

Broad river and clear peaks (page 212)

By Li Zai (died 1431)

Reign of the Xuande emperor (1426–1435)

Hanging scroll, ink on silk

H. 165.2 cm (65.04 in.), W. 90.4 cm (35.59 in.)

Palace Museum, Beijing

The prior rift between the artistic styles and themes of the elite and those of the common people began to give way during the Xuande reign. The Ming monarch fostered a fusion of interests and did not conform to the traditional judgment that identified highbrow idealism as supreme and popular themes as trivial and ugly. Responding to this dual aesthetic, Ming academicians came to recognize divergent tendencies in their practice of art.

Li Zai's landscape painting exemplifies this syncretism by combining traditional idealism with realistic elements. Three groups of figures of varying social status appear in the picture, differentiated by

certain activities. At the water's edge in the foreground, fishermen in boats entertain themselves by drinking wine and playing the Chinese flute. Upstream, on a hillside overlooking the water, an educated man in a pavilion reads books. Even farther up, in a mountain house at the center of the painting, a host greets a guest, followed by a boy servant carrying a zither. Presumably they are gathering for a concert and tea tasting.

The treatment—with deer-horn- and crab-claw-like branches and whirling, cloud-shaped textural strokes—reflects Li Zai's growing interest in the classical tradition. This is married to a rustic rendering and

vigorous ink washes. Li Zai's spirited, economical style, his intellectual approach to human figures, and his insistence on harmony in composition won him second position, under Dai Jin (see cat. no. 119), among landscape painters of his time.

Signature. The name *Guo Xi* 郭熙 has been inserted over the original signature. HL

119

宣德／天順朝　戴進繪　雪山行旅圖軸　絹本設色

Traveling in snowy mountains, approx. 1426–1462 (below)

By Dai Jin (1388–1462)

Hanging scroll, ink and colors on silk

H. 144.2 cm (56.77 in.), W. 78.1 cm (30.75 in.)

Palace Museum, Beijing

Dai Jin gained distinction as a court painter by emphasizing the Southern Song (1127–1279) tradition. Dai produced many landscapes but particularly valued mountain climbing as a theme, probably motivated by his persistent longing to find religious fulfillment, or "the way," deep in the mountains. In this winter scene, nine travelers—seven on horseback and two servants on foot—take a long journey toward temples perched on high mountain cliffs. The giddy mountain paths have separated the travelers. A forward party has reached the mountain gate, leaving the others behind, who are struggling across a narrow wooden bridge built on stilts.

Unlike Dai Jin's conventional compositions, here a heavily laid foreground extending up the left side of the painting provides a counterpoint to the open, largely vacant space on the right. This imbalance lends a peculiarly dangerous mood to the mountain scene. The precipitousness of the cliffs are indicated by the deep, misty valleys between the tower gate and temples. All these elements make the journey seem especially perilous.

Technically, the crab-claw strokes of the weathered trees and the textural brushwork of the leaves in the foreground show Dai Jin's deft application of his Song training. But the exaggerated form and texture of the rocks in such an unbalanced layout break the usual harmony, signaling that the artist sought to revitalize the quiet styles favored by Song masters.

Dai's later experience of selling paintings to make a living in his hometown allowed him to move toward more varied modes of art (Shan Guoqiang 1993, p. 25). His later achievements confirmed a growing resolve to find his artistic identity outside the Ming academic style, as witnessed in this transitionary work.

Signature. *Painted by Dai Wenjin from Qiantang* 錢唐［塘］戴文進寫.

Seals. *The Dai's* 戴氏 [two characters are missing]; *Yuquan daoren* 玉泉道人.

HL

120

宣德/天順朝　周文靖繪　歲朝圖軸　絹本設色

A celebration of the New Year

By Zhou Wenjing (active 1426–1463)

Hanging scroll, colors on silk

H. 137.7 cm (28.23 in.), W. 71.7 cm (54.21 in.)

Shanghai Museum

This depiction of a New Year's celebration by Zhou Wenjing, a court painter who served in the Hall of Benevolence and Wisdom during the reign of the Xuande emperor (1426–1435), is likely based on the Song-dynasty painting *Banquet by Lantern Light* by Ma Yuan (*GGSHTL,* vol. 2, p. 163). The influence of the earlier artist is apparent in the use of a misty void as a compositional device and the positioning of the figures in the foreground. Zhou's innovation rests on his realistic presentation of the figures: some of them are in pairs, others in groups, some chatting, drinking, or gesticulating, and some arriving on horse. The details of their robes, hats, and uniforms show that the guests attending this celebration were all of high rank.

New Year's paintings were an important genre for court artists of the Song dynasty (960–1279) and one of the many Song traditions revived at the Ming court. These works depicted the celebrations hosted by the Ming emperors every first lunar month as a demonstration of their desire for dynastic peace and prosperity. During these New Year celebrations, all the buildings in the Forbidden City would be hung with colorful banners and lanterns. Banquets, operas, and acrobats would also be part of the extravaganza. Outside the palace, people would visit each other, bearing presents to help smoothe a professional relationship or climb the official ladder. In general, paintings of these scenes were intended as seasonal interior decoration for homes of the wealthy or influential.

This painting has a particularly interesting provenance. Two seals of Ma Yuan (active 1189–1225) were stamped on the lower left, after Zhou Wenjing's time. As a result, in the eighteenth century this work was attributed to the Song-dynasty artist. The Qianlong emperor's inscription at the top of the painting reinforced its historical importance.

Colophon. The top of the painting bears a ten-sentence poem in semicursive script, describing a pleasant celebration of the New Year among noble and wealthy classes. Signed *Yuti* [the Qianlong emperor, reigned 1736–1795] *on the second day of the first lunar month of the year Geng-Zi* [1780].

Seals. *Zhou Wenjing* 周文靖; *Ma Yuan, Ma Yuan zhiyin* [both forgeries]. HL

121

明中期　劉俊繪　雪夜訪普圖軸　絹本設色

The first Song emperor visiting Zhao Pu on a snowy night (page 216)

By Liu Jun (active approx. 1450–1500)

Hanging scroll, ink and colors on silk

H. 147 cm (29.53 in.), W. 75 cm (57.87 in.)

Palace Museum, Beijing

This fifteenth-century painting illustrates a well documented historical incident highlighting the unusual relationship between Emperor Taizu (reigned 960–976), founder of the Song dynasty, and his Grand Councillor, Zhao Pu (922–992). The erudite, taciturn, and kindhearted Zhao Pu had had a beneficial influence on Emperor Taizu during his formation of the Song government. Soliciting Zhao's advice, the emperor often stopped by his subordinate's home unexpectedly after court hours. To prepare for the emperor's unscheduled appearances, Zhao would usually not change from his court uniform

into more relaxing attire until late at night. However, on the night of a heavy snowfall, sometime between 964 and 969, Zhao, not expecting the emperor to brave the freezing weather, decided to put on a comfortable gown. His Majesty's unpredictable visit caused a sudden domestic commotion. Grilling meat and warming wine on a charcoal brazier, Zhao and his wife received the emperor in a panic (*Songshi,* chap. 256, p. 708).

The court artist Liu Jun recounts the incident with imaginative and realistic details. He sets the stage in an open residence situated in the chilly hills. Liu portrays the

seated emperor as a mighty ruler wearing a dragon robe; Zhao Pu's pose is one of utter respect. Zhao's wife stands by the door as lady in waiting, ready for service. Four royal bodyguards, holding a banner, a crosier and the emperor's horse, stand shivering in the cold outside the courtyard. Liu Jun's elegant colors and smooth modeling hark back to the style of Song academic art.

Signature. *Painted by Liu Jun, Commander of the Embroidered Uniform Imperial Bodyguard* 錦衣都指揮劉俊寫. HL

122

成化十二年（1476年）　姚綬繪　秋江漁隱圖軸　紙本設色

Fishing in seclusion on an autumn river, 1476 (page 217)

By Yao Shou (1422 or 1423–1495)

Reign of the Chenghua emperor (1465–1487)

Hanging scroll, ink and colors on paper

H. 162.2 cm (23.23 in.), W. 59 cm (63.83 in.)

Palace Museum, Beijing

This work, comprising a poem and a painting, attests to a friendship between two scholar bureaucrats, both of whom found themselves committed more to nature and art than to government. Yao Shou's dream of serving state affairs dissipated shortly after he joined the Ming bureaucracy. At a trial over a case of libel, he was demoted from the central government to a local administrative post. Resigning from the bureaucracy at age forty-eight, he devoted the rest of his life to literature and art in his hometown. There, Yao found that solitude nurtured his soul. The fifty-five-year-old Yao Shou dedicated this work to his friend Zhang Bi (1425–1487), a military officer better known for his excellent calligraphy. Zhang's cursive script, especially works he created when drunk, rose to prominence in the mid-fifteenth century.

Without extremes of emotional intensity, Yao Shou reflects on his former high rank

in this image of a man wearing a red uniform and black silk hat, fishing alone in tranquility. The composition utilizes flat water, glazed between green hills and hazy mountains diluted in the distance. As in the poem inscribed at the top, Yao conveys a deep appreciation for the simplicity of a sequestered fishing life. His tranquil setting anticipates the work of the elites who thirty years later flourished in the Wu school.

Colophons. In a long poem written in semicursive script in the upper part of the painting, Yao Shou describes how the beauty around rivers inspired an official, who would get drunk on wine traded for the fish he caught and then paint the lyrical scene when sober. He also explains that his painting was based on a much earlier painting with the same title by Zhao Mengfu (1254–1322), whose work he had come to admire the most. Having recently acquired this painting, Yao studied it "from the morning

to evening" until gaining the confidence to master Zhao's brushwork.

A colophon by Dong Qichang (1555–1636), also written in semicursive script at the top of the work, states that the painting was created by Yao and dedicated to Zhang Bi's Qingyun Mountain Villa when Yao visited him in Guyang.

Signature. *Respectfully presented to Master Donghai* [Zhang Bi 張弼] *for his delicate appreciation in Qingyun Mountain Villa, inscribed by Dayun Yao Shou on the fourth day of the lunar first month in the year Bing-Shen of the Chenghua reign* [1476] 奉寄東海翁作慶雲山莊清賞／成化丙申建子月四日／大雲姚綬書.

Seals. Yao Shou's *Yundong xianguan* 雲東仙館 [Sacred studio on east clouds]; *Zixia biyue feng* 紫霞碧月風 [Rose clouds and the blue moon in wind]. Dong Qichang's *Zongxue boshi* 宗學伯士; *Dongshi xuanzai* 董氏玄宰. HL.

姚雲東侍御出
東海翁畫卷時此
五度雲山莊作為
是雲東過訪谷陽
時筆三公天下士稱
墨法傳皆五千古
子固寶藏尤貴
祖為之友風流如
昨蕉文孫程子
董其昌

紅葉滿目深江樹葉在林江上青漁者
硯硯謝朝簪武言鈞徒張志和奇
舟曰之尋煙波西塞山前飛白鷺拖
小舩肥漁船我呼鶴灣頭
住崖時持竿鈎魚多漁童逢青少
工人細而槭頭如鶯處得魚換酒
凍死添醒來臨跨湖州丹青是
漁陰一綠茗齊掃長江結嘴子秋湖
頑畫高自候好人弗如古擲筆金
壺中竹前湯作漁蓑還起蔡
兮晚章醉愛松雲趄永昏劇
法近浮其私江漁隱園朝夕玩
繹自謂瀾舟所向一目些古鼎
蔫碧窓雲罷臨晉帖用紫翠
硯台梅類二子龍奄見小澗朱鉛
書客
東海翁作雲慶雲山莊情賞
戚化丙申堵字月曰大雲如緩公

123

成化/弘治朝　鍾欽禮繪　雪夜出艇圖軸　絹本水墨

Boating on a snowy night

By Zhong Qinli (active 1465–1505)

Hanging scroll, ink on silk

H. 170 cm (66.93 in.), W. 102.5 cm (40.35 in.)

Palace Museum, Beijing

As suggested by the signature on this painting, the court artist Zhong Qinli devoted this work to a peculiar friendship between two fourth-century elites. Wang Huizhi (died 386) lived in a simple, very sparsely furnished house in Kuaiji (Zhejiang province), which he saw as an unpolluted environment for self-cultivation. His mentor, the renowned scholar-artist Dai Kui (died 395), also lived in Kuaiji but at a distance from him on the river. Antagonistic toward the bureaucracy, Dai had ignored an imperial edict calling for his service and instead chose to live for art and music. On a heavily snowing night, suddenly struck by a desire to venture into the cold and see his friend, Wang Huizhi boated along the river to Dai's house. Just before reaching it, Wang decided to return home without seeing Dai Kui; the impulse that had sparked his visit had passed. Wang's subsequent saying, "going impromptu and returning at heart's content," is regarded as a romantic metaphor of high virtue. His boating on a snowy night has remained a popular subject in art for over a thousand years.

In that spirit, Zhong Qinli tapped a variety of sources: literary and poetic references, his accumulated studies of old masters, and his own fertile imagination. He constructed the scene as three successive planes: the foreground is composed of Wang Huizhi and his young servant in the boat, traveling upriver; the middle ground reveals Dai's thatched house built on stilts over water; and the background is a mountain scene, open to the left with peaks in the distance. The thin lines on weathered branches and dark textural strokes forming rocks and tree trunks all reflect Zhong's sensibility, in particular his interest in Zhe-school techniques. The most remarkable effect is the subtlety of the fallen snow and the feeling of the chilly air shot through with moisture and permeated by mist. Zhong's lyric statement proclaimed great moral conviction for the principles of the waning Zhe school.

Signature. *Painted in a place where dirt cannot reach, by Kuaiji shanren, Zhong Qinli* 會稽山人鍾欽禮書于一塵不染處. HL

124

弘治朝　呂纪、呂文英合繪　竹园壽集圖卷　絹本設色

Elegant Gathering in the Bamboo Garden, 1499 (pages 219 – 221)

By Lu Wenying (active 1488 –1505) and Lū Ji (died 1504 or 1505)

Reign of the Hongzhi emperor (1488 –1505)

Handscroll, ink and colors on silk

H. 33.8 cm (13.31 in.), W. 395.4 cm (155.67 in.)

Palace Museum, Beijing

This work recorded an actual sixtieth birthday party in 1499 for three eminent officials at the Hongzhi court. The exceptional significance of this painting lies in the unique collaboration of two famous court painters. Also important are the colophons at the beginning and end of the handscroll, written by high-ranking guests who describe the event from different viewpoints. A preface brings into focus the inspiration for this work, an early-fifteenth-century painting called *Elegant Gathering in the Apricot Garden*.

Beginning from top right, page 221, the event unfolds in seven episodes: three boy servants prepare tea just outside a house (a); two officials watch dancing cranes led by a boy (b) ; a guest extends congratulations to one of the birthday elders with presents held by two boys (c); a minister composes phrases on bamboo (d); another paints or writes on a handscroll at a stone table (e); Lu Ji points out details of a painting to Wenying (f); and, at far left, servants carry supplies and presents toward the garden (g). The officials all wear black silk hats, belted formal robes, and court badges. Above the head of each is a cartouche with name and title.

The painting incorporates influences from earlier artists into its realistic description of the garden setting. It is filled with delightful elements—green bamboo and pine, pink lotus, blossoming peach, fungus, a red antique table and incense burner, Taihu rock and gray stone—that enhance the viewer's appreciation of the scene as a real-world event filled with joy. The execution shows different working methods. The splendid colors and precise rendering of the figures and plants mark the typical academic style of Lu Wenying, while the brief notations of strokes for the swallows and rocks were more frequently used in Lu Ji's work. One study has suggested that the work was probably chiefly executed by Wenying under the supervision of the senior Lu Ji (Yang Lili 2004, pp. 106 –109).

Colophons. Names above the noblemen read (from right to left), *Luˉ Zhong* 侶鐘, *Xu Gongjin* 許進, *Zhou Jing* 周經, and his two sons *Lu* 魯 and *Meng* 孟, *Li Mengyang* 李孟暘, *Gu Zuo* 顧佐, *Tu Yong* 屠滽, *Wu Kuan* 吳寬, *Wang Ji* 王繼, *Min Gui* 閔珪, *Qin Minyue* 秦民悅, *Lū Ji* 呂纪, and *Lū Wenying* 呂文英.

A title in clerical script by Tu Yong reads, *Gathering on a birthday in a bamboo garden*, and is signed *Danshan* [Tu].

The preface, written in standard script by Wu Kuan, verifies that Tu Yong, Zhou Jing, and Lu Zhong cohosted a party at Zhou's residence on the fourth day of the fifth lunar month in the year 1499 to celebrate their sixtieth birthdays. There, Tu Yong expressed his admiration for the earlier *Apricot Garden* painting and suggested that the two guests, Lu Ji and LuWenying, record the occasion in a similar fashion.

Ten other inscriptions and poems by attendees remark on the celebration's significance, equating it with the large number 180 as represented by the three sixty-year-olds; and the fact that the guests came from *east, west, south, and north, to reenact the gathering in the Apricot Garden*.

Seal. *Tongjian luo zhencang shuhua* [Treasured collection of calligraphy and painting of Tongjia Studio] 同鑒樓珍藏書畫 from the Qing dynasty. HL

b

e

g

a

d

c

f

125

弘治朝　丁某繪　五同會圖卷　紙本設色

Gathering of the Five Commonalities, 1505

By Ding ? (given name unknown)

Reign of the Hongzhi emperor (1488–1505)

Handscroll, ink and colors on silk

H. 41 cm (16.14 in.), W. 181.7 cm (71.54 in.)

Palace Museum, Beijing

This long handscroll commemorates the last meeting of five renowned court officials at a private residence in Beijing, 1505. The gathering was in fact a literati salon whose members shared philosophical and political interests and activities. The five officials gathered under the umbrella of five commonalities—united by the era in which they lived, the Wu region (Suzhou) where they were born, the court they served, the bureaucracy they worked in, and the inclinations they shared. Such "meetings of commonality" became a popular activity among high-ranking officials in the optimistic and tolerant climate of the Hongzhi reign. Their intentions of promoting culture and purifying bureaucracy had a positive influence on the government.

The five salon members wear official robes of red, blue, and green. Around them are boy servants presenting tea, books, and a zither, and a porter carrying a wine jar and supply of food. A chessboard, books, an inkstone, and brushes lie on a table behind them. The meticulous brushwork, high-toned color, and polished finish of the painting reflect the artist's assimilation of the academic painting style. Although his exact identity is unknown, he was a professional painter, also from Suzhou, with the surname Ding.

The work shown here is one of five original copies that had been made—one for each of the five group members to keep. Only two have survived; the other copy is in the Shanghai Museum. When this depiction was presented to the Qing court in 1806, all the colophons were missing. During a restoration undertaken at the palace, Qing academicians used existing documents to reproduce the original colophons, and they added their own complimentary annotations, giving a detailed historical background of the gathering.

Colophons. A total of nineteen colophons by sixteen people begin with the prefaces and poems of Wu Kuan 吳寬 (1436–1504) and Wang Ao 王鏊 (1450–1524), written by Junior Compiler Yan 顏 in 1806. These are followed by more inscriptions, poems, and annotations by the descendants of Chen Ju 陳璚 and by Qing academicians, including Weng Fanggang 翁方綱, Qin Ying 秦瀛, and Fa Shishan 法式善, from 1807 to 1810. HL

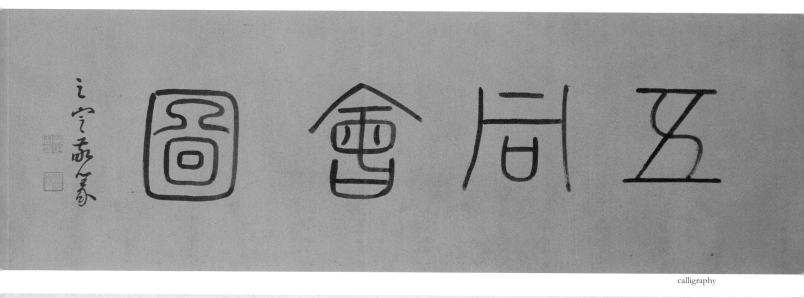

五同會圖

calligraphy

五同會序

126

宣德／弘治朝　呂紀繪　寒香幽鳥圖軸
絹本設色

Pairs of birds in winter

By Lu Ji (died 1504 or 1505)

Hanging scroll, ink and colors on silk

H. 141 cm (55.51 in.), W. 51.1 cm (20.19 in.)

Shanghai Museum

The New Year season is celebrated in this winter scene. Surrounded by traditional symbols of happiness and long life, three pairs of birds perch on a rock and branches. They huddle together to ward off the cold. Birds in pairs are synonymous with harmony and intimacy. Longevity is represented by the Three Friends of Winter: bamboo, plum, and Chinese wolfberry, which substitutes for the more common pine. Wolfberry was admired for its red fruit, which contrasts nicely with the green bamboo and white plum. The composition is unique for Lu Ji—he most often set his birds under or against waterfalls. Here the darkly painted rock and plum branch on which the birds sit are far above the dimmed mountain and stream.

Lu Ji's major patrons were members of the Ming court and aristocracy, and his style is representative of the flower-and-bird school they preferred. As seen in the bamboo and plum flowers, the artist employed a formal approach of creating outlines with refined ink strokes and filling the areas within with colors. Known in Chinese as *gongbi,* this meticulous style was made popular by the professional artists Huang Quan (903–965) and his son Jucai (born 933) from Sichuan. Lu's subtle use of colors and elaborate brushwork for the feathers of the birds and other details reflect a full awareness of the court painters of the Northern Song dynasty. For rocks and trees, Lu Ji employed sweeping, coarse brushstrokes that convey freedom and directness, recalling techniques made popular by Ma Yuan (active 1189–1225) during the Southern Song dynasty.

　　Signature. *Lu Ji* 呂紀.

　　Seals. *Lu Ji* 呂紀; *Siming Lu Tingzhen yin* 四明呂廷振印.　HL

127

弘治朝　王諤繪　踏雪尋梅圖軸　絹本淡色

Searching for plum blossoms in the snow

By Wang E (active 1488–1521)

Reign of the Hongzhi emperor (1488–1505)

Hanging scroll, ink and colors on silk

H. 106.5 cm (41.93 in.), W. 62 cm (24.41 in.)

Palace Museum, Beijing

This painting is based on the play *Searching for Plum Blossoms in the Snow* about the Tang poet Meng Haoran (689–740). Written in the early fifteenth century by Zhu Youdun (1379–1439), the play was staged at the palace to the amusement of the Xuande emperor. In the play, the iron-faced Meng has a refined passion for plum blossoms, a winter flower symbolizing an indomitable spirit. On a snowy day, guests come to Meng's mountain villa for a poetry competition. A bundle of blossoming plum branches is placed in the courtyard, and Meng begins to extemporize verses about flowers with one of his guests, Li Bai (also known as Li Po, 701–762). Meng versifies about plum blossoms, while Li, playing devil's advocate, versifies about the peony. Returning home with greater appreciation for the talented and well-informed Meng, Li Bai highly recommends him to the emperor.

Fifty years later, Wang E depicted the story in a manner consistent with the ideological regime of a wise emperor who could identify and use virtuous and able men in government. As in the painting by Liu Jun (cat. no. 121), the metaphorical content and style of Wang's work are associated with classicism. In a diagonally divided composition, the poetic execution of ink and forceful textural strokes used to define the cliffs and tree trunks embody characteristics developed earlier by Ma Yuan (active 1189–1225). Wang's first-rate brushwork makes use of a technique known as "leaving whiteness," in which a motif is rendered on untouched paper or silk by painting just its outlines or background with ink. This allows the plum tree in the front of the picture, as well as the pines trees and rocky peaks, to capture the chill beauty of the snow. The signature and seal marks on this work indicate that the artist created this piece for the Hongzhi emperor, who once acknowledged Wang E as the "Ma Yuan of our time."

Signature. *Painted by Your Subject Wang E* 臣王諤寫.

Seals. *Seal of Imperially Treasured Paintings* 御府寶繪之記; *Zhongzhi* 弘治; *Treasure of Vast Fortune* 廣運之寶; *Seal of Chen* [?] *ping* 陳 [?] 平印 [one character is missing or illegible]; *Clear Shadow in Eastern Forests* 東林清蔭. HL

128

弘治朝　吳偉繪　道釋賞月圖　絹本水墨

A monk enjoying a moon painting

By Wu Wei (1459–1508)

Hanging scroll, ink on silk

H. 138.6 cm (54.57 in.), W. 81 cm (31.89 in.)

Palace Museum, Beijing

This image shares a certain kinship with several of Wu Wei's other works on the theme of seeking self-cultivation in seclusion (*ZGHHQJ,* vol. 12, pp. 58–59). An element of liberty and humor infuses the painting: a loosely dressed monk, with his chest exposed and two hands holding an opened scroll bearing a painted moon, saunters on a slope dotted with an old tree. He appears to be far from an urban setting. The romantic atmosphere is attenuated by the rough straw sandals on his feet, underlining the artist's intent to make him look awkward. Blobs of ink were painted with violent strokes, giving the figure a random quality. The desolate country in the background is painted with rapid brushstrokes. In contrast to emperors' portraits of the period, executed in lifeless court styles, Wu Wei's figures— usually hermits, fishermen, peasants, geisha girls, and other representatives of the lower or middle classes—express their personalities. Wu's ability to communicate deep human experiences and human character places him among the most outstanding artists of the Ming dynasty.

The image certainly reflects his itinerant lifestyle. Traveling from one town to another in pursuit of freedom, wine, and entertainment, Wu chose to base himself in Nanjing most of the time. He was honored by two emperors with prestigious titles, including "Number One Painter," and was twice appointed to paint for the imperial court. Nevertheless, the position could not keep him in Beijing nor subdue his dissolute temperament, which he indulged by drinking with geishas. When drunk, his vigorous brushstrokes and bold splashes were far removed from the highly controlled techniques of many of his associates. Just as Wu himself departed from the main current, so did his art, which according to his contemporaries, expressed "insolence" or a "fighting spirit like the soldiers" (Shan Guoqiang 2000, pp. 13–15).

Signature. *Xiaoxian* 小僊.

Seal. *Xiaoxian Wu Wei* 小僊吴偉. HL

129

景泰/天順朝　周臣繪　長夏山村圖　紙本水墨

A mountain village in the long summer

By Zhou Chen (active 1472–1535)

Hanging scroll, ink on paper

H. 113.5 cm (23.31 in.), W. 59.2 cm (44.69 in.)

Shanghai Museum

In this work, Zhou Chen chose to depict the popular subject of officials seeking seclusion in remote mountains. The landscape derives its special charm from a setting in a mountain valley, with an open-sided building set over a stream. A member of the educated elite occupies the center of the villa. Even in this remote location, the gentleman wears the hat and long robe of his official rank as he leans on the railing, gazing upon the flow of water.

A native of Suzhou, the center of several art movements among the Ming educated elite, Zhou Chen integrated elements from these movements with the styles popular at court. In this work, the misty stream and heavily modeled peaks and trees that enclose it reflect the influence of the Song court painter Li Tang (approx. 1050–1130). The gray and black texturing on the mountain rocks incorporates a variety of brushstrokes (known as cord-, ax-, and nail-shaped) developed by court artists during the Southern Song dynasty. Yet the relaxed mood, rich ink tones, and multiple applications of dots and lines on the foliage speak to the styles favored by the elites of his day.

Zhou's embrace of elements from both court painting traditions and the art of the educated elite influenced his contemporaries, including Tang Yin (1470–1524) and Qiu Ying (approx. 1482–1559). Tang Yin inscribed a romantic poem in semicursive script on the upper right of this painting, expressing admiration for Zhou's lyric depiction and subtle disdain for the life of bureaucrats behind "the red door":

High flow of spirit for poetry arises in a peaceful
mountain village for the long summer
Always finding a spot by a blue stream to shelter myself
from summer heat
Pine shadows on the earth fill the air with green
All can drive beings out the red door to drift with the tide
like a bamboo hat
　　　　　　　—Inscribed by Tang Yin at Su Terrace

Signature. *Dongcun Zhou Chen xie* [Painted by Zhou Chen of Eastern Village] 東村周臣寫.

Seals. *Dongcun* 東村. Collectors' seals: *Xuzhai miwan* [Secret Plaything for Void Studio] 虛齋秘玩; *Wuxing Pangshi zhencang* [Highly treasured by the Pang] 吳興龐氏珍藏 [seal of Pang Yuanji, 1864–1949, from Wuxing, Jiangsu]. HL

130

景泰/天順朝　周臣繪　亭林消夏圖
絹本設色

Summer gatherings in mountain pavilions

By Zhou Chen (active 1472–1535)
Hanging scroll, ink and colors on silk
H. 134 cm (52.76 in.), W. 79 cm (31.1 in.)
Shanghai Museum

A magnificent landscape depicts the escape of educated elites to remote mountains for the summer holidays. Bizarre rock formations divide the perspective into five levels. Following the zigzag path of the river, each level can be assigned a theme suggested by the figures' activities: walking into the mountains in the right foreground; fishing from a boat on the left; resting in a thatched pavilion at the center; crossing a bridge at the upper left; and gazing at a waterfall from a mountain villa at the top right. The entire composition succeeds in conveying height, depth, and distance, as sought by Song masters. The brushwork encompasses a range of techniques. Figures are drawn in refined lines. Dense foliage is individually outlined, speckled, or blurred in a mass. Rocks standing by rivers have a solid, substantial quality. The gradation of ink tones—from very dark, to gray, to light washes—is used effectively for definition or gradual fading.

Artist Zhou Chen was a scrupulous professional painter from Wuxian (Suzhou) in southeast China, an area that fostered many great academicians and literati. Although he never entered the court, a short stay in Beijing influenced his early academic training, especially time spent studying painters from the Song to the Ming, including the founder of the orthodox Zhe school, Dai Jin (see cat. no. 119). Zhou's works evidence his technical mastery of court styles. Subjects were chosen to reflect the emperors' inclinations, which leaned largely toward religion and philosophy. One of the more established themes in Song court art depicted the cultivated pursuits of urbanites in sacred mountains. Zhou adopted the theme but married it with his own creative inspiration.

Signature. *Dongcun Zhou Chen* 東村周臣.

Seals. *Dongcun* 東村; *Shunqing* 舜卿. Collectors' seals: *Studio of Xubai* 虛白齋; *Treasured by Wu Ziyu family from Fengxi* 豐溪吳子璵氏家珍藏. HL

131

明中期　杜菫繪　十八學士圖屏四幅　絹本設色

Eighteen imperial academicians (below, page 230)

Attributed to Du Jin (active approx. 1465–1500)

Set of four screens, ink and colors on silk

Each: H. 134 cm (52.76 in.), W. 79 cm (31.1 in.)

Shanghai Museum

The theme of eighteen imperial academicians was a traditional one serving to glorify the imperial system. It refers to a group of Tang dynasty scholars remembered as the "Zhenguan Eighteen" for their service to Emperor Taizong during his reign of Zhenguan (627–649). The emperor divided the eighteen scholars into three groups on daily duty, advising him at his behest. To match the achievements of the eighteen became the goal of all Chinese bureaucrats. Emperor Taizong ordered Yan Liben (approx. 600–673), a famed court artist, to create portraits of two members of this group. The work was accompanied by a preface by Chu Suiliang (596–658), a calligrapher favored by the emperor. Although the original painting has been lost, an early surviving version of the subject, dating to the Song dynasty, is now in the National Palace Museum, Taipei. A comparative study of the Song painting and later versions has attributed this set of screens to Du Jin (Shan Guolin 2002).

The series depicts the eighteen academicians engaged in the four pursuits that dominated the leisure time of the educated elite: music, board games, literature, and painting. Each of the eighteen wears a formal uniform or a casual loose gown without insignia, and each is posed according to his role or profession. Thirteen servants in shorter robes see to their masters' needs. The scenes take place within a palace complex on a platform that is separated from gardens by a ledge. Each group sits in front of a wood-framed screen painted with ocean or fishing motifs.

Consistent with the subject and the styles of court painting, the artist's polished technique combines thick flat coloring with succinct lines. In keeping with earlier court traditions, beveled forms mark both starting and ending points of each brush line on the figures.

Seals. *Tang Yin siyin* 唐寅私印; *Tang Bohu* 唐伯虎; *Nanjing jieyuan* 南京芥園.
HL

132

明中期　杜菫繪　仕女圖卷　絹本設色

Court ladies in the inner palace (below, pages 232–234))
Attributed to Du Jin (active approx. 1465–1500)
Handscroll, ink and colors on silk
H. 31.4 cm (12.36 in.), W. 520.1 cm (204.76 in.)
Shanghai Museum

In this handscroll, Du Jin has grouped female figures in gardens that stretch along a series of palaces and ponds. The scroll is to be read from the right, with each group representing a specific activity: washing fruit (a), posing for portraits (b), playing with a doll (c), listening to a music recital (d), resting alone (not shown), drowsing in the afternoon (not shown), serving snacks (e), playing a golf game (f), gathering for reading and music (not shown), kicking a ball (g), putting on makeup (h), and playing a musical duet (i). Du's skill as figure painter is shown in his sure handling of the bright colors, and in the minute details of the fabrics and ornaments.

Du Jin adapted the subject and details of early paintings by Zhou Wenju (approx. 917–967), who was active at the Southern Tang court in Nanjing. During the tenth century, court artists painted portraits of the imperial family as well as commissions for the upper class. Thousands of court women, ranging from empresses to concubines, ladies in waiting, female officials, and servants, served at the whim of the emperor, isolated from the outside world. Paintings like this, done for members of the imperial household, focused on their beautiful appearance and pleasant lives. This splendor often hid tragedies and tears.

Du Jin followed the expected path of China's educated elite—studying the classics, taking part in the imperial examination system, and pursuing the highest possible degrees. However, he was unsuccessful in his ambitions to serve as a court official and turned to painting. After studying the styles of painting popular at the Beijing court, he settled in Nanjing, where he remained until his death.

While Du painted in traditional court styles, he also added contemporary interpretations. He emphasized the movement of his figures. Each woman in this work is dressed in the high fashion of the time, and all the details are depicted with delicate and refined brushwork.

Colophons. Zhang Xianghe wrote the first two colophons, the latter one dated 1861. Noting that this work once belonged to Lord Wang in 1783–1784, Zhang misidentifies the artist who produced this painting as Qiu Ying. The last colophon is by a twentieth-century person, Liu Tuo, who corrects Zhang's misidentification and attributes the work to Du Jin's copying of Zhou Wenju's *Illustrations of the Inner Palace*.

Seal. *Qingxia ting* 青霞亭. HL

a

c

e

g

b

d

f

h

i

Title of work

133

明隆慶二年（1568年） 尤求繪 漢宮春曉圖卷 紙本水墨

Enchanting spring at the Han court, 1568 (above, pages 236, 237)

By You Qiu (active approx. 1540–1590)

Handscroll, ink on paper

H. 27.3 cm (10.75 in.), W. 822.7 cm (323.9 in.)

Shanghai Museum

The Suzhou born painter You Qiu chose to depict the court life of Han Emperor Chengdi (reigned 51–7 BCE) to imply the risk of decline posed by the excessive grandeur that had arisen at court during the sixteenth century. The painting focuses on the lives of Zhao Feiyan (died 1 BCE) and her sister Hede (died 7 BCE). Entering the Han palace as a court entertainer, Zhao won the name Feiyan, which means Flying Swallow, for her excellent dance and music skills. Her beauty captured the heart of the emperor and crippled the court as she ultimately gained control over state affairs. Zhao was made empress in 16 BCE, and later Hede was named Lady of Bright Deportment, a high court position. They assassinated several newly born imperial sons to secure their places at court and to prevent the possibility of an heir from another woman. They also interfered in the granting of imperial monopolies (a major source of funds for the imperial family). The emperor squandered so much on gifts to them—from gold, pearls, jades, and gems to wagons, boats, and palaces—that the imperial household was brought to a state of privation. After the death of Emperor Chengdi, Zhao was expelled from the palace and committed suicide. Six years later, Hede, accused of assassinating the new emperor, killed herself in prison. You Qiu uses this episode as a warning, which is reinforced by his contemporaries in their cautionary tales at the beginning and end of the scroll.

In its fluid lines, delicate shades, and simple composition, this work evokes the refined drawing style of the Song academician Li Gonglin (1049–1106). The detailed treatment of figures with attention to facial expressions is in You Qiu's customary mode.

Colophons. Beginning the scroll is a prologue titled "The Two Swallows at the Han Court," written in clerical script by the Suzhou elite Wen Peng (1498–1573). Following it is a story titled "Unauthorized Biography of Zhao Feiyan," written in standard script written by the Suzhou literatus Zhou Tianqiu (1514–1595).

The scroll ends with several accounts of the Zhao sisters, including Zhou Tianqiu's "Legend of Zhao Feiyan" and "Complementary Biographies of Zhao Feiyan and Hede" by the Kunshan calligrapher Yu Yunwen (1512–1579).

Signature. *Painted by You Qiu from Changzhou* [Suzhou] *as a compliment on the tenth day of middle summer in the year Wu-Chen during the reign of Longqing* [1568] 長洲尤求/隆慶戊辰孟夏.

Seals. *You shi zi Qiu* 尤氏子求; *Feng Qiuzi* 鳳丘子. Five collectors' seals. HL

235

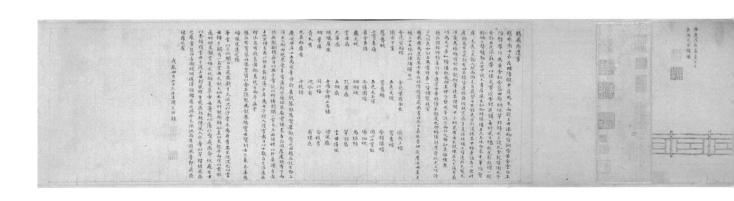

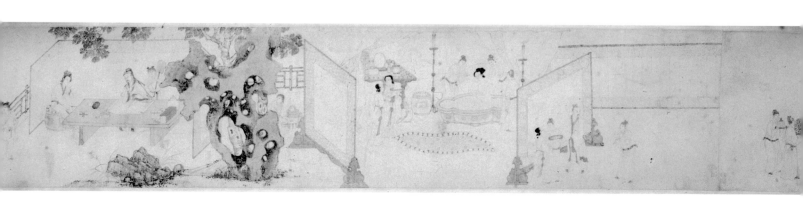

134

嘉靖朝九年（1530年）　文徵明繪　東園圖卷　絹本設色

Scenery of the Eastern Garden, 1530

By Wen Zhengming (1470–1559)

Reign of the Jiajing emperor (1522–1566)

Handscroll, ink and colors on silk

H. 30.2 cm (11.89 in.), W. 126.4 cm (49.76 in.)

Palace Museum, Beijing

The Eastern Garden, also known as the Supreme Mansion Garden, was owned by Xu Da (1332–1385), one of the founders of the Ming dynasty. Located in east Nanjing, the garden was maintained for over a hundred years by the Xu family, and survives as a suburban villa. This 1530 painting by Wen Zhengming commemorates a farewell party hosted in the garden in 1527 by Xu Taishi, one of Xu Da's descendants. Prominent guests at the gathering included the guest of honor, Chen Yi, an academician who was departing for a new position in Jiangxi, and Zhan Ruoshui, head of the Nanjing Ministry of War, known for imposing traditional forms of government based on Confucianism.

Designed to represent a microcosm of the universe, the garden embraces harmony through its fusion of the five elements in nature—metal, wood, fire, water, and earth. A bird's-eye view of the garden unfolds from right to left. A river runs by the outer garden, flowing down from a foothill. The front area, where main halls are located, is a typical southern-style garden with plants and cavernous Taihu rocks. Thatched pavilions and tea rooms stand on stilts along a pond, designed to be the central feature of the garden. Other note-worthy aspects

include nicely built brown stone dikes, and red lacquered railings and doors that make a pleasing contrast with the green trees, which number more than a dozen in species. Two masters, followed by a servant with a wrapped zither instrument, have just crossed a bridge and are walking on cobbled paths toward the garden. Inside the main hall, four figures sitting around a table work on their poetry and painting; outside by a rock, two boy servants are preparing the tea. Across the pond on the left, two gentlemen sitting in a pavilion enjoy the scenery. From the rear bamboo grove emerges a tea master with a utensil tray.

Encouraged by patrons' interests in the daily life of gentlemen, Wen painted over twenty thematic gardens from 1515 to 1558. A work from 1520 was said to have marked Wen's turning away from a four-teenth-century style he previously had focused on. In the 1530s, his artistry matured to develop its own sophistication (Yu Peijin 1991). This had much to do with his resignation from the court in 1526, using an excuse of health problems. In fact, his decision to return home to Jiangnan was prompted by the shake-up within the bureaucracy due to the great rites controversy (see cat. no. 147), which included the dismis-

sal of several of his mentors (Xiao Yanyi 1995). In Jiangnan he was able to devote his free spirit to art.

Colophons. In standard script at the end of the painting, Zhan Ruoshui wrote the prose titled "A Record of the Eastern Garden" to commemorate the party. An introduction to the garden's owner, Xu Taishi, claims that Xu was an honorable *jinshi* graduate, a reader in waiting, and an advisor on state affairs appointed by the court. Following Zhan, Chen Yi wrote a verse titled "A Record of a Banquet Tour at the Eastern Garden," which verifies that Xu Taishi hosted a farewell party at the Eastern Garden for the occasion of Chen's moving to a new position in Jiangxi in 1527. The following year, Chen composed another verse in semicursive script recalling the gathering.

Signature. *Scenery of the Eastern Garden. Produced by Wen Zhengming in the fall of the year Geng-Wu of the Jiajing reign* [1530] 東園圖／嘉靖庚寅秋／徵明製.

Seals. *Seal of Wen Zhengming* 文徵明印; *Zhengzhong* 徵仲; *Tingyun* 停雲; *Seal for the Magnolia Studio* 玉蘭堂印. HL

c   b

135

成化／嘉靖朝　仇英繪　職貢圖卷　絹本設色

Tribute bearers (pages 240–243)

By Qiu Ying (approx. 1482–1559)

Handscroll, ink and colors on silk

H. 29.5 cm (11.61 in.), W. 580 cm (228.35 in.)

Palace Museum, Beijing

This monumental work records a magnificent procession of frontier minorities and foreign envoys bringing gifts of tribute to the Chinese imperial court. The original picture was created during the reign of the Liang emperor Xiao Yan (reigned 502–549) to celebrate a meeting of alliance of thirty tribes and states. As an expression of the empire's exalted position among nations, the subject remained a popular painting theme for over a thousand years. Qiu Ying re-created the historical procession with imaginary episodes set in an intriguing landscape.

This was one of several works commissioned by the wealthy Chen Guan, also known as Huaiyun. Qiu executed it in Chen's peaceful mountain villa, where he was invited to stay and work (Xu Guohuang 1989; Yu Peijin 1991). The handscroll depicts

approximately 427 figures—including envoys, bearers, guards, servants, and female attendants—ascending cloud-covered peaks, as they would have reached China after crossing over many mountains. Eleven sections unfold from the right:

a. A group of forty-eight, with a banner reading "Lords from Nine Streams and Eighteen Caves" leading the way, is loaded with rocks, horns, boxes, and trunks.

b. With the banner "Sons of Han," thirty-nine people, probably from the northwest, are driving a flock of sheep and horses.

c. A group of thirty-nine from Bohai (Shandong and Liaodong peninsulas) is led by a musical band and followed by porters.

d. Thirty-seven from the northeastern nomadic state of Qidan bring horses and tribute carried by camels and pole-porters.

e. Forty-three from the northwestern state of Kunlun line up with horns, jades, hunting trophies, and products from the mountains.

f. Thirty-eight from a country governed by women, headed by a lady walking before a textile screen, lead male servants carrying piles of silkworm cocoons, yarns, and colorful textiles.

g. Coral jardinières and lions on lotus pedestals are presented by a group of fifty-one from the Three Buddhists Temple, thronging behind three men distinctively dressed in red, blue, and black robes.

h. Twenty-eight from the cold north, with a banner reading "Tribute," gather before a bridge leading various types of horses.

i. A dragon boat on a white elephant's back guarded by thirty-eight people from

a

the "Network of Ascending Zenith" is ready to cross a bridge.

j. A group of about thirty-eight people from the northwest kingdom of Xixia offer a salute with utmost respect toward the mountain to bless their long journey.

k. The last group, a party of twenty-eight from the northeast, marked by the banner "Chaoxian" (Joseon), emerges from rugged mountain paths.

The figures are naturally distributed in dense clusters with enough details to give a balanced compositional effect. By using sharply contrasting colors, Qiu Ying called attention to the leading persons from each group, established their ethnic identities, and staged interesting dramas involving the figures and the gifts they carry. The complexity of the landscape illustrates Qiu

Ying's development of the traditional blue-and-green landscape style. The alizarin reds of the rocks set off the malachite greens of the moss, which are softly diluted to the viridian greens of the sloped borders. Qiu infused the blue-and-green landscape with a literati spirit, for which he was credited by Dong Qichang (1555–1636) as the first and only artist in five hundred years to have achieved both the excellent technique and lyricism of the Southern Song master Zhao Boju (Dong Qichang; Shan Guolin 1989, p. 22).

Colophons. Xu Chushu wrote the title at the beginning of the scroll, *Tributes from Tribes and Minorities* 諸夷職貢.

Wen Zhengming, at the end of the painting, cites the historical source for Qiu Ying's subject, a depiction of a gathering

of chiefs from 630 leagues that was hosted at the Tang court. Wen also acclaims the quality of Qiu's work, comparing it to the superb achievements of tenth-century artist Hu Xiang (known for figures and horses in wild fields).

Peng Nian inscribed the scroll in 1552, writing that Qiu executed this painting at a mountain villa, Yanyi 燕翼, for its owner, Chen Guan.

Colophons by modern-day people include Zhang Daqian (1899–1983) and Wu Hufan (1894–1967).

Signature. *For Huaiyun, produced by Qiu Ying Shifu* 仇英實父為懷雲製.

Seals. *Nanyang* 南陽; *Liang Qingbiao* 梁清標; *Huai Yun* 懷雲; and the Qing imperial household. HL

e

h g

k j

d

f

i

243

136

弘治／正德朝　胡聰繪　柳陰雙駿圖軸　絹本設色

Two horses under a willow and plum tree

By Hu Cong (active approx. 1425–1525)

Hanging scroll, colors on silk

H. 102.2 cm (40.24 in.), W. 50.5 cm (19.88 in.)

Palace Museum, Beijing

In this painting, two well-posed horses are hitched to a willow tree enclosed in a hilly paddock. Both are white, with one showing contrasting colors in its mane, tail, and lower legs. They are most likely of a northern breed. Although not saddled, they are styled fashionably with bright red tassels on their bridles and ribbons gracefully tying up their tails.

Hu's precise portrayal and thick color application on the animals maintain a link with traditions of horse painting exemplified in the fourteenth century (*GGSHTL*, vol. 4, pl. 199, p. 209). But Hu's setting, different from the wild fields seen in most earlier horse paintings, was a recently developed theme, reflecting the scale and practices of Ming imperial horse pasturage as managed under the Ministry of War. The famous zoo and park complex rebuilt by the Yongle emperor on the northern outskirts of Beijing was the largest ranch of that time. A variety of animals and birds were kept on the hilly property, which was intersected by seventy-two streams (Gao Shouxian 2006). Used by members of the royal family for hunting, competitive racing, and other sports, it appears to have been a source for academic paintings on the subject of regal hunting.

Hu Cong deliberately changed the traditional setting to a cultivated ranch with artistically designed elements. There the twisted green willow of summer and the pinkish blossoming plum tree of winter appear side by side, regardless of their different thriving seasons, their intertwined branches providing the horses with shade. The horizontal trimming of the top of the willow was also seen in early sixteenth-century paintings (*GGSHTL*, vol. 7, p. 323). The small flowers and bamboo growing among rocks in the foreground are typical motifs from a southern-style garden. Hu's unrealistic rendering was done to celebrate dynastic glory.

Signature. *Painted by Hu Cong from the eastern Gao* [Rugao, Jiangsu], *serving at the Hall of Military Valor* 直武英殿東皋胡聰寫. HL

137

弘治/正德朝　朱端繪　煙江晚眺圖軸
絹本設色

Looking at a misty river at dusk

By Zhu Duan (1441–after 1500)

Hanging scroll, ink and colors on silk

H. 168 cm (66.14 in.), W. 107 cm (42.13 in.)

Palace Museum, Beijing

This panoramic view shows two sages seated on a hill in the foreground, looking over distant mountains; standing by is a servant. Across a misty river, fishing boats expose their masts in heavy weather, and an elder drags a boy across a bridge in a fishing village. At the top of the picture, dramatic cliffs stretch up to the sky, in contrast to the uninspiring summits of the mountains on the right. Zhu Duan intensified both the imaginative interpretation and the visual perspective of nature.

The artist's mastery of contrasting techniques is evidenced on the one hand by the crisp, dense strokes that formalize the rock structure, and on the other hand by the fluidity of the soft ink application for the mists. Harsh textural strokes that might have lent the painting a compelling energy were deliberately avoided. Thus the painting was given a physical presence imbued with peace.

Called upon to paint at court, Zhu was hampered by the need to adopt the classical style favored there. As in this large-scale scene, he mainly expanded on the model set by Northern Song master Guo Xi (approx. 1001–1090), emphasizing the grandeur of the mountain. Yet, fascinated by the exchange of reflections between the peaks above and the water below, Zhu came to conceive of the painting as a magnificent view with an elegant substance transmitted by dim mists.

Signature. *Zhu Duan* 朱端.

Seals. *Kezheng* 克正; *Manifested gentleman of the year Xin-You* [1441] 辛酉徵士 [an important seal indicating Zhu Duan's birth year]; *The Yiqiao Book granted by the imperial court* 欽賜□樵圖書. Collector seals include *Treasure of Prince Yi* [died 1730] 怡親王寶; and *Seal mark for calligraphy and painting of Mingyi Hall* 明義堂覽書畫印記. HL

138

明中期　安正文繪　岳陽樓圖軸　絹本設色

The Yueyang Tower

By An Zhengwen (active approx. 1425–1525)

Hanging scroll, colors on silk

H. 162.5 cm (63.98 in.), W. 105.5 cm (41.54 in.)

Shanghai Museum

This hanging scroll is one of the few paintings focusing on architecture to survive from the Ming dynasty. It is also an important example of the Ming court's interest in ancient buildings. It features the Yueyang Tower, completed in 716 on the shore of Lake Dongting in Hunan province. Famous for its spectacular views, the tower became a destination for travelers from all parts of China. Among these visitors were a number of well-known poets: the Tang dynasty poet Du Fu (712–770) saw "heaven and earth floating" while inspecting the view from the top, while Li Bai (also known as Li Bo, 701–762), famous for his consumption of alcohol, "received the wine cup from the heavens" during one of his visits. In the prose composition "A Record of the Yueyang Tower" written by Fan Zhongyan in 1046, the tower became associated with national

virtue. In a famous line, Fan states that men "should not satisfy themselves with material things, or feel despair for their own misfortune," but "should consider the world's problems their priorities and indulge in comforts last, after the world's beings."

Existing records indicate the tower had been a subject for painters since the tenth century (*GGWWYK* 2004, no. 251, p. 82). The current scroll, by the court painter An Zhengwen, shows the tower as viewed from the lakeside and includes a wharf under a gate of wooden pillars. Some of the compositional devices, such as the diagonal emptiness in the background, recall the works of Southern Song artists like Ma Yuan (active 1189–1225).

An divides the architecture into individual components and takes different lines of sight when depicting them: the

front is seen with a bird's-eye view, while the lower point of view taken for the tower gives it a grandiose look. Stone, brick, and wood alternate in buildings, lending the picture complex qualities. An open hall at the top of the tower is packed with travelers, shown as clusters of mingling people. Below is a busy embarkation for a ferry service; the galley and its crew are about to pull into shore.

Signature. *Painted by An Zhengwen, an Embroidered Uniform Battalion Commander in Honest Wisdom Hall* 直正智殿錦衣千戶安正文寫.

Seal. *Rijin qingguang* [When daytime comes, the light gets clear] 日近清光．　HL

139

嘉靖三十一年（1552年）　謝時臣繪
溪亭逸思圖軸　紙本設色

Leisurely Thinking in a River Pavilion, 1552
By Xie Shichen (1488–after 1567)
Reign of the Jiajing emperor (1522–1566)
Hanging scroll, ink and colors on paper
H. 190.2 cm (74.88 in.), W. 65.2 cm (25.67 in.)
Palace Museum, Beijing

This monumental composition sets cultivated scholars in pavilions along a river. On the riverbank, softly tinted mists form pale clouds, while lush green and brown autumn trees stand firm or slightly bend. A waterfall pouring straight down from rocks makes its way to swiftly flowing currents. From the hills, a shallow stream flows slowly across pebbles. At the peak, in a basinlike space, a pagoda surrounded by temples stretches toward a cloudy white sky.

Since the tenth century, isolation in remote mountains represented a kind of intensely subjectified naturalism and personal idealism that educated scholars pursued and expressed in landscape painting. The depiction of such seclusion and an intellectual appreciation of nature was generally part of the repertoire of scholars' painting. Many artists—both court and literati painters—sought a duality or multiplicity in subjects and technique. Xie Shichen, who spent most of his life in Suzhou and never served the court, was among them. His references to the Ming dynasty often blend styles and elements of Dai Jin, representative of the orthodox Zhe school, with those of the literati Wu school.

Xie's work reveals many influences from old masters as well as from his own contemporaries. As he noted himself, he strove to imitate Yuan literati artist Wang Meng (approx. 1308–1385), whose influence is found in the massive building of peaks, the increased height of mountains, and the accumulation of foliage. Yet the various forms employed in the rendering of tree branches and leaves, the short, dark textural strokes of the rocks, and the informal execution of architectural structures all seem more directly inspired by painter Dai Jin.

Colophon. *Leisurely thinking in a river pavilion* 溪亭逸思. *The Chu* [a tree] *immortal Xie Shichen imitated Wang Shuming's* [Wang Meng's] *inkwork* 樗仙謝時臣仿王叔明用墨.

Seal. *Free spirit under Gusu Terrace* 姑蘇臺下逸人, *at age sixty-six in the year Ren-Zi of the Jiajing* [1552] 嘉靖壬子時年六十有六. HL

140

萬曆三十年（1602年）　吳彬繪　普賢佛像圖軸　紙本設色

Buddhist deity Samantabhadra (Puxian) on a white elephant, 1602 (page 250)

By Wu Bin (active 1568–1627)

Reign of the Wanli emperor (1573–1619)

Hanging scroll, ink and colors on paper

H. 128 cm (50.39 in.), W. 65.4 cm (25.75 in.)

Palace Museum, Beijing

The celestial bodhisattva Samantabhadra (Sanskrit for "the all-good one") sits on his elephant and receives a foreign monk, who presents inscribed bodhi leaves held between two palms. Four attendants face the central deity, poised at the four directions. Each has an assigned task: one arranges flowers in a standing basin; one prepares a low table for the deity to lean on; one holds an alarm staff; and another holds an alms bowl. The heavy, squat white elephant occupies a large space in the picture. It is cadenced by the standing figures and high flowering trees on the sides, representing distinct color gradations from cardinal red to umber, pinkish, and white. All seem to create a central focus on the bodhisattva in a stabilized composition.

In many ways, this work epitomizes Wu Bin's art. He succeeds in integrating Chinese and non-Chinese artistic elements to accommodate his peculiar taste. The six figures appear to be of four or more ethnicities; notably the face of the flower-arranging monk is similar to that of another in Wu's work, which is thought to have been modeled after a Manichean statue built by Persians in the thirteenth century (Shih 1998,

p. 64). During the Ming dynasty, except for a few instances when seaports were blocked, boats from all over the world anchored in Quanzhou, in Wu's native Fujian province. There, he was fascinated by foreigners, and used them as models for his arhat (*luohan*) paintings, as witnessed in the 1591 example now in the Metropolitan Museum of Art, New York. His ethnic hybridization persisted and evolved through early 1602, as seen in his more sophisticated handling of the Buddhist figures inside the famous temple on the outskirts of Nanjing (*GGSHTL*, vol. 8, p. 275). Later that winter, Wu created this depiction of a deity surrounded by flowers; no one else in Chinese Buddhist art had ever done this, suggesting once again a foreign influence. His cutting-edge images earned Wu the nickname "magic miracle" from his contemporaries.

Signature. *Respectfully painted by Wu Bin with a sacrificial heart, lay Buddhist of Branch Hidden Temple, in the winter of the year Ren-Yin* [1602] 壬寅孟冬枝隱庵頭陀吳彬齋心拜寫.

Seals. *Lay Buddhist of Branch Hidden Temple* 枝隱菴頭陀; *Wenzhong shi* 文中氏. HL

141

明中晚期　明人繪　金盆撈月圖軸　絹本設色

Scooping the moon from a golden basin, 1475–1644

Hanging scroll, ink and colors on silk

H. 187.2 cm (73.7 in.), W. 140.1 cm (55.16 in.)

Shanghai Museum

This undated work is similar to a painting titled *Washing the Moon* (approx. 906–960), now in the National Palace Museum, Taipei, whose subject has been identified as the worship of the moon and moon goddess Chang'e (*GGSHTL*, vol. 1, p. 135). In Chinese popular religion, Chang'e was believed to live in the moon, and she was closely associated with immortality. According to the annual cosmological cycle, Chang'e's *yin* force would radiate the full moon on the fifteenth day of the eighth lunar month. On that date, Chinese families, especially women, would worship the moon to receive Chang'e's magical strength.

The method of representing this theme in the work shown here is quite different than that of *Washing the Moon*. In the tenth-century version, Chang'e is given a sacred air. In the Ming version, the atmosphere is cheerful and secular. Here a woman shakes a shallow water-filled basin held by a servant to better show the perfectly round moon reflected in it. Her companions are fashionably dressed ladies. The details that surround them—an altar with wine, food, and an incense burner, set under a Chinese parasol tree in a courtyard filled with peonies and other seasonal blossoms, bamboo, and rocks—all have auspicious meanings. The scene is animated with a pair of dancing cranes and a fuzzy cat which crouches on a stool to observe the ceremony.

The artist who created this remarkably well-preserved work has combined elements of the elaborate, finely delineated style known as *gongbi* with elements from the fresco tradition of the tenth century. Individual details are closely observed, from the textures of textiles and feathers, to the precisely rendered jewelry and inlays in the metal objects, to the colors and characteristics of the flowers and plants. HL

142

萬曆四十年（1612年）　丁雲鵬繪　玉川煮茶圖軸　紙本設色

A Depiction of Yuchuan Brewing Tea, 1612

By Ding Yunpeng (1547– after 1628)

Reign of the Wanli emperor (1573–1619)

Hanging scroll, ink and colors on paper

H. 138 cm (54.33 in.), W. 64.9 cm (25.55 in.)

Palace Museum, Beijing

The court painter Ding Yunpeng continued to paint historical characters who played an important role in the political establishment of the early Ming, a subject of particular interest to imperial collectors. This lively and crisp scene of brewing tea was based on the story of the eccentric master Lu Tong (died 835) from Hebei (*Xin Tangshu*, chap. 176, p. 26). The free-spirited Lu turned down callings to serve the court, and styled himself as self-taught poet while traveling widely. He bitterly lashed out against corrupt politicians in satirical verse, yet he associated with a few eminent officials who admired his writing. Lu secluded himself in mountain solitude with two companions at a shabby house. He brewed tea when reading and composing, with water taken only from a spring along the Long River, which was later renamed Jade River (Yuchuan) after Lu's nickname, "Son of Jade River."

The artist Ding Yunpeng recorded the story with a creative sense of humor. Sitting on a blanket over blue rocks, master Lu, dressed in a typical eighth-century-style costume—a two-winged black headdress and a loose, side-opened gown with a round collar—stares at teaware on a tripod oven that is the focus of the picture. To his right, an old woman in bare feet offers a tea-leaf basket. The number of wrinkles on her skin rivals that of the drapery folds lining her red outer jacket. On his left, a long-bearded servant carrying a pot of water walks to the teaware. The backdrop is set off by cavity-riddled rocks and massive green plantains with orange blossoms. The presentation is characteristic of the artist's odd taste. Ding's colorful exploration of settings and dramatized expressions of humanity were significant contributions to Ming figure painting. For his extraordinary talent, Ding Yunpeng was called "the most incomparably skillful master in three hundred years."

Colophon. *A depiction of Yuchuan brewing tea, for Master Xunzhi, painted in the living quarters at Huqiu monastery* [Tiger Hill, Jiangsu] *on a winter day of the year Ren-Zi* [1612] 玉川煮茶圖/壬子冬日為遜之先生寫於虎丘僧寮. The person nicknamed *Xunzhi* 遜之, to whom this painting is dedicated, was the then-twenty-year-old Wang Shimin 王時敏 (Li Shi 1989).

Seals. *Yunpeng* 雲朋[鵬]; *Nanyu* 南羽. Collectors' seals: *Seal of Shen Shuyong* 沈樹鏞印; *San Tianzi duwaichen* [Subject outside the capital of the three Sons of Heaven] 三天子都外臣; *Examined and appraised by Yunchu* 韻初審定. HL

143

崇禎元年(1628年)　董其昌繪　嵐容川色圖軸　紙本水墨

Misty Aspects of Mountains and Rivers, 1628

By Dong Qichang (1555–1636)

Reign of the Chongzhen emperor (1628–1643)

Hanging scroll, ink on paper

H. 111.3 cm (43.82 in.), W. 43.5 cm (17.13 in.)

Palace Museum, Beijing

This groundbreaking work was painted by the seventy-four-year-old Dong Qichang, a court official and scholar from Songjiang (Shanghai). Dong wrote in the inscription at the top that he painted the work after an idea of artist Shen Zhou, who attempted to have an opposite style from that of the Four Yuan Masters. Thus, instead of the heavy over-lapping of traditional ink washes, Dong used economic variations of dry strokes. More than ten types of trees stand visually clear and colorless here, in contrast to the various agitated layers found in landscapes by the Four Yuan Masters. The usual rock structure is broken by inconsistent strokes—straight, cloven, sinuous, or horizontal—without coherent gradations. Viewers' expectations about perspective are not satisfied because the foreground, midground, and even far mountain peaks were all evenly applied with delicate strokes in monotone ink. Dong believed that "to paint trees was to cast iron; to paint mountains was to lay sand." Only by getting rid of "sugary vulgarity" could one gain the true "spirit of literati."

Born to a wealthy family, Dong worked his way up the ranks of court officials to a high position. Evidence suggests that his promotion was not driven by politics, although he used his power and position to live a life of art and luxury (Shih 1994). For him, painting was primarily a means of cultivating oneself. On one hand, he was a classicist, preaching perfection in classical art. On the other hand, he freed himself to completely be an individual, and sought to overturn the traditions of the past by setting out different methods of brushwork and providing reviewers with the conceptual tools to comprehend unrealistic landscapes.

Colophon. *Misty aspects of mountains and rivers. The Huang family from the Wu city of Liangxi has a painting by Shen Nanqi* [Shen Zhou], *handed down from past generations, which is in opposition to the styles of the Four Yuan Masters. I once saw it. Later a meddlesome one bought it away. I revived the idea here from my memory. Inscribed in the middle fall of the year Wu-Chen* [1628]. *Xuanzai* [Dong Qichang] 戊辰中秋題/玄宰. 已巳仲春贈/元霖汪丈/玄宰重題. HL

144

清初順治　陳洪綬繪　童子禮佛圖軸　絹本設色

Boys worshipping the Buddha, probably 1650

By Chen Hongshou (1598–1652)

Hanging scroll, ink and colors on silk

H. 150 cm (59.06 in.), W. 67.3 cm (26.5 in.)

Palace Museum, Beijing

The worshipping of a Buddha statue is set outdoors by cavernous rocks. Unlike usual portrayals, the Buddha here is not the central figure; it sits on a rock to the side, playing a small supporting role to four boys. With square chins and bulbous noses, the Buddha and the boys look very much alike. The four boys all sport the same fashionable hairstyle—a shaved head with a peach-shaped tuft of hair, which could be tied up—and carry out their duties seriously. One on his knees brushes a multiple-story pagoda; another kneeling boy holds his palms together, prostrating; a standing boy bows deeply, presenting a flower vase to the Buddha; and the littlest one bumps his head to the ground, with chubby buttocks spilling from his slipping pants. Genteel, graceful lines with delicate colors reveal rhythmic movements. In a geometric composition, the presentation is permeated with a clean freshness and psychological feeling. Chen's "high archaism" and "extreme delicacy" are thought to represent an inventive revival in Chinese figure painting (Xue Yang 1999).

Traditionally on the fifteenth day of the seventh lunar month, the Chinese celebrate a festival of the dead, following ancient rites mutually observed by Buddhism and Taoism. Families go on pleasure outings or to street fairs and lantern shows, and they set up sacrificial altars and burn incense at their residences. According to regional annals from 1573, children would be treated with the noisy sound of gongs and drums around ceramic pagoda-shaped lamps. Born to a Buddhist family, Chen must have had these experiences during his childhood. But a peaceful life was not his fortune. His early loss of loved ones, unhappy service in the bureaucracy, and narrow escape from the Manchus' occupation all led Chen to become itinerant and eccentric. Despite his religious beliefs, he never ceased to paint, drink, or love women and flowers (Wang Yaoting 1991). Two years before his death, Chen observed this festival of the dead on a mountain peak in Hangzhou (Wei Dong

1991). It brought up sentimental memories of his hometown. He then created this unforgettable work, peculiar not only for its subject but also for its departure from traditional rules of formality and proportion in figure paintings.

Signature. *Painted by Laolian* ["Old Lotus"] *Hongshou in Thatched House to Protect Orchids* [Hulan Caotang, Chen's studio in Hangzhou] 老蓮洪綬畫於護蘭草堂中.

Seals. *Seal of Chen Hongshou* 陳洪綬印; *Zhanghou* 章侯. HL

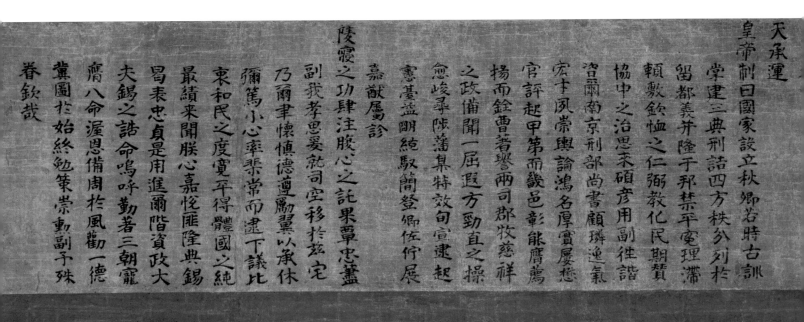

145, 146

明嘉靖二十三年（1544年）　明人繪

南京刑部尚書顧璘　顧璘夫人像　紙本設色

Portraits of Minister Gu Lin and Lady Shen, 1544 (pages 257, 258)

Reign of the Jiajing emperor (1522–1566)

Hanging scroll, colors on paper

H. 209 cm (82.28 in.), W. 106 cm (41.73 in.)

Nanjing Municipal Museum

In a typical placement for Chinese traditional portraiture, this married couple, dressed in matching formal robes, sit in the center of the composition. Painted portraits such as this were usually executed from life, on hanging scrolls. After the subjects' death, their portraits would be hung on the wall behind an altar table with incense burners; family members would kneel in front of the table to worship. The figures evince a dignified attitude with their bodies concealed beneath layered costumes. As a simple backdrop, their chairs were covered with sumptuous green floral textiles with auspicious brownish cloud patterns, providing contrasting accents to the red robes. On such commemorative portraits for the glorification of a family's ancestors, the artist would not leave his signature, which might attenuate the solemnity.

Gu Lin (1476–1565), Minister of Justice of Nanjing, poses sternly with one hand grasping his belt and the other resting on his thigh. His consort, Lady Shen, sits in a reverential pose with her hands crossed inside loose-fitting sleeves. The fine depictions focus on the symbolic heraldries they wear. His black silk hat with two semitranslucent petals, a staple of the official uniform since the fifth century, represents a common style for Ming officials. The square on his chest is a civil servant's badge, with the insignia of cranes and flying clouds indicating the first rank. Other emblems of high rank include the gold plaques on his belt and green tassel hanging from his waist. Consorts of officials in the top two ranks were allowed to wear the insignia of their husbands. Lady Shen also wears an elaborate "phoenix crown" decorated with gemstones, pearls, gold, and feathers arranged in noble motifs of foliage, clouds, and phoenixes. Long strings of jewelry dangle from the mouths of the two phoenixes.

The work was painted on the fifteenth of the fifth lunar month, 1544, to certify the honorable title and awards issued by the Jiajing emperor to the Gus. The account was written in standard script on the upper part of the painting, reading vertically from right to left. The inscription for Gu Lin begins with words of blessing for the emperor's long-lasting power and goes on to proclaim the significance of legal principles. This is followed by a summary of Gu Lin's life and personality which describes him as a leading legalist who has wielded immense political influence and shaped Ming laws with honesty and justice. Known for his kind and caring personality, Gu remained highly popular with the people, and became a virtuous model in the court. As a favor from the Jiajing emperor for his trustfulness and loyalty, Gu was awarded a new title, Grand Master.

In accordance with the Ming civil service system, high officials were permitted to confer the same rank on their first wives. Noble-born Lady Shen, according to the inscription, was well educated, and she had aided her husband in fulfilling laws. In addition to her previously given titles of Lady and Elegant Lady, she was granted the title of Consort. HL

257

147

嘉靖朝　明人繪　興獻王朱祐杬著袞服翼善冠坐像軸　絹本設色

Portrait of Prince Zhu Youyuan in ceremonial uniform, 1521–1524 (page 260)

Reign of the Jiajing emperor (1522–1566)

Hanging scroll, colors on silk

H. 108.3 cm (42.64 in.), W. 76 cm (29.92 in.)

Palace Museum, Beijing

Zhu Houcong, the Jiajing emperor, must have commissioned this official portrait of his birth father, Zhu Youyuan, sometime between 1521 and 1524 for the purpose of issuing new hereditary titles. In 1521, Zhu Houcong was brought in to succeed to the throne because his cousin, the Zhengde emperor, had died with neither a son nor a brother. According to the Ming hereditary order, Zhu Houcong had to be named the adopted son of the Zhengde emperor's father, the Hongzhi emperor, in order to be in the direct line of succession. However, Zhu Houcong did not want to acknowledge the Hongzhi emperor as his "imperial father," preferring instead to honor his true filial ties by giving that title to his actual father, Youyuan (Prince Xingxian), who had died in 1519. The Jiajing emperor's breaking with traditional hierarchy encountered vehement protests from hundreds of officials and subjects. The conflict, known as the "great rites controversy" (*da liyi*), resulted in bloody bureaucratic purges. In the fall of 1524, the Jiajing emperor issued a special dispensation to posthumously elevate Youyuan to the status of emperor, with a lower title going to the Hongzhi emperor.

Zhu Youyuan is depicted in the primary uniform, officially redesigned in 1383, for an enthroned emperor to wear at a formal ceremony. In a front view, he is seated in a dignified pose with his hands, unexposed beneath loose sleeves, crossed above the waist. The black silk hat he wears was a return to Tang fashion, known as the "crown with wings of kindness" for the resemblance of its two top wings to the Chinese character for "kindness" (*shan*). His yellow robe with green dragon medallions against a cloud-patterned background is a ceremonial garment with traditional symbolic motifs arranged in specific formations. The shoulders are symmetrically adorned with a clear white moon and fiery red sun; at the side of each sleeves is a pair of noble birds. Rendered on the lower apron, from the top downward, are six auspicious symbols, all reserved for imperial use: blue vessels, green algae, red fire, white rice, blue axes, and blue bows. The only furniture here is the wooden chair he sits on, decorated with red lacquer and gold patterns.

Two original tags are attached to the painting. On one is written the identity of the subject: *Prince Xingxian of the Ming* 明朝興獻王. The other confirms the painting was registered by the Qianlong imperial households: *Seal for calligraphy and painting of Baoji Hall* 寶笈樓書畫鋼. HL

148

明中晚期　明人繪　宮廷貴婦著紅雲鳳袍像軸　絹本設色

Portrait of a court lady in a red phoenix gown, approx. 1500–1600

Hanging scroll, colors on silk

H. 162 cm (63.78 in.), W. 99.8 cm (39.29 in.)

Palace Museum, Beijing

Although no clues exist to confirm the exact identity of the woman depicted here, certain elements in the portrait associated with nobility indicate that her social status was no doubt that of a court lady. Having lost most of her youthful charms, she is presented as a dignified woman according to the high fashion of the time. She sits imperturbably forward, with unexposed hands as is typical in aristocratic portraiture. She wears a blue enameled crown with five long-tailed birds at the front and two gold phoenixes at the top; the phoenixes suspend long strands of ornaments down each side of her head. This arrangement indicates that she was an imperial member at a lower position than the empress, who was allowed to wear an even more elaborate crown of four phoenixes. The design of her earrings, with exquisite figures in multiple-story pavilions, is derived from popular Taoist religion, as was the case for the pair of golden earrings from the late Ming (cat. no. 9).

She is dressed in standard attire for noblewomen, which comprises a widely sleeved gown and long inner skirt. The red gown has a cloud-patterned background and gold phoenixes on each side of the shoulders. Her inner skirt, exposed at the lower train, is made of a textile with black floral scrolls against an eggshell-green background, and rendered with a wide golden flowery hem. To match her gown, a golden belt is attached with casein-colored jade medallions. The chair behind her shows green meander designs representing "longevity," and is covered with crimson brocade.

The lady is waited on by a young servant holding a cosmetic box. The touches of pretty polychrome in her hairpins and clothing add vibrancy. On the right side stands a black lacquered table inlaid with mother-of-pearl, bearing a viridian bronze vessel, a porcelain vase of peony blossoms, and a Buddhist sutra container, demonstrating the interest the artist took in composing these details. This work exemplifies a transitional mode of the early seventeenth century, deriving its special charm from decorative settings. HL

149

天啟朝　明人繪　熹宗朱由校朝服像軸　絹本設色

Portrait of the Tianqi emperor in court costume

Reign of the Tianqi emperor (1621–1627)

Hanging scroll, colors on silk

H. 111.2 cm (43.78 in.), W. 75.7 cm (29.8 in.)

Palace Museum, Beijing

Unlike the pose in the commemorative portrait of Zhu Youyuan (cat. no. 147), the Tianqi emperor, Zhu Youjiao (1605–1627), sits relaxed on an elaborate dragon chair, surrounded by objects evoking the rich interior of an imperial library. He wears a golden robe with dragon medallions, his hands crossed inside the sleeves, and a black silk hat adorned with two golden dragons and red flaming pearls. On the emperor's shoulders are woven patterns of a gleaming white moon and blazing red sun, representing his supreme being. On his waist is a cardinal red belt with umber-colored appliqués suggesting jade plaques. The emperor was emphasized in size by being placed before a screen sitting on a scholar's table. The screen, depicting two dragons, is bordered by a wooden frame with double dragons on each side at the top; from the mouth of each outer dragon, a string of jewelry is suspended. On the red lacquered table with gold scrolls sit vases of pink peonies symbolizing prosperity, a ritual bronze vessel in honor of imperial classics, a blue-and-white porcelain vessel to represent peace, and books symbolizing knowledge.

Surviving portraits of the Tianqi emperor are rare in comparison to those of other Ming rulers. This painting presents a warm quality, more decorative in tone than the academic configurations of other official portraits. Executed by an unknown portraitist familiar with techniques of scenery and poses, and especially skilled in capturing the qualities of objects and furniture, it has the look of a work done by a refined courtly painter. Stylistically it combines echoes of earlier portraits employing a traditional frontal composition with more recently developed elements of a detail-filled backdrop found in depictions of later monarchs.

During the Tianqi reign, the Ming was no more impervious to the dynastic cycle than previous times had been. The economy continued to decline, and the government showed signs of collapsing from inner pressures and frequent uprisings. Seventeen years after Zhu Youjiao's death, the 276-year-long dynasty was overthrown by the Manchus from the northeast, marking the end of the last native-ruled dynasty in China's history.

Seal. *Seal for calligraphy and painting of Baoji Hall* 寶笈樓書畫鋼 [Qing imperial household]. HL

GIVEN NAME	LIFE DATES	POSTHUMOUS NAME	TEMPLE NAME	REIGN NAME	REIGN DATES
Zhu Yuanzhang 朱元璋	1328 – 1398	Gao Di 高帝	Taizu 太祖	Hongwu 洪武	1368 – 1398
Zhu Yunwen 朱允炆	1377 – 1402	Hui Di 惠帝	None	Jianwen 建文	1399 – 1402
Zhu Di 朱棣	1360 – 1424	Wen Di 文帝	Taizong, Chengzu 太宗，成祖	Yongle 永樂	1403 – 1424
Zhu Gaochi 朱高熾	1378 – 1425	Zhao Di 昭帝	Renzong 仁宗	Hongxi 洪熙	1425
Zhu Zhanji 朱瞻基	1398 – 1435	Zhang Di 章帝	Xuanzong 宣宗	Xuande 宣德	1426 – 1435
Zhu Qizhen 朱祁鎮	1427 – 1464	Rui Di 睿帝	Yingzong 英宗	Zhengtong 正統 Tianshun 天順	1436 – 1449 1457 – 1464
Zhu Qiyu 朱祁鈺	1428 – 1457	Jing Di 景帝	Daizong 代宗	Jingtai 景泰	1450 – 1456
Zhu Jianshen 朱見深	1447 – 1487	Chun Di 純帝	Xianzong 憲宗	Chenghua 成化	1465 – 1487
Zhu Youyuan 朱祐樘	1470 – 1505	Jing Di 敬帝	Xiaozong 孝宗	Hongzhi 弘治	1488 – 1505
Zhu Houzhao 朱厚照	1491 – 1521	Yi Di 毅帝	Wuzong 武宗	Zhengde 正德	1506 – 1521
Zhu Houcong 朱厚熜	1507 – 1567	Su Di 肅帝	Shizong 世宗	Jiajing 嘉靖	1522 – 1566
Zhu Zaihou 朱載垕	1537 – 1572	Zhuang Di 莊帝	Muzong 穆宗	Longqing 隆慶	1567 – 1572
Zhu Yijun 朱翊鈞	1563 – 1620	Xian Di 顯帝	Shenzong 神宗	Wanli 萬曆	1573 – 1619
Zhu Changluo 朱常洛	1582 – 1620	Zhen Di 貞帝	Guangzong 光宗	Taichang 泰昌	1620
Zhu Youjiao 朱由校	1605 – 1627	Zhe Di 悊帝	Xizong 熹宗	Tianqi 天啟	1621 – 1627
Zhu Youjian 朱由檢	1611 – 1644	Zhuang Lie Min 莊烈愍帝	Sizong 思宗	Chongzhen 崇禎	1628 – 1643

THE HONGWU EMPEROR

THE YONGLE EMPEROR

THE XUANDE EMPEROR

THE CHENGHUA EMPEROR

THE HONGZHI EMPEROR

THE ZHENGDE EMPEROR

THE JIAJING EMPEROR

THE LONGQING EMPEROR

THE WANLI EMPEROR

An Zhengwen 安正文, active approx. 1425–1525. Little is known of An Zhengwen's life besides the fact that he was a court painter who held the prestigious title of Battalion Commander in the Embroidered Uniform Guard at Honest Wisdom Hall.

Chen Hongshou 陳洪綬, 1598–1652 (zi: Zhanghou 章侯; hao: Laolian 老蓮, Laochi 老遲, Heichi 悔遲). A child prodigy who started painting at age four, Chen Hongshou was born to a wealthy family in Zhuji (present-day Zhaoxing), Zhejiang, but lost his father during his boyhood, and his mother and wife while still relatively young. Early in his career, Chen received instruction in sketching nature from Lan Ying (1585–1664) and was influenced particularly by the Song academic approach. Having passed the *xiucai* degree in 1616, he was appointed to serve in the Imperial Academy in 1640, with the title Houseman. Three years later, Chen resigned from the bureaucracy and went back to Zhejiang. In the pandemonium following the Manchu (Qing) takeover of China, he escaped to a Buddhist monastery and lived as a monk for a time. Refusing to paint for Qing nobles or bureaucrats, he secluded himself in poverty until his death. Chen Hongshou's eccentric personality and extreme intelligence are expressed in many of his paintings of religious figures, women, flowers, birds, and rocks. His art—distinctive, exaggerated, uncanny, and classically archaic— had a deep impact on later painters, especially those of the Jinling and Shanghai schools.

Chen, Lady 陳氏, 1589–1647. Lady Chen and her husband, Tong Bonian (佟卜年), were natives of Liaoyang, Liaoning province. Tong passed the *jinshi* degree and served as an army inspector in Shandong. Dismissed from his service on an unjust charge, he was exiled in 1622 and died in a prison in Hubei in 1625. Following her husband, Chen suffered from the stress and instability of living in exile. Years later, after her death, Tong was proven innocent. The court allowed Chen to be reburied in Nanjing and granted her the posthumous title Lady of Chaste Beauty.

Chen Yi 陳沂, 1469–1538. A native of Jinling (Nanjing) and a 1517 *jinshi*, Chen served as a bureaucrat in Jiangxi prefecture and later Shandong, but he was eventually pushed out to an inferior position. With a passion for eighth-century poetry and classics, he mastered painting and the seal and clerical scripts of calligraphy. By studying the work of Ma Yuan (active 1189–1225), he achieved simple, lyric effects in the subjects of famous mountains and rivers. Along with his contemporary Gu Lin (q.v.) and Tang-dynasty scholar-artist Wang Wei, Chen was admired as one of the Three Gentlemen of Jinling.

Dai Jin 戴進, 1388–1462 (zi: Wenjin 文進; hao: Jingan 靜庵, Yuquan shanren 玉泉山人). A native of Qiantang (Hangzhou), Zhejiang province, the young Dai Jin gained a solid artistic foundation in goldsmithing and jewelry crafting which he would later use to pursue a successful career in painting. Growing up in Hangzhou, the Southern Song capital, Dai Jin visited Nanjing for the first time by his twenties, and later lived in Suzhou for a short time. In middle age, Dai moved to Beijing and worked as a court painter for about twelve years. His mastery of Southern Song traditions, to which he had been introduced during his early life in Hangzhou, brought him acclaim. Given the title of Editorial Assistant, he met with the Xuande emperor (s.v. Zhu Zhanji) a few times and was appointed to paint in the Hall of Benevolence and Wisdom. Dai was eventually pushed out by court painters who were jealous of his talents. Retiring from service in 1442, he moved back to his hometown and made a living selling paintings until his death. Dai Jin is traditionally credited as the founder of the Zhe school, a group of Ming academic painters with close connections to the Southern Song academy of painting.

Ding Yunpeng 丁云鵬, 1547–after 1628 (zi: Nanyu 南羽; hao: Shenghua jushi 聖華居士, Huangshan laoqiao 黃山老樵). A native of Xiuning in Anhui province, Ding Yunpeng was a highly skilled painter in various subjects, particularly Buddhist figures and landscape. Building upon the artistic foundation he inherited from his family, he developed his own artistic style and went on to surpass the accomplishments and reputation of his father, Ding Zan. Ding Yunpeng's signature use of solid, fluid, and graceful lines reflects his training in the calligraphy of Wang Xizhi (303–379) and in the *baimiao* method of ink drawing used by old masters Wu Daozi (approx. 710–760) and Li Gonglin (approx. 1049–1106). Ding's close association with prominent elites—including Dong Qichang (q.v.), Chen Jiru (1558–1639), and inkmaker Cheng Junfang (active approx. 1600)—greatly influenced his philosophy and use of particular art forms. A recent study disputes the common idea, based on a statement by Gu Wenbin (1811–1889), that Ding Yunpeng served as a court painter for ten-plus years; although Ding's works were certainly presented to the Wanli court from 1583 to 1596, he may not have actually lived at the court during this period (Wu Meifeng 2005).

Dong Qichang 董其昌, 1555–1636 (zi: Xuanzai 玄宰; hao: Sibai 思白, Huating 華亭). A native of Songjiang (Shanghai) and a 1588 *jinshi*, Dong rose through the ranks of the Ming bureaucracy, from his initial appointment as Bachelor and Junior Compiler, to the post of Minister in the Nanjing Ministry of Rites (1625–1626). He became an excellent calligrapher in semicursive and standard scripts by age thirty. Simple and innocent, his calligraphy was often grouped with that of Zhao Mengfu (1254–1322). In landscape he began by copying Huang Gongwang (1269–1354) but soon developed a preference for the tenth-century masters. As was typical of literati artists, he adapted techniques established earlier in landscape painting to create his own style. Today Dong Qichang is viewed as a key figure in the renaissance of literati art. More specifically he is regarded as a late Wu-school master and the leader of the Songjiang (or Huating) school, which in the late Ming overshadowed the Wu school. In his influential writings on aesthetics and art history, he borrowed from Chan (Zen) Buddhism to develop the theory, first forwarded by Mo Shilong (died 1587), of dividing Chinese landscape painting into two different schools: a Southern school, represented by Wang Wei (699–759) and Dong Yuan (died 962); and a Northern school, represented by Li Sixun (651–716), Ma Yuan (active 1189–1225), and their Zhe-school successors. Dong Qichang belonged to the former and was one of the artists responsible for the domination of literati-style painting in the late Ming.

Du Jin 杜堇, active approx. 1465–1500 (original surname: Lu 陸; zi: Junan 懼男; hao: Gukuang 古狂, Qingxia tingchang 青霞亭長). A native of Dantu in Jiangsu province, Du lived in Beijing for many years in his middle age. After repeatedly failing to pass the examinations for the high *jinshi* degree (1463–1487), he returned to his native province, settling in Nanjing, where he devoted his life to painting. Along with Wu Wei (q.v.) and Zhou Chen (q.v.), he was considered one of the top three figure painters in the south at that time. He was described by Ming writers as a talented poet, a classical scholar, and an artist who followed the principled approach of the orthodox academic school. His landscapes display the style established by Southern Song painters, especially Li Tang (approx. 1050–1130) and Liu Songnian (approx. 1150–after 1225). Du Jin was also skilled in painting architectural and flower-and-bird scenes.

Gu Lin 顧璘, 1476–1545 (zi: Huayu 華玉; hao: Dongqiao jushi 東橋居士). The Suzhou-born Gu Lin made his reputation in Nanjing as an able statesman and a talented writer-poet, earning his place as one of Three Gentlemen of Jinling (Nanjing). After getting a *jinshi* degree in 1496, Gu started his bureaucratic service as governor of Guangping county. He was eventually promoted to the highest position at the Ministry of Justice in Nanjing. A year before his death, Gu was granted the title Grand Master (Daifu) by the Jiajing emperor. Gu's wife, Lady Shen, won her share of honorable titles, with Lady (Anren), Elegant Lady (Shuren), and the highest, Consort (Furen).

Han Ximeng 韓希孟, active 1600–1644 (also known as Han Lady Embroidery 韓媛繡). Han Ximeng was the wife of Gu Shouqian (顧壽潛), grandson of Shanghai-born Gu Mingshi (顧名世), who gained a *jinshi* degree in 1559 and served at the Directorate of Palace Seals. Upon his retirement to Shanghai, Mingshi built a garden estate named Dew Fragrance Garden (露香園), which became the renowned Gu embroidery shop, with the family artisans Lady Miao (繆), Mingshi's daughter-in-law; Han Ximeng; and Gu Lanyu (顧蘭玉), Mingshi's great-granddaughter. Han's mastery of stitches was acclaimed as "painting" with needle and thread. Dong Qichang (q.v.), who taught painting to her husband, commented in 1639 that Han's work was a marvelous rival to the flower-and-bird painting of Huang Quan (903–965). Only careful examination by experts could reveal that her work was embroidery.

Hu Cong 胡聰, active approx. 1425–1525. A native of Rugao, Jiangsu, Hu Cong served as a court painter in the Hall of Military Valor. His primary subject was horses, and his style, characterized by clear and precise lines, was inspired by Song horse paintings. Hu's rocks and trees directly evoke Ma Yuan's brushwork.

Kang Maocai 康茂才, 1313–1369. A native of Qizhou, Hubei, and an elite scholar of classics and Confucianism, Kang served in the late Yuan army as a mid-ranking officer. In the last stand against the Ming troops at Jiqing in Jiangsu province, he was forced to surrender to Zhu Yuanzhang. Switching sides, Kang continued his military career as a Ming naval commander. He followed Xu Da (q.v.) to the central plains in 1368 and died the next year on the way back to Nanjing from a successful mission. Kang Maocai was known posthumously as the Duke of Qi.

Li Wenzhong 李文忠, 1339–1384. A native of Xuyu, Jiangsu, and nephew of the Hongwu emperor, Li was known for his knowledge of military history and poetry. He was awarded the title Duke of Cao and (posthumously) Prince of Qiyang.

Li Zai 李在, died 1431 (zi: Yizheng 以政). A native of Putian, Fujian, Li Zai lived in Yunnan for a short time before entering the bureaucracy. Along with fellow court painters Dai Jin (q.v.) and Zhou Wenjing (q.v.), Li served as an Editorial Assistant in the Hall of Benevolence and Wisdom from 1426 to 1435. He was skilled at painting landscapes and figures. His refined and detailed brushwork demonstrates an affinity to Northern Song master Gui Xi (approx. 1001–1090), while his coarse, bold strokes evoke the style of Ma Yuan (active approx. 1189–1225). Li Zai was known for supervising the Japanese monk-artist Xue Zhou in landscape painting. Li was classified as the second highest landscape painter at the Xuande court, next to Dai Jin.

Liu Jun 劉俊, active approx. 1450–1500 (zi: Tingwei 廷偉). Little is known about Liu Jun's life except that he served as a court painter with the honorary title Commander of the Embroidered Uniform Guard in the fifteenth century. The Southern Song academic style seems to have provided inspiration for his painting. Liu's figures and landscapes in particular received critical acclaim.

Lu Ji 呂纪, died 1504 or 1505 (zi: Tingzhen 廷振; hao: Leyu 樂愚). A native of Yin (present-day Ningbo), Zhejiang province, Lu Ji entered the court during the Hongzhi reign (1488–1505) and served as a Commander of the Embroidered Uniform Guard at the Hall of Benevolence and Wisdom. Initially he studied Tang and Song painters, the delicate technique of Bian Jingzhao (active 1426–1435), and ink paintings by Lin Liang (active 1488–1503). Later, Lū developed his own unique style and was very popular during his time. His flower-and-bird paintings took two forms: the first, stressing color and precision, was luxuriantly beautiful; the second was characterized by sweeping, coarse brushstrokes, conveying freedom and directness. Lū Ji was also skilled at figures and landscapes, and his style can be traced to that of Southern Song painters Ma Yuan (active approx. 1189–1225) and Xia Gui (active approx. 1195–1230). Lū's flower-and-bird paintings, quite influential at court, garnered an impressive following.

Lu Wenying 呂文英, active 1488–1505. A native of Kuocang (present-day Lishui), Zhejiang province, Lu Wenying, along with mentor Lū Ji (q.v.), served as a Commander of the Embroidered Uniform Guard in the Hall of Benevolence and Wisdom. The two were known respectively as "Little Lu" and "Big Lu." Revealing Southern Song academic influence, Lu Wenying's figures and landscapes presented precise lines and rather bright colors. He is recognized as one of the leading artists of the Zhe school.

Miu Fu 繆輔, active 1426–1435. A native of Suzhou, Jiangsu, Miu Fu served as a court painter during the Xuande reign with the title of Judge in the Embroidered Uniform Guard in the Hall of Military Valor. He carried on the elaborate painting style established by Huang Quan (903–965), applying careful attention to the details of his subjects, which were chiefly water scenes with fish and aquatic plants. He gained a reputation as an outstanding court painter of realism. Not much about his life is known, and not many of his works survive.

Mu Changzuo 沐昌祚, died 1625. Son of Mu Chaobi and a ninth-generation descendant of Mu Ying (q.v.), Changzuo took over the family's hereditary title, Duke of Qian, in 1572, and was named Grand Guardian of the Heir Apparent, one of the Three Preceptors of the royal heir, in 1584.

Mu Rui 沐叡, died 1609. Son of Mu Changzuo (q.v.) and a tenth-generation descendant of Mu Ying (q.v.), Rui held the official rank of Vice Commissioner-in-Chief in addition to the family title, the hereditary Duke of Qian, which he took in 1573. He spent the last years of his life in prison for involvement in a legal violation and died there in 1609. His tomb was located outside Zhonghua Gate on Mount Jiangjun, on the outskirts of Nanjing.

Mu Sheng 沐晟, 1368–1439. The second son of Mu Ying (q.v.), Sheng was described as being similar to his father—smart, humble, and quiet. His successes in subduing tribes in Hunan and capturing the King of Annam (northern Vietnam) brought him honors, including the hereditary titles Marquis of West Subjugation and Duke of Qian (Yunnan and Guizhou), with a yearly endowment of three thousand dan of rice (over 165 US tons). At a court banquet celebrating his victory over Annam in 1408, the Yongle emperor (s.v. Zhu Di) awarded Mu Sheng a jade belt and a golden plaque, along with his own handwritten poem. Failing in military missions during the later years of his governorship of Qian, Mu lost favor from the court and returned to Nanjing, dismissed from service.

Mu Ying 沐英, 1345–1392 (originally Mu Wenying 沐文英). A native of Dingyuan, Anhui province, Mu Ying was not only a skilled military general but also a literary scholar and art collector. Orphaned at age eight, he was adopted by Empress Ma and the Hongwu emperor, Zhu Yuanzhang. For his success in conquering the frontiers, Mu Ying's name was placed sixth among the twenty-one engraved on the triumphant stele at the Imperial Merit Temple, built by Zhu Yuanzhang in 1369. In 1377 the renowned Ming general was granted the title Marquis of West Subjugation, with a yearly endowment of 2,500 dan of rice (almost 138 US tons). Gravely affected by the death of his dear adoptive mother, Empress Ma, in 1392, he suddenly became seriously ill and died that same year at age forty-eight. The Hongwu emperor honored him by naming him posthumously Prince of Qian Tranquility. The governorship of Qian (present-day Yunnan and Guizhou) became a hereditary title that passed down through the next twelve generations of Mu's family, until the last Ming reign. The emperor also married his own granddaughter, Princess Chang Ning (1386–1408), to Mu Ying's youngest son, Mu Xin.

More distinguished in fame is the Mu family art collection. Begun by Mu Ying, it is considered one of the best in quality of all Chinese private collections. Ming elite Wang Shizhen (1526–1590) recorded that the Mu collection was well known for its huge size, which was "close to that in the imperial households." According to a 1999 inventory, the Mu family collection includes fifty-two paintings from the Song and Yuan dynasties (Lin Lina 1999).

Qiu Ying 仇英, approx. 1482–1559 (zi: Shifu 實甫, 實父; hao: Shizhou 十洲). Together with Shen Zhou (1427–1509), Tang Yin (1470–1523), and Wen Zhengming (q.v.), Qiu Ying is regarded as one of the four masters of the Wu school. A native of Taicang, Jiangsu, Qiu started out as a lacquer craftsman. He moved to Suzhou, where he began painting under Zhou Chen (q.v.) while becoming acquainted with Wen Zhengming and other Wu-school elites. With a mastery of technical principles, coloring, drawing, and ink washes, he successfully established himself as a professional painter of landscape, flower-and-bird, architectural, and figural subjects. Qiu was especially skilled at copying classical masterpieces; his copies were often mistaken for the originals. His female images were compared to those of Tang master Zhou Fang (approx. 730–800). While trained in the classically disciplined traditions of the Song academy, Qiu absorbed the individualistic mentality of the Wu school. His dual characteristics—combining the well-trained Song approach with more expressive styles derived from literati painting—attracted attention and won praise.

Wang E 王諤, active 1488–1521. Wang E served as a court painter in the Hall of Benevolence and Wisdom during the Hongzhi reign, and was promoted to Battalion Commander in the Embroidered Uniform Guard by the Zhengde court. Wang initially learned landscape painting from a teacher in his native Fenghua. Later he became interested in Tang and Song landscape paintings, and intensively pursued the brush techniques established by Song masters Li Tang (approx. 1050–1130), Ma Yuan (active approx. 1189–1225), and Xia Gui (active approx. 1195–1230). Wang employed refined brushwork in his depiction of rocks, trees, and mountains, for which he was hailed as a Zhe-school master.

The Hongzhi emperor's patronage and praise of Wang E as the "Ma Yuan of our time" ensured his position at court. When he resigned due to illness, Wang was about eighty.

Wang Xingzu 汪興祖, 1338–1371. A native of Chaoxian, Anhui, Wang Xingzu was adopted by the famous naval leader Zhang Desheng (died 1360) and became a great military general in his own right. In 1369 Wang won honor as one of the seven meritorious subjects commemorated in the Imperial Ancestral Temple (Taimiao). Wang assisted Xu Da (q.v.) in conquering the central lands, and eventually made his way up to the position of Chief Military Commissioner of Shanxi. Falling in battle from an attack of thrown stones in Sichuan, Wang was posthumously awarded the title Marquis of East Triumph. His tomb is located in Zhangjiawa, outside the Central Gate, Nanjing.

Wen Zhengming 文徵明, 1470–1559 (zi: Zhengzhong 徵仲; hao: Hengshan jushi 衡山居士). Born to a family from Changzhou (present-day Suzhou) with a long history of imperial service, Wen was described as having grown up slowly, unable to talk until the age of eight, shy, reticent, and prudent. At twenty he started painting with the Wu-school master Shen Zhou, later studying calligraphy with Li Yingzhen and literature with Wu Kuan. After failing the civil service examinations ten times by the age of fifty-four, Wen was recommended to the court in 1523 and given the post of Editorial Assistant in the Hanlin Imperial Academy. In 1526 he resigned and resettled in his hometown; there he made a livelihood as a professional artist until his death. With a solid training in Northern Song academic techniques, Wen focused on Zhao Mengfu's style. Such training enabled him to develop a certain freedom in his brushwork and arrangement of compositions. Precision and careful attention to detail characterized his earlier painting style, while during his middle years, the style shifted to one that was broader, coarser, and less inhibited. Late in life, Wen rendered his works in a balanced approach that combined those two styles. He painted mostly lake and mountain scenes from his native Jiangnan region, as well as famous gardens and the life of the literati. Together with Shen Zhou (1427–1509), Tang Yin (1470–1523), and Qiu Ying (q.v.), Wen Zhengming is recognized as one of four masters of the Wu school during the middle Ming.

Wu Bin 吳彬, active 1568–1627 (zi: Wenzhong 文中; hao: Zhixian 質先, Zhian fazeng 枝庵法僧, Zhiyin anzhu 枝隱庵主). A native of Putian, Fujian province, Wu moved to Jinling (Nanjing) in 1568 or earlier, and was appointed to serve the Wanli court as Secretariat Drafter in the Ministry of Works. Despite the fact that his paintings and calligraphy were admired and collected by the Wanli emperor, Wu's outspoken nature made him powerful enemies, who plotted a bureaucratic purge to dismiss him from his position. Because of his peculiar aesthetic, Wu's art has been linked by critics to the Jinling school and the "transmogrificationists," including Chen Hongshou (q.v.), Cui Zizhong (died 1644), and Ding Yunpeng (q.v.). Emphasizing abstract forms, his landscapes took issue with formulated structuralism. His Buddhist figures often had bizarre-looking, distorted faces, unseen in earlier times. His outline drawing was said to be a fantastic and unusual rival to that of Zhao Mengfu (1254–1322). Wu Bin's exotic interests, mastery of brushwork, and inventive conceptions made him one of the most important artists of the late Ming.

Wu Cheng 吳誠, active 1426–1435. Director of the Directorate of Ceremonial, Wu Cheng was a prestigious eunuch on the imperial household staff and the trusted masseur of the Xuande emperor (s.v. Zhu Zhanji). Wu played a key role in the organization of state ritual affairs and the manufacture of goods for imperial household use, including foreign tribute. In 1428, Wu directly supervised the Xuande emperor's orders to the Ministry of Works to produce quantities of improved ceremonial utensils, using Song official wares as models (Wen Peng 1534).

Wu Jing 吳经, active 1505–1517. A high-ranking court eunuch during the reign of the Zhengde emperor, Wu Jing used the power given him to lead an imperial tour to the south to extort large sums of money, luxuries, and slaves from peasants. For that abuse of trust, Wu was expelled from the court to a garrison force at the imperial graves in Nanjing.

Wu Wei 吳偉, 1459–1508 (zi: Shiying 士英, Ciweng 次翁; hao: Lufu 魯夫, Xiaoxian 小僊). Born to a poor family in Jiangxia (Wuchang), Hubei province, Wu Wei wandered to Haiyu (Jiangsu) and was adopted by a family to tutor boys. His talents were recognized by Nanjing noblemen, who promoted his paintings to generous patrons. Wu subsequently received invitations and commissions to paint for the upper class, including some from royal families. Prince Zhu Gongyan called him "Little Immortal Xiaoxian," while the Chenghua emperor acclaimed his painting as "true magic brushwork" and later granted him the positions of Editorial Assistant and Judge of the Embroidered Uniform Guard. Wu was known in his youth for his dissolute ways and frequent self-indulging in wine and women. His improper behavior at court caused his demotion to Nanjing. Shortly after, Wu was recruited by the new Hongzhi emperor and given a higher title, Company Commander of the Embroidered Uniform Guard, along with the seal "Number One Painter" and a residence in Beijing. Unhappy and "sick" with the constraints of bureaucracy, Wu chose to earn a living as a freelance painter in Nanjing. He died from causes related to alcoholism on his way to the capital, having been called by the Zhengde emperor. Wu Wei was regarded as the leader of the Jiangxia school, which traced its lineage to the Zhe school. He and his followers focused on Southern Song styles and flourished until the early sixteenth century.

Xie Shichen 謝時臣, 1488–after 1567 (zi: Sizhong 思忠; hao: Chuxian 樗仙). A native of Wuxian (Suzhou, Jiangsu), Xie began his painting studies learning the styles of Shen Zhou (1427–1509), the leading master of the Wu literati school. He later launched a professional career in landscapes by combining the literati philosophy with elements of the academic Zhe school. His water-and-mountain scenes are rendered with vigorous brushwork and delicate colors.

His large compositions are dominated by a use of dashing strokes, yet sensitive ink washes. Xie continued to produce paintings after the age of eighty.

Xu Da 徐達, 1332–1385. Born to a poor farmer in Haozhou, Anhui, Xu Da was the most powerful military leader of the Ming army. Following many successes in taking important spots from the Mongols, Xu Da captured the Yuan capital of Beijing in 1368, for which the Hongwu emperor placed his name first among the twenty-one engraved on the triumphant stele at the Imperial Merit Temple in 1369. In the emperor's own words, Xu was the "only one who goes to missions on my order, returns to me with success . . . , behaves nobly without foppery, performs honestly like the son and the moon." In addition to generous awards of gold and silk, the Hongwu emperor also granted Xu several honorable titles including Duke of Prestige Kingdom, Duke of Wei, and, posthumously, Prince of Central Mountains. Two of Xu's four sons were given the title of duke, and three of his daughters were married to princes. His eldest daughter was chosen to marry Prince Zhu Di (q.v.); together they provoked an uprising against the Jianwen emperor (reigned 1399–1402), and she became Empress Xu when her husband took the throne in 1403 as the Yongle emperor. Xu Da's grave is close to the imperial grave at the foot of Purple Mountain (Zijinshan, also known as Zhongshan), Nanjing.

Xu Fu 徐俌, 1450–1517. A fifth-generation descendant of Xu Da (q.v.), Xu Fu took the hereditary title Duke of Wei in 1465. Fu served as a highly respected Commissioner-in-Chief in charge of the Nanjing-based Left Army beginning in 1479, and the Middle Army in 1496. He gained a reputation as a loyal and honest official. He was honored as Grand Mentor of the Heir Apparent in 1510 and received three posthumous titles. His tomb, located one hundred meters east of Xu Da's tomb, was excavated in 1982 (Wenwu 1982, no. 2, pp. 28–33).

Xu Qin 徐钦, died 1424. The oldest grandson of Xu Da (q.v.), Qin inherited the family title, Duke of Wei, in 1421. He was later dismissed from the court for his involvement in a political scandal, and lived as a nonentity until his death.

Yao Shou 姚綬, 1422/1423–1495 (zi: 公綬; hao: Songyun 松雲, Danqiusheng 丹丘生, Gu'an'zi 谷庵子, Yundong yishi 雲東逸史). A native of Jiaxing, Zhejiang, Yao Shou earned the top grade at the regional civil service examinations in 1453. He was appointed to the position of Censor in 1464. His career in the bureaucracy lasted only four years. In 1467 a case of libel forced Yao to leave the court, and he was sent to govern Yongning prefecture in Jiangxi. He took an early retirement in 1469 and spent his later life with his mother in their hometown, painting and composing. As a calligrapher, Yao switched from his early practice of classical calligraphy in the tradition of Zhong Gun and Wang Xizhi to studying Tang works. His writing style encompassed both power and grace. In painting, he studied Yuan masterpieces, especially those he collected by Ju Ran (approx. 960–985), Wu Zhen (1280–1354), Zhao Mengfu (1254–1322), and Wang Meng (approx. 1308–1385). Several of his collected works bear his inscriptions. Yao's poetic ink washes and textural stokes influenced the literati who later formed the Wu school.

You Qiu 尤求, active approx. 1540–1590 (zi: Ziqiu 子求; hao: Fengqiu 鳳丘, Fengshan 鳳山). A native of Changzhou (present-day Suzhou, Jiangsu province), You Qiu was said to have been a relative (some say nephew, some say son-in-law) of Qiu Ying (q.v.). You moved to Taicang, a small town not far from Changzhou, where he spent his later years painting. He was well known for a wide range of subjects in painting, from human figures to landscape. His baimiao, or outlined ink drawings, were of a style close to Qiu Ying's.

Zhang Bi 張弼, 1425–1487 (zi: Rubi 汝弼; hao: Donghai weng 東海翁). A native of Huating (Shanghai), Zhang earned a jinshi degree in 1466 and was appointed Vice Director at the Ministry of War to govern Nan'an. Well known for calligraphy, he wrote wild cursive script when drunk.

Zheng He 鄭和, 1371–1433 (originally Ma Sanbao). Zheng came from the Semur minority, who practiced Islam and had come centuries ago from Central Asia to settle in Yunnan in southern China. A eunuch, he was a close confidant of the Yongle emperor (s.v. Zhu Di), who gave him the honored name Zheng He for his distinguished military service and made him admiral of his treasure ships. Between 1405 and 1433, Zheng, commanding the largest fleet in the world at that time, led seven major expeditions to Southeast Asia, India, Persia, Arabia, and the eastern coast of Africa. Gavin Menzies, a retired British Navy commander, claims that Zheng He even traveled to the Americas long before Christopher Columbus (Menzies 2003).

Zhong Qinli 鍾欽禮, active 1465–1505 (also known as Zhong Li 鍾禮; hao: Nanyue shanren 南越山人, Kuaiji shanren 會稽山人). A native of Shangyu, Zhejiang, Zhong Qinli served as a court painter in the Hall of Benevolence and Wisdom during the reigns of the Chenghua and Hongzhi emperors. After early brush training with Zhe-school master Dai Jin (q.v.), Zhong became known for distinctive landscapes; his snowy and cloudy scenes were particularly admired by the emperors. He also painted delicate insects, grass, and flowers, though few examples have survived. In calligraphy he followed modes set by Zhao Mengfu (1254–1322). Zhong was among the last representative figures of the Zhe school, just as the Wu school was coming to dominate Ming painting.

Zhou Chen 周臣, active 1472–1535 (zi: Shunqing 舜卿; hao: Dongcun 東村). A professional painter from Suzhou, Jiangsu, Zhou Chen was skilled at figure and landscape painting. Ming documents record that Zhou practiced the classical styles of Song masters, especially court painters Li Tang (approx. 1050–1130) and Ma Yuan (active approx. 1189–1225). He studied in the studio of a townsman, landscape painter Chen Xian (1405–1496). With detailed composition, his art was also influenced by Ming court painter Dai Jin (q.v.), the founder of the orthodox Zhe school. For his synthesis of styles, Zhou was credited by his contemporaries as a master academic painter outside the court. But his name was overshadowed by two of his pupils, Qiu Ying (q.v.) and Tang Yin (1470–1523). The famous artist Li Rihua (1564–1635) wrote that Zhou Chen's brushwork was dense and maturely powerful, while Tang Yin's was elegant and romantic.

Zhou Wenjing 周文靖, active 1426–1463. A native of Putian (some say Fuzhou), Fujian province, Zhou served as a court painter in the Hall of Benevolence and Wisdom during the Xuande reign. During his court service, he proved himself capable of mastering the orthodox style and techniques he had studied in his early training, especially time spent copying works in the style of Ma Yuan (active approx. 1189–1225), Xia Gui (active approx. 1195–1230), and Wu Zhen (1280–1354). He won first place in the imperial examinations for his painting Withered Trees with Winter Birds. He was especially adept at landscapes, besides painting a wide range of subjects: figures, flowers and birds, bamboo and rocks, animals, and architecture.

Zhu Di 朱棣, 1360–1424 (the Yongle emperor, reigned 1403–1424). The fourth son of the Hongwu emperor, Zhu Di had been given the title Prince of Yan (the Beijing area) in his youth and, as such, proved himself to be an able military commander. When his father died in 1398, he left the throne to grandson Zhu Yunwen, Zhu Di's nephew. Zhu Di, however, believed that as the son of the Hongwu emperor, he himself was the more rightful heir. He dispatched troops in 1399 to "ferret out the evils" of his nephew, the Jianwen emperor, and seized the throne in 1403. As the Yongle emperor, he moved the capital from Nanjing to Beijing and built the Forbidden City. During his reign, the Ming navy, led by eunuch Zheng He (q.v.), gained control of the trade route to India and the Islamic world. Zhu Di displayed an ongoing enthusiasm for Tibetan Buddhism and Taoism, evidenced by his invitation of Halima and other important Buddhist leaders from Tibet to Nanjing, and by his worship of the Taoist deity Zhenwu. He enhanced Hanlin Imperial Academy by filling positions with prominent scholars. His wife, Empress Xu, was the oldest daughter of Xu Da (q.v.) and an outstanding female intellectual of her time.

Zhu Duan 朱端, 1441–after 1500 (zi: Kezheng 克正; hao: Yiqiao 一樵). A native of Haiyan, Zhejiang, Zhu Duan entered the bureaucracy as a professional painter and calligrapher during the Hongzhi reign, and was appointed to be a Commander in the Hall of Benevolence and Wisdom during the Zhengde reign. He took the nickname Yiqiao ("the woodcutter") from an imperial seal granted to him by the court. Zhu adapted a wide range of classical elements: his landscape technique was rooted in the Song tradition; his figure painting was derived from the Yuan master Sheng Mao (active 1320–1360); his flower-and-bird painting was based on the approach of Lu Ji (q.v.); and his bamboo painting, on Xia Chang (1388–1470).

Zhu Youjiao 朱由校, 1605–1627 (the Tianqi emperor, reigned 1621–1627). The eldest son of the Taichang emperor (Zhu Changluo, 1585–1620), Zhu Youjiao ascended the throne at age fifteen as the Tianqi emperor and died less than seven years later. His complete dependence on the ruthlessly ambitious eunuch Wei Zhongxian (1568–1627) further weakened an already deteriorating Ming government and civil service bureaucracy. Wei enriched himself at the government's expense and abused honest officials by dismissing, jailing, or even executing them. The young emperor's powerlessness put his throne in danger and left the Ming court vulnerable to growing rebellions.

Zhu Youyuan 朱祐杬, 1476–1519. The fourth son of the Chenghua emperor and father of the Jiajing emperor, Zhu Youyuan was granted the title Prince Xing in 1487 and given the territory of De'an (Anlu in Hubei) in 1491. Living simply, he spent most of his time studying literature and history. Awarded the posthumous title Prince Xian, he was elevated to the status of emperor a few years after his death to settle the "great rites controversy" over his son's line of succession to the throne.

Zhu Zhanji 朱瞻基, 1398–1435 (the Xuande emperor, reigned 1426–1435). The eldest grandson of the Yongle emperor (s.v. Zhu Di), Zhu Zhanji was installed as the Crown Prince in 1411 and enthroned as the fifth emperor of the Ming dynasty in 1426. During his time as a prince, he learned much about military and state affairs from the Yongle emperor, and his early experiences on the battlefield and with the building of the capital in Beijing made him a strong monarch. In the Ming orthodox history (Mingshi), Zhu Zhanji is regarded as a capable and conscientious emperor, and his Xuande reign a time of peace, stability, and prosperity. His dethroning of Empress Hu for his favorite concubine, who would become Empress Sun, earned him the reputation of being a libertine. Zhu Zhanji was also a talented poet, painter, calligrapher, and a patron of bronze and ceramics; the wares produced in his imperial factories were held in high esteem for the rest of the Ming through the Qing dynasty. He was trained in calligraphy at the school of the Shen family from Huating (near Shanghai), and practiced painting in the subjects of landscape, figures, animals, and flowers. When giving away his own paintings as gifts or rewards, he always inscribed the work with the recipient's name and date, along with official seals. He gave himself the Taoist name "Genuine Person for Lasting Spring" (長春真人).

Zhu Zhizheng 朱稚征, active 1573–1619 (hao: Sansong 三松). Son of Zhu Ying (Xiaosong) and grandson of Zhu He (founder of the Jiading bamboo art school), Zhu Zhizheng became a substantial celebrity in his native Jiading, Jiangsu province, for his talents in painting and bamboo carving. His depictions of landscapes, plants, and donkeys show he was clearly inspired by the spirit of the literati culture. With bamboo Zhu created a wide range of subjects and forms. Brush pots, arm rests, crabs, frogs, and vegetables were especially appealing to his contemporaries. Bamboo works by the Jiading school masters were collected in the imperial household and continuously used by royal members. Even three hundred years after Zhu's death, the Qianlong emperor composed poems to praise Sansong's superb carving techniques.

REFERENCES

Asian Art Museum. 1994. *Selected Works*. Seattle: University of Washington Press.

———. 2007. *Later Chinese Jades*. San Francisco: Asian Art Museum.

Barnhart, Richard M. 1993. *Painters of the Great Ming: The Imperial Court and the Zhe School*. Dallas: Dallas Museum of Art.

Bartholomew, Terese Tse. 2006. *Hidden Meanings in Chinese Art*. San Francisco: Asian Art Museum.

Bowers Museum of Cultural Art. 2003. *Tibet: Treasures from the Roof of the World*. Santa Ana, CA: Bowers Museum of Cultural Art.

Cahill, James. 1978. *Parting at the Shore: Chinese Painting of the Early and Middle Ming Dynasty, 1368–1580*. New York: John Weatherhill.

———. 1982. *The Distant Mountains: Chinese Painting of the Late Ming Dynasty, 1570–1644*. New York: John Weatherhill.

Cao Zhi (192–232 CE). Mingdu pian [The Famous Capital]. Repr. in vol. 1 of *Lidai shige xuan* [Poetry of Historical Periods], ed. Ji Zhenhuai, 166. Beijing: Zhongguo qingnian chubanshe, 1980.
曹植(192–232)：名都篇 收入季鎮淮等編註，歷代詩歌選．中國青年出版社1980．

Chang Shana. 2000. *Zhongguo zhixiu fushi quanji* [Corpus of Chinese Fabric, Embroidery, and Finery]. Tianjin: Renmin chubanshe.
常沙娜主編，中國織鏽服飾全集，天津人民美術出版社2000．

CHC: The Cambridge History of China. Vols. 7–8, *The Ming Dynasty, 1368–1644*, ed. Frederick W. Mote and Denis Twitchett. Cambridge: Cambridge University Press, 1988.

Chen Menglei. 1723–1727. *Gujin tushu jicheng* [Collections of Books from Ancient to Modern Periods]. Repr., Taiwan: Dingwen shuju, 1977.
陳夢雷1723–1727：古今圖書集成．台灣鼎文書局1977版．

Chen Nan. 2005. Ming Chengzu Zhu Di yu daci fawang Shijia yeshi [Ming Emperor Chengzu, Zhu Di, and the Lokapala of Great Compassion, Sakya Yeshe]. *Journal of the Palace Museum Studies* 2: 233–243.
陳楠：明成祖朱棣与大慈法王釋迦也失，故宮學刊2005，第二輯．

Ch'ien Chai. 1992. Mingjian fengge xiao yijing [The elegant style of a popular genre of a lacquer shop]. *GGWWYK*, no. 94: 74–79.
潛齋：民間風格小益精——漆園偶撷，故宮博物院月刊1992.94．

Cleary, J. C., ed. 1991. *Worldly Wisdom: Confucian Teachings of the Ming Dynasty*. Boston: Shambhala.

Clunas, Craig. 1997. *Pictures and Visuality in Early Modern China*. Princeton, NJ: Princeton University Press.

———. 2004. *Elegant Debts: The Social Art of Wen Zhengming*. Honolulu: University of Hawaii Press.

———. 2007. *Empire of Great Brightness: Visual and Material Cultures of Ming China, 1368–1644*. Honolulu: University of Hawaii Press.

DMB: Dictionary of Ming Biography, 1368–1644, ed. L. Carrington Goodrich and Chaoying Fang. 2 vols. New York: Columbia University Press, 1976.

Dong Qichang (1555–1636). Huayan [The eye for painting]. Repr. in *Mingren huaxue lunzhu* [Essays by Ming people on painting theories], vol. 12 of *Yishu congbian*, ed. Yang Jialuo, 17–53. Taipei: Shijie shuju, 1962.
董其昌：畫眼，收入楊家駱編：明人畫學論著，藝術叢編，12冊．臺北世界書局1962．

Dongnan wenhua [Southeast Cultures]. Quarterly journal. Nanjing: Jiangsu Provincial Museum. 南京博物院，東南文化．

Elman, Benjamin A. 2001. *From Philosophy to Philology: Intellectual and Social Aspects of Change in Late Imperial China*. Los Angeles: UCLA Press.

Ershiwu shi [Histories of the Twenty-five Dynasties]. Taipei: Kaiming shudian zhuban, 1962–1969. 二十五史，開明書店鑄版1962–1969．

Feng Zhao. 1999. *Treasures in Silk: An Illustrated History of Chinese Textiles*. Hong Kong: Costume Squad.

Fong, Wen C. 1995. Imperial portraiture in the Song, Yuan, and Ming periods. *Ars Orientalis* 25: 47–60.

Fong, Wen C., and James C. Y. Watt. 1996. *Possessing the Past: Treasures from the National Palace Museum, Taipei*. New York: Metropolitan Museum of Art / H. N. Abrams.

Gao Shouxian. 2006. Mingdai huangjia siyang de zhenxi dongwu he chongwu [Rare animals and pets raised by the Ming imperial household]. *Zijincheng* [Forbidden City Magazine], no. 2: 89. 高壽仙：明代皇家飼養的珍稀動物和寵物，紫禁城2006.2．

Geng Baochang et al. 2002. *Gugong bowuyuan cang Mingchu qinghuazi* [The Collection of Early Ming Blue-and-White Porcelain from the Palace Museum]. 2 vols. Beijing: Zijincheng chubanshe [Forbidden City Press]. 耿寶昌：故宮博物院藏明初青花瓷．北京紫禁城出版社2002年．

271

GGBWYYK: Gugong bowuyuan yuankan [Palace Museum Journal]. Quarterly journal. Beijing: Zijincheng chubanshe [Forbidden City Press]. 故宮博物院院刊，北京紫禁城出版社.

GGSHTL: Gugong shuhua tulu [The Collection of Calligraphy and Paintings in the National Palace Museum]. 18 vols. Taipei: National Palace Museum, 1989–2002. 台北故宮博物院：故宮書畫圖錄.

GGWWYK: Gugong wenwu yuekan [National Palace Museum Monthly of Chinese Art]. Monthly journal. Taipei: National Palace Museum. 台北故宮博物院：故宮文物月刊.

GGXSJK: Gugong xueshu jikan [National Palace Museum Research Quarterly]. Quarterly journal. Taipei: National Palace Museum. 台北故宮博物院：故宮學術季刊.

He Jiying. 2002. Shanghai Mingdai muzang gaishu [A survey of Ming graves in Shanghai]. *Shanghai bowuguan jikan* [Bulletin of the Shanghai Museum] 9: 653–66. 何繼英:上海明代墓葬概述，上海博物館集刊2002年九期，上海古籍出版社.

He Li. 2006. *Chinese Ceramics: The New Standard Guide.* London: Thames & Hudson.

Ho, Wai-kam, ed. 1980. *Eight Dynasties of Chinese Painting: The Collections of the Nelson Gallery-Atkins Museum, Kansas City, and the Cleveland Museum of Art.* Cleveland: Cleveland Museum of Art.

———, ed. 1992. *The Century of Tung Ch'i-ch'ang, 1555–1636.* 2 vols. Kansas City: Nelson-Atkins Museum of Art.

Hunan Provincial Museum. 1973. *The Han Tomb No. 1 at Mawangtui, Changsha.* Beijing: Wenwu Press. 湖南省博物館：長沙馬王堆一號漢墓，北京文物出版社1973.

IA-CASS: Institute of Archaeology-Chinese Academy of Social Sciences, with the Ding Ling Museum and Archaeological Team of the City of Beijing. 1990. *Ding Ling: The Imperial Tomb of the Ming Dynasty.* 2 vols. Beijing: Wenwu Press.

Ji Shijia. 1984. Mingdu Nanjing chengyuan luelun [A discussion of the city wall of the Ming capital Nanjing]. *GGBWYYK,* no. 2: 70–81. 季士家：明都南京城垣略論，故宮博物院院刊1984.2.

Kaogu [Archaeology]. Monthly journal. Beijing: Wenwu chubanshe. 考古，北京文物出版社.

Laing, Ellen Johnston. 1997. Qiu Ying's other patrons. *Journal of the American Oriental Society* 117, no. 4: 686–92.

Lam, Joseph S. C. 2002. Musical Confucianism: The case of jikong yuewu. In Wilson 2002, 134–72.

Lan Pu. 1815. *Jingdezhen taolu* [Records of Ceramics in Jingdezhen]. Repr. in *Zhongguo taozi mingzhu huibian* [A Collection of Famous Essays on Chinese Ceramics], 1–85. Beijing: Zhongguo shudian, 1991. 藍浦：景德鎮陶錄. 中國陶瓷名著匯編，中國書店1991年.

Lefebvre d'Argencé, René-Yvon, ed. 1978. *Great Centers of Art: Asian Art in the San Francisco Bay Area.* Germany: Edition Leipzig.

Li Dongyang et al. 1587. *Daming huidian* [Complete Encyclopedia of the Great Ming Dynasty]. Repr., Taipei: Dongnan shubaoshe, 1963. 李東陽等：大明會典. 再刊，台灣東南書報社1963.

Li Jingze. 2007. Guoyuan chang xiaokao [Textual research on Orchard Workshop]. *Shanghai Wenbo* [Shanghai Culture and Museums], no. 1: 33–39. 李經澤：果園廠小考，上海市文物管理委員會主辦：上海文博2007年1月. 上海辭書出版社.

Li Jingze and Hu Shichang. 2001. Hongwu tihong qiqichutan [An initial study of red lacquer wares of the Hongwu]. *GGWWYK,* no. 220 (July): 56–71. 李經澤，胡世昌：洪武剔紅漆器初探，台北故宮博物院：故宮文物月刊2001.220.

Li Shi. 1989. Ding Yunpeng Yuchuan zhucha tu [*Brewing Tea by Jade River* by Ding Yunpeng]. *GGBWYYK,* no. 1: 89–91. 李湜：丁云鵬玉川煮茶圖，故宮博物院院刊1989.1.

Li, Thomas Shiyu, and Susan Naquin. 1988. The Baoming Temple: Religion and the throne in Ming and Qing China. *Harvard Journal of Asiatic Studies* 48, no. 1 (June): 131–188.

Li Zhaoxiang. Approx. 1547. *Longjiang chuanchang zhi* [Records of the Treasure Ships on Dragon River]. Repr., Jiangsu: Guji chubanshe 1999. 李昭祥：龍江船廠志，江蘇古籍出版社1999.

Liang Sicheng. 1984. Taiji jianshuo [A brief discussion of pedestals]. Repr. in *Liang Sicheng wenji* [Collected articles by Liang Sicheng], chap. 2. Beijing: Zhongguo jianzhu gongye chubanshe. 梁思成，梁詩正文集，卷二. 中國建築工業出版社1984.

Lin Lina. 1999. Mingdai Mushi jiazu zhi shengping jiqi shuhua shoucang [The Biography and Collection of the Mu Family of the Ming Dynasty]. *GGWWYK,* no. 101: 48–77. 林莉娜：明代沐氏家族之生平及其書畫收藏，故宮文物月刊1999.101集.

Little, Stephen. 1985. The demon queller and the art of Qiu Ying (Ch'iu Ying). *Artibus Asiae* 46, no. 1/2: 5–128.

Liu Xinyuan. 1996. Jingdezhen zhushan chutu de Mingchu yu Yongle guanyao zhi yanjiu [A study of excavated imperial porcelain from the Yongle and Xuande stratum in Jingdezhen]. In *Hongxi Wenwu* [Relics from the Hongxi Collection], 9–49. Taipei: Hongxi Foundation for Arts, Culture, and Education. 劉新園：景德鎮珠山出土的明初与永樂官窯之研究，鴻禧文物. 臺灣鴻禧藝術文教基金會1996.

Ma Chengyuan et al. 1991. *Chugoku no bihō* [Beautiful Treasures of China]. Tokyo: Nihon Hoso; Shanghai: Renmin meishu chubanshe. 馬承源等：中國の美寶. 東京，日本放送 § 上海人美1991.

Mao Yuanyi. Approx. 1620s. *Wubei zhi* [Records of Military Equipment]. Repr. in vol. 73 of Chen Menglei 1723–1727, 988–93. 茅元儀(崇禎)，武備誌. 收入陳夢雷1723–1727: 古今圖書集成，73冊，戎政典.

Menzies, Gavin. 2003. *1421: The Year China Discovered America.* New York: William Morrow.

Mingshi [A History of the Ming Dynasty]. Approx. 1739. Repr. in vol. 9 of *Ershiwu shi* [Histories of the Twenty-Five Dynasties]. 1969. 明史(乾隆4年)，收入二十五史，開明書店鑄版1969.

Mu Yiqin. 1988. *Mingchu huihua yu yuanti zhepai* [Early paintings by Ming academics and the Zhe School]. In vol. 6 of *ZGMSQJ, huihua bian,* 15–21. 穆益勤：明初繪畫与院体、浙派，中國美術全集六卷，1988.

Murray, Julia K. 2002. Varied views of the sage: Illustrated narratives of the life of Confucius. In Wilson 2002, 222–64.

———. 2007. *Mirror of Morality: Chinese Narrative Illustration and Confucian Ideology.* Honolulu: University of Hawaii Press.

Nagoya Municipal Government. 1989: *Zhongguo nanjingshi bowuguan Mingchao wanggong guizu wenwuzhan* [An exhibition of cultural relics of the Ming monarchy and aristocracy from Nanjing]. Nagoya: Municipal Government. 名古屋市政局，中國南京市博物館明朝王公貴族文物展，名古屋市政局1989.

Nanjing Municipal Museum. 2000. *Mingchao shoushi guanfu* [Accessories and Crowns of the Ming Dynasty]. Beijing: Kexue chubanshe. 南京市博物館編：明朝首飾冠服，科學出版社2000.

———. 2006. *Baochuan chang yizhi Nanjing Ming baochuan chang liu zuotang kaogu baogao* [The Ruins of Treasure-Ship Shipyard: Archaeological Reports on the Sixth Workshop of the Ming Treasure-Ship Shipyard in Nanjing]. Beijing: Wenwu chubanshe. 南京市博物館編：寶船廠遺址——南京明寶船廠六作塘考古報告，文物出版社2006.

Naquin, Susan. 2001. *Peking: Temples and City Life, 1400–1900.* Berkeley: University of California Press.

Needham, Joseph. 1986. *Science and Civilization in China.* Vol. 5.7, *Military Technology: The Gunpowder Epic.* Cambridge University Press.

Ohba, Shogyo. 1988. The *kyushitsu* technique demonstrated on a *natsume.* In *Urushi: Proceedings of the Urushi Study Group, June 10–27, 1985,* ed. N. S. Brommelle and Perry Smith, 91–94. Marina del Rey, CA: Getty Conservation Institute.

Park, Eun-Wha. 1995. Zhu Duan's winter landscapes. *Ars Orientalis* 25: 133–42.

Qian Hanshu [A History of the Former Han Dynasty]. Approx. 83 CE. Repr. in vol. 1 of *Ershiwu shi* [Histories of the Twenty-Five Dynasties]. 1969. 前漢書，收入二十五史，開明書店鑄版1969.

Riely, Celia Carrington. 1992. Tung Ch'i-ch'ang's life (1555–1636). In vol. 2 of Ho 1992, 387–457.

Shaanxi kaogu yanjiusuo [Institute of Archeology, Shaanxi province]. 1992. *Tangdai Huangbao yaozhi* [Excavation of a Tang Kiln Site at Huangpu in Tongchua]. Beijing: Wenwu chubanshe 1992. 陝西考古研究所：唐代黃堡耀州窯址，北京文物出版社1992.

Shan Guolin. 1989. Wumen huapai zongshu [A general discussion of the Wu painting school]. In vol. 7 of *ZGMSQJ, huihua bian,* 1–26. 單國霖：吳門畫派綜述，中國美術全集7明代繪畫，上海人美.

———. 2002. Hanging scrolls of the Ming painting *Eighteen Scholars. Shanghai bowuguan jikan* [Bulletin of the Shanghai Museum] 9. 單國霖：明十八學士圖屏考，上海博物館集刊2002年，九期.

Shan Guoqiang. 1993. Dai Jin zuopin shixu kao [A study of the chronological sequence of Dai Jin's works]. *GGBWYYK,* no. 4: 11–35. 單國強：戴進作品時序考，故宮博物院院刊1993.4.

———. 2000. Mingdai huihua xulun [Preface on paintings of the Ming dynasty]. In vol. 10 of *ZGHHQJ*. 單國強：明代繪畫序論，中國繪畫全集 卷10, 2000.

Shanghai WWGWH [Shanghai Administration of Cultural Relics]. 2001. *Shanghai chutu Tang Song Yuan Ming Qing yuqi* [Jade Wares of the Tang, Song, Yuan, Ming, and Qing, Unearthed from Shanghai]. Shanghai: Renmin chubanshe. 上海文物管理委員會：上海出土唐宋元明清玉器，上海人民出版社2001.

Shen Defu. 1606–1619. *Wanli yehuo bian* [Stories of Hunting from the Wanli Period]. Repr., Beijing: Zhonghua shuju, 1959. 沈德符1606–1619：萬曆野獲編，中華書局再版1959.

Shih, Shou-ch'ien. 1994. Dong Qichang Wanbian caotang tu jiqi gexin huafeng [Dong Qichang's Wanbian thatched house and his new revolutionary style]. *Lishi yuyan yanjiu suo jikan* [Bulletin of the Institute of History and Philology] 65: 306–332. 石守謙：董其昌婉變草堂圖及其革新畫風，歷史語言研究所集刊，第65冊，二分1994年6月.

———. 1998. You qigu dao fugu: 17 shiji Jinling huihua de yige qiemian [From "in praise of eccentricity" to "in pursuit of antiquity": A study of seventeenth-century Nanking painting]. *GGXSJK* 15, no. 4 (Summer): 33–76. 石守謙：由奇古到復古——十七世紀金陵繪畫的一個切面，故宮學術季刊1998,15卷4期.

Shoudu Bowuguan [The Capital Museum]. 2001. *Shoudu Bowuguan* [The Capital Museum]. Beijing: Yanshan chubanshe. 首都博物館編：首都博物館. 北京燕山出版社 2001.

Silbergeld, Jerome. 1985. In praise of government: Chao Yung's painting *Noble Steeds* and late Yuan politics. *Artibus Asiae* 56, no. 3: 159–202.

Simcox, Jacqueline. 2004. Ming festival badges. In *Celestial Silks: Chinese Religious and Court Textiles,* ed. Judith Rutherford and Jackie Menzies, 74–77. Sydney: Art Gallery of New South Wales.

Sommer, Deborah. 2002. Destroying Confucius: Iconoclasm in the Confucian temple. In Wilson 2002, 95–133.

Song Yingxing. 1637. *Tiangong kaiwu* [Exploitation of the Works of Nature], ed. Luo Zhenyu. Repr., Osaka: Sholin, 1927. 宋應星：天工開物. 大阪，再版書林1927.

Songshi [A History of the Song Dynasty]. Approx. 1345. Repr. in vol. 6 of *Ershiwu shi* [Histories of the Twenty-Five Dynasties]. 1969. 宋史，收入二十五史，6冊. 開明書店鑄版1969.

Su Bai. 1957. *Baisha Songmu* [A Song Tomb in Baisha]. Beijing: Wenwu chubanshe. 宿白：白沙宋墓. 北京文物出版社1957.

Sung, Hou-mei. 1989. From the Min-Che tradition to the Che school (part 2): Precursors of the Che school: Hsieh Huan and Tai Chin. *GGXSJK* 7, no. 1 (Autumn): 1–15.

———. 1990. The formation of the Ming painting academy. *Ming Studies,* no. 29 (Spring): 30–55.

———. 1993. Lu Chi and his pheasant painting. *GGXSJK* 10, no. 4 (Summer).

———. 1995. Eagle painting themes of the Ming court. *Archives of Asian Art* 48: 48–63.

———. 1998. The three Yin masters of the Ming court: Yin

Shan, Yin Xie, and Yin Hong. *Artibus Asiae* 58, no. 1/2: 91–114.

———. 1999. Liu Jun, the great master of figure painting in the Ming court. *Oriental Art* 45, no. 3 (Autumn): 65–78.

Suzuki Kei. 1968. Mindai kaigashi no kenkyu: Seppa [A study of Ming painting: The Zhe school]. *Toyo Bunka Kenkyujo Kiyo* [Memoirs of the Intitute for Oriental Culture], special issue.

Urban Council et al. 1989. *Imperial Porcelain of the Yongle and Xuande Periods Excavated from the Site of the Ming Imperial Factory at Jingdezhen.* Hong Kong: Urban Council. 香港市政局，景德鎮陶瓷歷史博物館聯辦：<u>景德鎮明御廠故址出土永樂宣德官窯瓷器展覽</u>，1989.

Vanderstappen, Harrie. 1956–1957. Painters at the early Ming court (1368–1435) and the problem of a Ming painting academy. *Monumenta Serica* 15: 258–302 (part 1); 16: 315–46 (part 2).

Wang Chenghua. 1998. Material culture and emperorship: The shaping of imperial roles at the court of Xuanzong. PhD diss., Yale University.

Wang Yaoting. 1991. Chen Hongshou bixia de Yuanming yizhi [Yuanming's seclusionism by brushwork of Chen Hongshou]. *GGWWYK,* no. 95: 96–109. 王耀庭：陳洪綬筆下的淵明逸致，<u>故宮文物月刊</u>95期，1991.

Wang Zhengshu. 1993. [A study of Ming burial furniture in Shanghai Museum's collection.] *Nanfang wenwu* [Relics from South], no. 1: 23–38. 王正書：上海博物館藏明代家具明器研究，<u>南方文物</u>1993.1.

Wei Dong. 1991. Chen Hongshou Yingxi tu chutan [Initial study of the depiction of boys playing by Chen Hongshou]. *Wenwu,* no. 11: 88–90. 畏冬：陳洪綬戲嬰圖初探，<u>文物</u>1991.11.

Weidner, Marsha, ed. 1994. *Latter Days of the Law: Images of Chinese Buddhism, 850–1850.* Lawrence, KS: Spencer Museum of Art, University of Kansas.

Wen Peng. 1534. Xuande dingyi pu [Illustrated Collection of Tripods and Vessels of the Xuande Reign]. Repr. in *Yushi guqi pulu* [Records of Books on Jade, Stone, and Antiques], vol. 35 of *Yishu congbian,* ed. Yang Jialuo, 109–244. Taipei: Shijie shuju, 1962. 文彭：宣德鼎彝譜，收入楊家駱再編：<u>玉石古器譜錄</u>，<u>藝術叢編</u>，35冊.臺北世界書局1962.

Wenwu [Cultural Relics]. Monthly journal. Beijing: Wenwu chubanshe. <u>文物</u>，北京文物出版社.

Wilson, Thomas A., ed. 2002. *On Sacred Grounds: Culture, Society, Politics, and the Formation of the Cult of Confucius.* Cambridge, MA: Harvard University Press.

Wu Meifeng. 2005. Jingqi yaofu wuyunlai, bushi qianqiu xi matai [The fluttering flags summon the five clouds, To what is not a hobby horse stage]. *Journal of the Palace Museum Studies* 2: 97–131. 吳美鳳：旌旗遙拂五雲來，不是千秋戲馬台，<u>故宮學刊</u>2005，第二輯，北京紫禁城出版社.

Xiao Yanyi. 1995. Youguan Wen Zhengming ciguan de liangtong shuzha [Two letters concerning Wen Zhengming's resignation of an official position]. *GGBWYYK,* no. 4: 45–50. 肖燕翼：有關文徵明辭官的兩通書札，<u>故宮博物院院刊</u>1995.4.

Xin Tangshu [New History of the Tang Dynasty]. Approx. 1060. Repr. in vol. 5 of *Ershiwu shi* [Histories of the Twenty-Five Dynasties]. 1969. <u>新唐書</u>，收入<u>二十五史</u>，5冊.開明書店鑄版1969.

Xu Dishan. 1999. *Daojiao shi* [A History of Taoism]. Repr., Shanghai: Shanghai guji. 許地山：<u>道教史</u>，上海古籍1999.

Xu Guohuang. 1989. Qiu Ying he tade huihua yishu [Qiu Ying and his art of painting]. *GGWWYK,* no. 74. 許郭璜：仇英和他的繪畫藝術，<u>故宮文物月刊</u>74號，1989.

———. 2003. Hanmei xueqin yu youlan [Winter prunus, snowy birds, and orchids], *GGWWYK,* no. 244: 58–71. 許郭璜：寒梅、雪禽與幽蘭——關於馬麟的花卉風格，<u>故宮文物月刊</u>244號，2003.

Xue Yang. 1999. A comparative study of figure paintings by Chen Hongshou and Ren Bonian. *Dongnan wenhua* [Southeast Cultures], no. 4: 72–76. 薛揚：陳洪綬与任伯年的人物畫比較，<u>東南文化</u>1999.4.

Yang Lili. 2004. Mingren Shi tongnian tu [Initial study of the Ming scroll painting *Shi tongnian tu*], *GGBWYYK,* no. 2: 100–12. 楊麗麗：明人[十同年圖]卷初探，收入<u>故宮博物院院刊</u>2004年2期總112期.

Yang Xin et al., eds. 1994. *Gugong bowuyuan cang Ming Qing huihua* [Ming and Qing Dynasty Paintings in the Palace Museum Beijing Collection]. Beijing: Zijincheng chubanshe [Forbidden City Press].

Yu Peijin. 1991. Cong Dukeyuantu kan Wen Zhengming yu Qiu Ying fengge de yitong [Different styles of Wen Zhengming and Qiu Ying, revealed in Dule Garden]. *GGXSJK* 8, no. 4: 85–117. 余佩謹：從獨樂園圖看文徵明與仇英風格的異同，<u>故宮學術季刊</u>1991,8卷4期.

Yuanshi [A History of the Yuan Dynasty]. Approx. 1370. Repr. in vol. 7 of *Ershiwu shi* [Histories of the Twenty-Five Dynasties]. 1969. 元史，收入<u>二十五史</u>，7冊.開明書店鑄版1969.

ZGGJWWJ: Zhongguo guojia wenwuju [State Administration for Cultural Heritage]. 1996. *Zhongguo wenwu jinghua dacidian* [An Encyclopedia of Masterpieces of Chinese Relics]. *Jinyin yushi* [vol. on gold, silver, jade, and stone]. Shanghai: Cishu chubanshe; Hong Kong: Shangwu yinshu. 中國國家文物局：<u>中國文物精華大辭典，金銀玉石卷</u>，上海辭書、商務印書館1996.

ZGHHQJ: *Zhongguo huihua quanji* [Complete Collection of Chinese Paintings]. Vols. 10–18, Ming. Hangzhou: Zhejiang meishu; Beijing: Wenwu chubanshe, 2000. <u>中國繪畫全集</u>，10–18 明.浙江美術 & 文物出版社2000.

ZGMSQJ: *Zhongguo meishu quanji* [Complete Collection of Chinese Art]:

———. Vol. 4, *Jianzhu yishu bian* [Architectural Art]. Beijing: Jiangong chubanshe, 1988. <u>中國美術全集</u>，4卷，建筑藝術編.北京建工出版社1988.

———. Vol. 7, *Yinran zhixiu* [Dyes, Textiles, and Embroidery]. Beijing: Wenwu chubanshe, 1987. 中國美術全集，7卷，印染織繡編. 北京文物出版社1987.

———. Vol. 10, *Gongyi meishu pian* [Crafts]. Beijing: Wenwu chubanshe, 1987. 中國美術全集，10卷，工藝美術編. 北京文物出版社1987.

———. *Huihua bian* [Painting section]. Vols. 6–8, *Mingdai huihua* [Paintings of the Ming Dynasty]. Shanghai: Renmin meishu chubanshe, 1988–1989. 中國美術全集，6–8卷，繪畫編明代繪畫，上海人美1988–1989.

ZGYSYJY: Zhongguo yishu yanjiu yuan [Chinese Academy of Arts]. 1999. *Zhongguo jianzhu shi* [Chinese Architectural History]. Beijing: Wenwu chubanshe. 中国艺术学院中国建筑艺术史编写组：中国建筑艺术史，北京文物出版社1999.

ZGYQQ]: Zhongguo yuqi quanji [Collections of Chinese Jade]. Vol. 5 [Jades of Sui, Tang, Yuan, Ming, and Qing Dynasties], ed. Yang Boda. Shijiazhuang: Hebei meishu chubanshe, 1993. 楊伯達主編：中國玉器全集，五冊. 河北人美 1993.

Zhang Xikong and Tian Jue. 1987. *Zhongguo lishi dashi biannian* [Chronology of Chinese Important Historical Events]. Vol. 4. Beijing: Beijing chubanshe. 张席孔，田珏：中国历史大事编年，卷四. 北京出版社1987.

Zheng Xuan (127–200 CE). *Liji zhengyi* [Correct Annotations on Record of Rites]. Repr. in vol. 2 of *Shisan jing zhushu* [Annotations on the Thirteen Classics]. Shanghai: Shanghai guji, 1997. 鄭玄：禮記正義. 投壺，收入十三經注疏，下冊. 上海古籍1997.

Zhou Xibao. 1984. *Zhongguo gudai fushi shi* [A History of Ancient Chinese Costume]. Shanghai: Zhongguo xiju chubanshe. 周錫保，中國古代服飾史，上海：中國戲劇出版社1984.

Zhou Xinhui. 1998. Mingdai banke lueshu [A brief discussion of woodblock prints of the Ming dynasty]. In *Mingdai banke tushi* [Annotations and Illustrations of Woodblock Prints of the Ming Dynasty]. 4 vols. Beijing: Xueyuan chuban. 周心惠：明代刻版略述，收入明代刻版圖釋，北京學苑出版社1998.

Zhu Jiajin and Xia Gengqi. 1995. *Ming dai qiqi gaishu* [An Overview of Ming Lacquers]. Vol. 5 of *Zhongguo qiqi quanji* [Lacquer treasures from China]. Fuzhou: Fujian meishu chubanshe. 朱家溍：明代漆器概述，中國漆器全集5，福建美術出版1995.

Zhu Yan. 1744. *Taoshuo* [A Story of Ceramics]. Repr. in vol. 9 of *Meishu congshu* [Series of Books on Arts], ed. Huang Binhong and Deng Shi, 61–218. Beijing: Yiwen yinshu, 1947. 朱琰：陶說，收入黃賓鴻、鄧實編美術叢書，九冊. 藝文印書1947.

Zijincheng [Forbidden City Magazine]. Monthly journal, Beijing: Zijincheng chubanshe [Forbidden City Press]. 紫禁城月刊，北京紫禁城出版社.

Zito, Angela. 1997. *Of Body and Brush: Grand Sacrifice as Text / Performance in Eighteenth-Century China*. Chicago: University of Chicago Press.

277

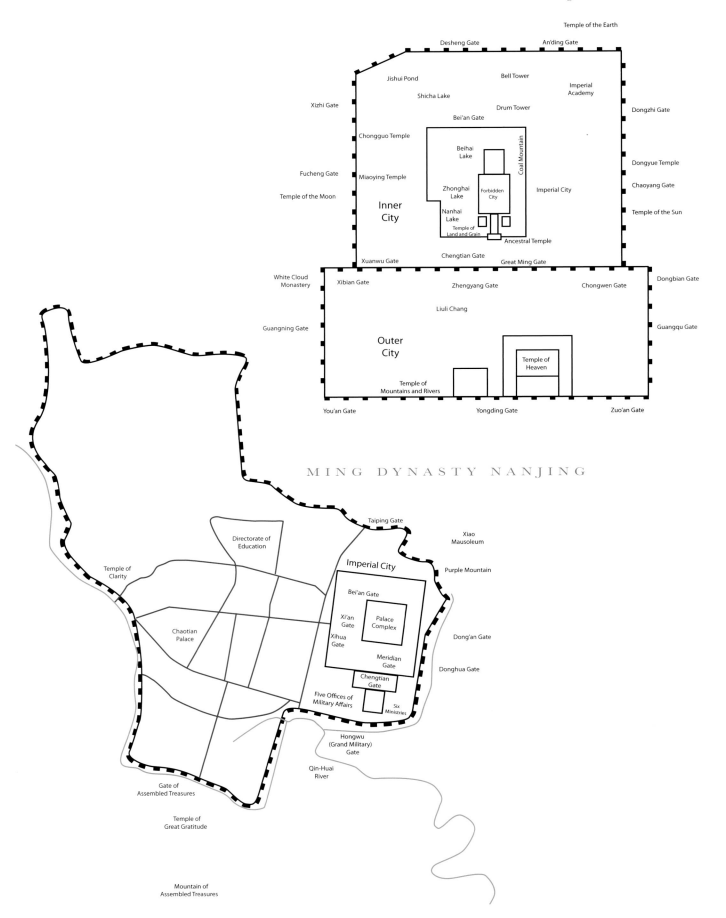

Temple of the Earth

Desheng Gate
An'ding Gate

Jishui Pond
Bell Tower
Imperial Academy

Xizhi Gate
Shicha Lake
Dongzhi Gate

Drum Tower

Bei'an Gate

Chongguo Temple
Coal Mountain
Dongyue Temple

Beihai Lake

Miaoying Temple
Chaoyang Gate

Fucheng Gate
Forbidden City
Imperial City

Zhonghai Lake

Temple of the Moon
Inner City
Temple of the Sun

Nanhai Lake

Temple of Land and Grain

Ancestral Temple

Xuanwu Gate
Chengtian Gate
Great Ming Gate

White Cloud Monastery
Xibian Gate
Zhengyang Gate
Chongwen Gate
Dongbian Gate

Liuli Chang

Guangning Gate
Outer City
Guangqu Gate

Temple of Heaven

Temple of Mountains and Rivers

You'an Gate
Yongding Gate
Zuo'an Gate

Taiping Gate

Xiao Mausoleum

Directorate of Education

Purple Mountain

Temple of Clarity
Imperial City

Bei'an Gate

Xi'an Gate
Palace Complex

Chaotian Palace
Xihua Gate
Dong'an Gate

Meridian Gate
Donghua Gate

Chengtian Gate

Five Offices of Military Affairs
Six Ministries

Hongwu (Grand Military) Gate

Qin-Huai River

Gate of Assembled Treasures

Temple of Great Gratitude

Mountain of Assembled Treasures